THEY TASTED GLORY

THEY TASTED GLORY

Among the Missing at the Baseball Hall of Fame

Wil A. Linkugel *and* Edward J. Pappas

with forewords by
GENE BUDIG   ERNIE HARWELL
SPARKY ANDERSON

McFarland & Company, Inc., Publishers
Jefferson, North Carolina, and London

Cover: Pete Reiser of the Brooklyn Dodgers steals home on April 18, 1946, as New York Giants catcher Ernie Lombardi reaches down to make the put-out, but Ump Dunn calls the runner safe. Gene Hermanshi, Dodger outfielder, is up at bat. (UPI/CORBIS-BETTMAN)

British Library Cataloguing-in-Publication data are available

Library of Congress Cataloguing-in-Publication Data

Linkugel, Wil A.
    They tasted glory : among the missing at the Baseball Hall of Fame
/ Wil A. Linkugel and Edward J. Pappas ; with forewords by Gene
Budig, Ernie Harwell, Sparky Anderson.
      p.   cm.
    Includes index.
    ISBN 0-7864-0484-1 (sewn softcover : 50# alkaline paper) ∞
    1. Baseball players — United States — Biography.   2. Baseball
players — Wounds and injuries — United States.   3. National Baseball
Hall of Fame and Museum.   I. Pappas, Edward J., 1931– .
II. Title.
GV865.A1L54   1998
796.357'092'273 — dc21
[B]   98-12340
                                          CIP

Manufactured in the United States of America

McFarland & Company, Inc., Publishers
  Box 611, Jefferson, North Carolina 28640

To our wives, Helen and Eunice

CONTENTS

ACKNOWLEDGMENTS

We express our gratitude to the Baseball Hall of Fame Library in Cooperstown, New York, for the use of its sources and its facilities. We thank the library's staff for the cheerful assistance they rendered. We also thank *The Sporting News*, St. Louis, Missouri, for their cooperation.

The pictures in the book are from the National Baseball Hall of Fame Library, the Corbis-Bettman Archives, New York City, and the Rochester *Democrat and Chronicle*.

We wish to acknowledge the professional assistance we received from James R. Cypher, Author's Representative. His helpful and congenial attitude was a constant. We thank Jackson Harrell, vice president of Halcyon, Inc., of Dallas, Texas, for his astute criticism of portions of the manuscript and for his keen appreciation of the project. David Hornstein, a Detroit writer, did valuable editing for us in the manuscript's early stages. We thank Steve Busby for the quality time he spent with us. And, finally, we extend heartfelt appreciation to the sports writers, too numerous to mention by name, from whose newspaper columns we drew information in writing this book.

Robin Holladay, Pamela Hickman, and Marilyn Figuieras were instrumental in producing copies of written materials. To them we say thank you.

Most importantly, we appreciate Helen and Eunice for their patience.

FOREWORDS

Professional life is often fragile, and we are reminded of that cruel fact in the highly competitive world of sports. There have been countless young athletes with unbridled optimism and enormous potential. And yet fate has claimed many of them.

They Tasted Glory provides a reality check for all of us who follow and care about Major League Baseball. The authors remind us of the game's many achievements and pressing needs.

There is no substitute for greatness in players. Baseball, if it is to survive and increase fan interest, must have marquee names like Ruth, DiMaggio and Musial. More than 60 million people each year frequent big league ballparks because of the stars and the way they play the game. That magic easily outdraws the other professional sports.

The authors remind us that there are few in the rarefied strata of Frank Thomas, Ken Griffey, Jr., and Barry Bonds. Not many will find their way to Cooperstown for induction and that fact will not change in the years ahead. Injury will claim some of the very best and shatter untold dreams.

They Tasted Glory serves as a stern reminder of reality and increases our collective appreciation for the uniqueness of player greatness. Immortality in sport requires great skill and uncommon luck.

GENE A. BUDIG
President
American League

*   *   *

The road to Cooperstown is a long one. The Baseball Hall of Fame is not easy to reach. There are too many potholes along the way.

To reach the zenith, players must be luckier than lucky and better than good. Many of my best friends — even heroes — were on the way to the Hall of Fame when suddenly they were side-tracked. In a lot of ways, their journeys make even more fascinating reading than the journeys of those greats who finally reached the Hall.

That's why you will enjoy these insightful sketches by Wil A. Linkugel and Edward J. Pappas. They tell us about the glory which slipped from the grasps of these great players.

I've personally followed the careers of all the players — except two, Vean Gregg and Joe Wood. I've read and heard about those two but never saw them in action. Joe Wood is a star who has fascinated me for many years.

Of the others, my special favorites are Pete Reiser, Herb Score and Mark Fidrych. I knew Reiser very well. He was with the Dodgers the year I broke into the big leagues with the Dodgers — 1948. Herb Score is one of my close friends among the big league announcers. Also, I admired his talent and courage when he pitched for the Indians. I broadcasted every game Fidrych pitched for the Tigers. He was the most charismatic player I've ever seen in my 50 years of big-league broadcasting. Whenever he pitched, the crowds increased at least 20,000 — whether the game was in Detroit or away.

All the other players in this book have a special appeal. They were on their way to greatness until fate somehow changed their courses.

These writers discern that appeal and make this book one which all of us will treasure.

ERNIE HARWELL
Broadcaster

*   *   *

Somehow the good ones usually make it into the line-up some way or another. Once in a while, though, the devil jumps up and snatches a career away when a player blinked just for a second.

We've all seen it happen, sometimes to young players who never really got the chance to get it going in the big leagues. How many times have bad arms stolen the chance of a lifetime from young pitchers who look like "can't miss" prospects?

I don't know if it's worse to lose it then or after the player gets a taste of big-time glory like some of the players featured in this book. If a taste of honey really is worse than none at all, then these players truly know the feeling.

But at least they were able to walk under the stars that most people don't even get a chance to see.

This book is a good wake-up call for everybody, not just the die-hard baseball fan. We all are blessed with certain talents. But, they're only ours to borrow. We must use them to the fullest advantage and always be aware that they can vanish in the wink of an eye.

Nothing in life should be taken for granted. We must appreciate what we have and be careful not to let it slip away. This book is about ball players. But there's a bigger lesson everyone can share. It's definitely worth the read.

SPARKY ANDERSON
Manager

INTRODUCTION

Baseball fans love to discuss current players and assess their chances of reaching the pinnacle of achievement: the Hall of Fame. They ask, "Who among current players will make the Hall?" We might mention Rickey Henderson and his record-breaking number of stolen bases, Barry Bonds and his 300 homers and 300 stolen bases, Tony Gwynn and his eight batting titles, Cal Ripken and his consecutive games played or Roger Clemens and his Cy Young awards and his strikeout records. When we think of the recent past, we recall Joe Morgan and Johnny Bench of the Big Red Machine, and Reggie Jackson and Catfish Hunter of the great Oakland teams that won three consecutive World Series. If we have an interest in the history of the game, we remember Joe DiMaggio, Ted Williams, Stan Musial, Mickey Mantle, Hank Aaron and Willie Mays. Or we can go back to the early part of the century and call to mind Ty Cobb, Babe Ruth, Christy Mathewson and Walter Johnson.

The greatest players of all time are already in the Hall of Fame at Cooperstown, New York. Election to the Hall of Fame is the game's highest honor, an achievement that requires a combination of skill and luck. One ticket to the Hall of Fame is greatness over a long period of time, such as Babe Ruth, Tris Speaker and Grover Cleveland Alexander. Another ticket is extended solid play and the achievement of some plateau, such as 3,000 hits, 300 wins or 500 home runs, levels reached by players such as Al Kaline, Willie McCovey, Harmon Killebrew and Steve Carlton.

But there is an element of luck as well in making the Hall of Fame. The hazards that stand between a talented player and making it to the Hall of Fame are many. Injuries are an inevitable part of every sport. Batters can be beaned. Fielders can collide with fences, or with each other. A pitcher's overhand throwing motion is unnatural, putting strain on his arm. Baserunners can suffer leg injuries if they don't slide the right way.

There are off the field dangers as well. Ballplayers are not immune to illness, accident or violence. The history of baseball has numerous examples of careers that were ended for these reasons.

There are players in the Hall of Fame whose careers were prematurely ended by illness, injury or death. They include Lou Gehrig, Dizzy Dean, Sandy Koufax, Roy Campanella, Mickey Cochrane, Roberto Clemente and Ross Youngs. All of these players lasted long enough to produce accomplishments that qualified them for Cooperstown. That is the third ticket to the Hall: Greatness over a shorter period, but marked with dramatic, notable achievements. How long is long enough? The careers of the above mentioned players range from Dizzy Dean's eight productive seasons to Lou Gehrig's 17.

Ballplayers profiled in this book are unlikely candidates for Cooperstown. The players were young, strong and talented. Each tasted stardom, glory and the adulation of fans. Each was felled by a pitch, a line drive, an illness or death. Some of the players profiled in this book enjoyed several seasons in the glaring spotlight of the media. For others, it was a single, shining season, a great accomplishment or feat that attested to the player's special ability.

This book is about players cut down in their prime before they were afforded the opportunity to play 15 seasons and make a run at 3,000 hits or 500 home runs or other benchmarks of greatness. These players tasted glory, but will never have a plaque in Cooperstown dedicated to them. They were going to be great, but their careers were prematurely, sometimes cruelly, ended by sore arms, injuries, illnesses and accidents.

This book is about what might have been. It is about promise and achievement, not career fulfilling accomplishments.

Seventeen players are featured. Their careers spanned almost the entire century, beginning with Smoky Joe Wood and ending with Kirby Puckett. We speculate about what might have been had they been able to enjoy a full, uninterrupted career. We have reviewed many accounts to capture observations about their performances, and their injuries or illnesses.

Pete Reiser's star shone brightly in the glorious 1941 season. In that year, he was the equal of Williams and DiMaggio, but his penchant for running into walls aborted his journey to Cooperstown. Herb Score was a worthy successor to Rapid Robert Feller, but a Gil McDougald line drive shelved Score's baseball career. Tony Conigliaro hit 100 home runs before his 25th birthday, more than anyone else in history, but a Jack Hamilton fastball prevented him from reaching milestones other sluggers were able to reach. We recall the brilliance of Mark Fidrych in 1976. How dominant might Detroit have been in 1984 had Fidrych joined Jack Morris, Dan Petry and Milt Wilcox? What might St. Louis's Gas House Gang have accomplished had Paul Dean's arm stayed healthy? What about the Reds in the early 1950s with

Ewell Blackwell pitching like he did in 1947? Might the Kansas City Royals, instead of the Yankees, have gone to the World Series in three successive years in the late 1970s had double no-hit Steve Busby not torn his rotator cuff?

As we consider Tony Oliva, Smoky Joe Wood and Vean Gregg, we wonder what else they might have achieved had fate not intervened. J.R. Richard was overpowering, Johnny Beazley was thrilling in the clutch and Kirby Puckett was a consistent model. Hal Trosky was a slugger in the Jimmie Foxx and Hank Greenberg mold, but illness interrupted his career. Both Foxx, who played 12 seasons, and Greenberg, who lost four years to the war, achieved enough to gain the attention of the electors and are enshrined in the Hall. Trosky is not. Puckett someday may be.

We know that Lyman Bostock's brief but promising career was not long enough to assess, nor can any conclusion be reached with regard to Boston's Boo Ferriss, whose two seasons of glory were as impressive as any two seasons of most pitchers in the Hall of Fame. The Yankees with Thurman Munson were able to win two world titles in 1977 and 1978, but his death ended the string.

This book is about promises and great expectations shattered by fate. The players profiled in this book deserve recognition for their accomplishments before their careers were cut short. Some of these players have become obscure to today's fans and the recognition they receive here is overdue. Their stories of stardom gone awry contain joy, agony, despair, courage and finally, an aura of mystery, for each of them left the game too soon, with an unknown amount of unfilled potential. Perhaps the pages of this book will return some of the glory they tasted all too briefly.

1 THE KANSAS CYCLONE

SMOKY JOE WOOD

> "There's no man alive who can throw harder than Smoky Joe Wood."
> WALTER JOHNSON

It was a classic encounter, played on September 6, 1912, in Boston's new stadium, Fenway Park. The contest, like popular boxing matches of that era, had a reigning champion, Walter Johnson of the Washington Nationals, pitted against a challenger, Smoky Joe Wood of the Boston Red Sox. Both pitchers stemmed from Kansas; Johnson from Humboldt, Wood from Ness City. Newspapers gave all the statistics of each competitor prior to the game: height, weight, arm span and general physical attributes as well as pitching numbers.

Early in the 1912 season, Johnson had a brilliant 16-game winning streak that went from July 3 to August 23. By September 6, Joe Wood was challenging that record. Wood had already won 13 straight, and 16 or more in a row seemed within reach. In order to pit Wood directly against Johnson and give the Big Train a chance to protect his record, Boston manager Jake Stahl moved Wood up in the pitching rotation from Saturday to Friday.

The fans jammed into Fenway Park early, and, as was usual then when the seats were filled, spectators were allowed to stand in the outfield behind ropes and along the sidelines of the infield. The crowd was so large that the players bench was abandoned, and the teams sat on chairs next to the foul lines. The park was packed an hour before the opening pitch, and, while there was no accurate attendance count, the crowd greatly exceeded the seating capacity of Fenway Park. People swarmed the field, so there was little room for the rival pitchers to warm up.

Johnson seemed to have things under better control than Wood early

Joe Wood and Walter Johnson. Both pitchers won 16 consecutive games in 1912
(NATIONAL BASEBALL HALL OF FAME LIBRARY, COOPERSTOWN, NY).

in the game. Washington loaded the bases against Wood in the third, but
Smoky Joe blazed a third strike past right fielder Danny Moeller to end the
inning. The Nats had runners on second in scoring position in the sixth,
eighth and ninth, but each time Wood retired the side without runs scoring, twice with strikeouts.

Boston, however, struck swiftly in the sixth inning when Tris Speaker hit a drive into the crowd in left field for a double. Duffy Lewis, who followed Speaker, hit a fly ball to right which the right fielder, Danny Moeller, barely touched, and the ball fell into the crowd for a run-scoring double. It proved to be the game's only run.

Washington						Boston					
	AB	R	H	PO	A		AB	R	H	PO	A
Milan, cf	3	0	1	0	0	Hooper, rf	4	0	0	0	0
Foster, 3b	3	0	1	0	0	Yerkes, 3b	4	0	1	0	0
Moeller, rf	4	0	0	3	0	Speaker, cf	2	1	1	2	0
Gandil, 1b	4	0	0	9	1	Lewis, lf	2	0	1	2	0
LaPorte, 2b	4	0	2	1	4	Gardner, 3b	3	0	1	0	1
Moran, lf	3	0	0	2	0	Engle, 1b	3	0	1	10	1
McBride, ss	4	0	1	4	2	Wagner, ss	3	0	0	2	4
Ainsmith, c	2	0	0	5	1	Cady, c	3	0	0	10	2
Johnson, p	3	0	1	0	2	Wood, p	3	0	0	1	5
TOTALS	30	0	6	24	10	TOTALS	27	1	5	27	13

												R	H	E
Washington	0	0	0	0	0	0	0	0	0	—	0	6	0
Boston	0	0	0	0	0	1	0	0	x	—	1	5	0

RBI — Lewis. Two Base Hits — McBride, LaPorte, Speaker, Lewis. DP — Wood, Wagner and Engle. Left on Base — Boston 4, Washington 8. Time of game 1:46. Umpires — Connelly and Hart.

	IP	H	R	ER	BB	SO
Wood	9	6	0	0	1	9
Johnson	8	5	1	1	1	5

Wood in 1912 had one of the greatest seasons any pitcher has recorded in the twentieth century. The *New York Herald Tribune* hailed him as "practically unbeatable — for one season." He was at the top or near the top in almost all pitching categories. He led the league in wins with 34 (Johnson had 32); his 34–5 record was the league's best winning percentage, .872; his 35 complete games led the league, as did his 10 shutouts.

He finished second to Johnson in four categories: strikeouts, 303 to 258; strikeouts per nine innings, 7.24 to 6.75; fewest hits per nine innings, 6.33 to 6.99; and earned run average, 1.39 to 1.91. He ranked third in innings pitched (344), and in total games pitched (43).

Between May 29 and September 15 of that year, his record was 24–1. A 4–3 loss to Eddie Plank on July 4 was his only defeat in almost four months. Wood even matched Johnson's 16 consecutive wins. His streak was broken on September 20, two days after the Red Sox had clinched the pennant. Detroit rookie Tex Covington outpitched Wood, 6–4, to end the spectacular streak. Wood was shaky from the beginning of the game and walked four straight batters at one point. Despite his wildness, it was rookie shortstop Marty Krug's dropped pop fly with the bases loaded that scored three runs and cost Smoky Joe the game and the streak. Wood won his next three starts and would have exceeded Rube Marquard's record of 19 straight had it not been for Krug's miscue. Marquard's record still stands.

When a reporter asked Walter Johnson whether he could throw harder than the Kansas Cyclone, as Wood was often called, the Big Train replied, "Can I throw harder than Joe Wood? Listen, my friend, there's no man alive who can throw harder than Smoky Joe Wood."

Joe Wood was born October 25, 1889, in Kansas City, Missouri, as the second son to John F. and Rebecca Stephens Wood. They named him Howard Ellsworth.

His father, a lawyer, was restless and moved his family often. He moved first to Chicago and then to Ouray, a small town in southwestern Colorado. The town was in the real "West" near such places as Lizard Head and Slumgullion Gulch, where at the turn of the century the stage coach, drawn by six horses with two guards sitting on top protecting the gold shipment from the mines, came by daily. John Wood took his two sons, Harley, the elder, and Howard, to the circus one day. The two youngsters were so impressed by two circus clowns that they decided to adopt the names of the clowns, and Harley became Pete and Howard became Joe.

Pete and Joe's father never settled down. He joined the Klondike gold rush in 1897 as a prospector but found no gold in the Yukon. Later, he prospected in Nevada and California and found no gold there either. With the gold fever finally out of his system, John Wood in 1906 moved his family to Ness City, Kansas, about 60 miles north of Dodge, where he resumed his legal career as a lawyer for the Missouri Pacific and Santa Fe railroads.

Young Smoky Joe, by now 16 years old, joined the town's baseball team. Town team baseball was popular in Kansas in the early part of the century. Every small town and most rural communities had ball teams. Ness City played such teams as Ellis, Bazine, High Point, Ransom and Scott City. The Sunday afternoon baseball game was a huge event and most of the community attended. Joe Wood was by at least two years the youngest member of the Ness City team, and he was the pitcher simply because he threw harder than anyone else. When he wasn't pitching, he played in the infield, mostly at shortstop.

In September 1906, a barnstorming team called the Bloomer Girls from Des Moines came to Ness City to play the local team in a highly touted ballgame. The game was advertised for weeks. A great crowd was on hand to witness the Ness City victory over the Bloomer Girls.

After the game, the manager of the Bloomer Girls offered Wood $20 to join his team as an infielder. Twenty dollars was a lot of money in 1906 to young Joe, but he did not want to join a girls' team. The manager persuaded him to sign on by informing him that the team already had four males wearing wigs who played regularly. When Wood refused to wear a wig, the manager told young Joe not to worry because his youthful face would let him get by without one. He did, until he rifled a throw from short to first. Then the word got out that the "girl" playing short was really a boy. Since all the games were exhibitions, nobody seemed concerned.

A few years later, Hall of Famer Rogers Hornsby also got his start as a professional ballplayer by playing for the Bloomer Girls.

Joe Wood's first real start in organized baseball came in 1907 at the age of 17. Belden Hill, who ran the Cedar Rapids team of the Three I League, visited the University of Kansas to sign a young pitcher named Lefty Holmes of Pittsburg, Kansas. Holmes' roommate was Harley Wood, Joe's brother. On learning that Hill was connected with professional baseball, he told him about his younger brother's baseball talents. Harley's story convinced Hill, and he gave him a contract to mail to young Joe. Joe signed the contract and had his father sign it and returned it to Belden Hill with a thank-you note expressing appreciation for the opportunity to play professional baseball.

When Hill discovered that Cedar Rapids did not have space on its roster for Wood, he turned the contract over to his friend Doc Andrews of Hutchinson, Kansas, of the Western Association. Joe Wood and his family were thrilled because Hutchinson was only 90 miles from Ness City.

Wood started as an infielder for Hutchinson, but he soon became a pitcher because of the way he threw the ball to first. He won 18 games for Hutchinson in 1907 at the age of 17. After the season, Andrews sold Wood to George Tebeau of the Kansas City Blues of the American Association for $1,000. Despite a disappointing 7–12 record in 1908, Wood's fastball and his 2.26 ERA were so impressive that before the completion of the season the Boston Red Sox decided to pick up the 18-year-old pitcher. He got into six games and finished with a 1–1 record in 1908, his first American League season.

It was soon after his arrival in Boston that Wood was given the nickname Smoky Joe (not Smokey as it is often written) by *Boston Post* sportswriter Paul Shannon. Shannon watched Wood throw on the sideline one day and remarked, "Gee, that fellow really throws smoke." From then on, he was known as Smoky Joe.

In his first two years with Boston, Wood gave no indication of what was to come. In 1909 Wood posted an 11–7 record, helping the Red Sox to a third-place finish, 10 games behind the pennant-winning Detroit Tigers. The Sox had finished fifth the year before. His earned run average in his first full major league season was an impressive 2.37. In 1910, young Joe Wood won 12 and lost 13 with a fine 1.68 ERA. In his second big league season, he had the seventh-best earned run average in the league.

Not only was Wood's mound work impressive but he also retained the fielding skills of a shortstop, his former position. Joe was quick in knocking down hard-hit balls up the middle, retrieving them and throwing runners out. His quickness and agility discouraged hitters from trying to bunt the ball. Smoky Joe was referred to as a bunt hawk because of his fielding finesse. Joe backed up all plays at every base he could reach in time. He was particularly adept at retrieving errant throws from the outfield and nailing baserunners trying to advance.

Wood was a hard worker with a passion for the game. Often in pregame warmups, he moved about continuously, chasing fly balls in the outfield, fielding ground balls at shortstop and flinging the ball across the diamond to first base. The player on first frequently complained about the velocity of his throws. Wood even would get behind the plate sometimes. He loved to fire the ball from home plate to second base. He could throw and he loved to do it. He threw so much that a remark frequently heard around the dugout was that "someday he will throw his arm away." Smoky Joe Wood had three great seasons before it happened.

In 1911, he broke the twenty victory level for the first time. He finished the season with a 23–17 record. He became the ace of the Red Sox staff and finished behind Cleveland's Vean Gregg and Washington's Walter Johnson in the ERA category with a nifty 2.02. He fanned 231 batters in 277 innings; only Ed Walsh fanned more. His top performance of the 1911 season occurred against the St. Louis Browns on July 29 when he no-hit the Browns in a 5–0 win. He struck out 12 batters.

St. Louis	AB	R	H	PO	A	Boston	AB	R	H	PO	A
Shotten, cf	4	0	0	1	0	Hooper, rf	4	0	0	0	0
Austin, 3b	4	0	0	1	4	Engle, 1b	4	0	2	8	1
Schweitzer, rf	3	0	0	1	0	Speaker, cf	3	1	1	2	0
LaPorte, 2b	3	0	0	3	2	Wagner, 2b	4	1	0	0	2
Hogan, lf	4	0	0	1	0	Carrigan, c	4	1	1	14	0
Stephens, c	2	0	0	4	2	Gardner, 3b	4	1	1	0	2
Black, 1b	3	0	0	10	2	Riggert, lf	3	0	1	1	0

	AB	R	H	PO	A		AB	R	H	PO	A
Wallace, ss	3	0	0	1	2	Yerkes, ss	3	1	1	1	1
Lake, p	1	0	0	2	5	Wood, p	3	0	0	1	2
Criss, ph	1	0	0	0	0	TOTALS	32	5	7	27	8
TOTALS	25	0	0	24	15						

Criss batted for Lake in 9th.

				R	H	E
St. Louis	0 0 0	0 0 0	0 0 0	—	0	0	4
Boston	0 1 0	0 1 2	0 1 x	—	5	7	0

Errors — LaPorte, Stephens, Black, Wallace. Two-base hit — Engle. Three-base hit — Gardner. Home run — Speaker. Sacrifice hit — Stephens. Stolen base — Gardner. Double play — Yerkes and Engle; Austin, LaPorte and Black. Left on base- Boston 5; St. Louis 2. Time —1:48. Umpire — O'Loughlin.

	IP	H	R	BB	SO
Wood	9	0	0	2	12
Lake	8	7	5	2	4

The 1912 season is memorable for Boston baseball for several reasons. Its American League team that previously had been known as the Pilgrims, Americans and Puritans was renamed the Red Sox and moved into a brand-new home. The team had been playing at the Huntington Avenue Grounds in a 9,000-seat facility built on an old carnival site in 1901 when Ban Johnson, the first president of the American League, awarded Boston an American League franchise. Construction of a new ballpark commenced in 1911 in a marshy area known as "The Fens," and it was ready for the opening of the 1912 season. Club President John I. Taylor (whose father, Charles Taylor, was said to have bought the club for his son to give him something to do) named the field Fenway Park in honor of its location. Fenway Park had an irregular contour because of the space on which it was constructed. It featured a single-decked grandstand. It had wooden bleachers in left field, a wooden pavilion in right and wooden bleachers in extreme right and center fields. There was a ten-foot embankment in front of the left-field fence which in time became known as "Duffy's Cliff" in honor of Duffy Lewis, who learned to play the cliff with great finesse. The seating capacity of the park was 27,000.

The quality of the Red Sox team was a second reason why 1912 is memorable in Boston. Tris Speaker hit .383 to finish third in hitting, trailing only Ty Cobb's .410 and Joe Jackson's .395. Speaker led the league in home runs with 10. The Gray Eagle was exceptional in the field, finishing second in the league with 372 putouts and throwing out an American League record–tying 35 base runners. (Chuck Klein holds the National League record with 44.)

It was on the mound where the Red Sox shone. They had three 20-game winners: Buck O'Brien at 20–13, rookie Hugh Bedient with a 20–9 record and Smoky Joe Wood with an unbelievable 34–5 mark. Wood literally overwhelmed American League batters. He started 38 games, pitched in relief in five others, and finished the season with an ERA of 1.91. Only Johnson's 1.39 was better. In 344 innings, Wood fanned 258 and led the league in shutouts with 10. Wood was so effective that Duffy Lewis said, "Joe Wood in 1912 was the best pitcher I ever saw pitch." Teammate Harry Hooper agreed: "I've seen a lot of great pitching in my lifetime but never anything to compare with Wood in 1912."

The Red Sox, with a 105–47 record, won the pennant by 14 games over Walter Johnson and the Washington Senators. No other Boston team has ever won as many games as did Wood's team in 1912.

In the senior circuit, the Giants of John McGraw won their second consecutive pennant, almost matching the Red Sox by winning 103 and losing 48, beating Honus Wagner's Pirates by 10 games. The two teams were ready for a great World Series that would feature Christy Mathewson, who had already won 312 big-league games in his career and had won 30 or more four times.

The Boston team was eager to show off its young sensation with the romantic-sounding name, Smoky Joe Wood. The Giants' team batting average was .286, the best in baseball, contrasted to the Red Sox, who batted a respectable .277.

The series opened in the Polo Grounds, October 8. Wood was matched against Jeff Tesreau, who had gone 17–7 during the season but who had led the league with a 1.91 ERA. The Giants took the lead in the third inning with two runs, but the Red Sox, after scoring one in the sixth, came back with three in the seventh to take a lead they were able to hold. The Giants scored one run in the bottom of the ninth, but Wood was able to put down the Giants, and the Red Sox drew first blood, with Smoky Joe fanning 11.

The second game ended in a 6–6 tie when, after 11 innings, the game was called because of darkness. Mathewson went the distance for New York but was unable to win because his teammates committed five errors, allowing the Red Sox to score four unearned runs. In the third game, New York evened the series with a 2–1 victory behind Rube Marquard's brilliant pitching. Josh Devore made a great catch with two out and two on in the bottom of the ninth. In game four, the series moved back to New York, with Joe Wood again beating Jeff Tesreau, this time 3–1. Wood fanned eight and drove in one of the runs with a single. Boston narrowly beat Mathewson in game five, 2–1, but the Giants bounced back in game six behind Rube Marquard to win 5–2.

Wood had a sensational 1912 season, winning 37 games, including three World Series victories (NATIONAL BASEBALL HALL OF FAME LIBRARY, COOPERSTOWN, NY).

Game seven was played October 15, and again Wood was pitted against Tesreau. This time the Giants got to Wood in the first inning, scoring six runs and knocking the Kansas Cyclone out of the box. The Giants won the game 11–4, setting the stage for a dramatic conclusion to the 1912 World Series to be played in Boston. For the first time since the first World Series, there was an eighth game, and the Giants' ace was ready to win the series for the New York team. Mathewson was well rested and faced big right-handed Hugh Bedient, who had handcuffed the Giants in the fifth game, holding them to just three hits.

Bedient matched Mathewson slant for slant for the first seven innings. The Red Sox, down 1–0, tied the score in the bottom of the seventh. In the eighth, Manager Jake Stahl made a pitching change for the Red Sox, bringing in once again his ace pitcher who was nine days shy of his 23rd birthday. At last, the sensational young righthander was matched against his famous rival, Christy Mathewson. Both the eighth and ninth innings were scoreless. In the top of the tenth, the Giants scored and seemed poised to claim the championship. The Red Sox, trying to come back against the crafty Mathewson who had held them to eight hits, began their inning with pinch-hitter Clyde Engel batting for Wood. Engel sent a routine fly ball to Fred Snodgrass, who misjudged the ball and dropped it for a two-base error. Snodgrass partially redeemed himself with a great catch, and Yerkes followed with a walk of Mathewson. Speaker then hit a foul ball between Fred Merkle and catcher Chief Meyers, and unbelievably the ball fell between them. Speaker, given life, then singled home Engle with the tying run. Now the Red Sox had the opportunity to seal the win and the championship. After an intentional walk to Duffy Lewis, Larry Gardner lifted a long fly to right field. Yerkes tagged and scored the winning run. Abetted by the Giants' sloppiness in the field, the Red Sox won their second World Series. Smoky Joe Wood won his third game of the Series, a feat only five have equalled since.

When the wins were tallied after the series, Wood's overall record for 1912 was 37 victories and only 5 losses, one of the finest seasons in the history of baseball. No one with 30 wins has ever topped his winning percentage. Smoky Joe Wood seemed destined to take his place alongside the all-time great pitchers of the game.

Walter Johnson said during the 1912 season that he feared Wood would hurt his arm because of the "snap ball" he threw. Wood was known for the remarkable strength and size of his pitching hand and wrist, and he delivered the ball with terrific wrist snap, which put great movement on his fastball, and it enabled him to throw a devastating, almost impossible to hit, curveball. Wood contended that he had arrived at his pitching style naturally, that no one had taught him anything, and he could curve a baseball when he was 7 years old. Johnson believed that Joe should alter his delivery to place less strain on his wrist and arm.

In the spring of 1913, Joe's spirits were high; he expected to have a great year. Then it happened. With typical exuberance, Wood sought to field a ground ball on wet grass, slipped and fell on his right thumb. He broke it. It was placed in a cast for three weeks. In Wood's own words, "I don't know whether I tried to pitch too soon after that, or whether maybe something happened to my shoulder at the same time. But whatever it was, I never pitched again without a terrific amount of pain in my right shoulder. Never again." He had injured more than his thumb; something had torn in his right shoulder as well. When he tried to pitch, the zip was gone from his fastball. It didn't hop like it used to when people referred to his "snap ball." He won 11 games in 1913 while losing only 5, and he struck out 9 men a game. But the pain worsened in his shoulder sufficiently during the season that it kept him from pitching regularly.

In the 1914 season, Wood pitched even less — just 113 innings — and struck out only 67 batters, winning 9 and losing 3 with a 2.62 ERA.

In the 1915 season, Wood improved slightly. He pitched 157 innings, compiling a fine 15–5 record with an excellent 1.49 ERA. However, his arm now hurt so badly after each game he pitched that it would be days before he could even lift his arm. After the season, he was desperate. He had been examined by doctors the previous three years, but no one had the answer. Being told that a chiropractor in New York could help him, every week in the winter of 1915-16 Wood commuted to New York for treatment. It was, as Wood put it, "very hush hush — an unmarked office behind locked doors — because in those days it wasn't legal for a chiropractor to practice."

After each treatment, the chiropractor wanted Joe to throw as long and as hard as he could. So Wood went to Columbia University where he worked with baseball coach Andy Coakley. Wood threw hard until the pain was greater than he could endure. "After an hour I couldn't lift my arm as high as my belt," Joe later reported. "Had to use my left hand to put my right into my coat pocket. And if I'd go to a movie in the evening I couldn't get my right arm up high enough to put it on the arm rest."

His arm problem kept him from playing in 1916. He retired to the farm, but he soon became restless. He was only 26 years old, about the age most ballplayers reach their prime. He pondered if his career had gone up in smoke. He vowed to keep that from happening. He put up a trapeze in his attic and hung on it for hours to stretch his arm, hoping that it would help bring it back. It didn't.

He then decided, "Doggone it, I was a ballplayer, not just a pitcher." He recalled that he had hit .290 the year he had won 34 games. Maybe he could come back as an outfielder. He called his best friend, Tris Speaker, now with the Cleveland Indians. Speaker put in a word for Wood with Cleveland's management, and on February 24, 1917, the Indians conditionally purchased Wood from Boston for a price reportedly ranging from $5,000 to $15,000. *The Baseball Encyclopedia* reports $15,000. The purchase of Wood by the Indians gave Smoky Joe what he wanted: a chance to play baseball again. He reported to spring training and tried to impress the club with his desire to succeed. "I played in the infield during fielders' practice, I shagged flies in the outfield, I was ready to pinch-run, to pinch-hit — I'd have carried the water bucket if they had water boys in baseball," Wood told Lawrence S. Ritter, author of *The Glory of Their Times*.

While Wood pitched in five games for Cleveland in 1917, it was the following year that he launched a second career as an outfielder. He played 95 games in the outfield and 19 at second base. He also played a few games at first base, demonstrating rare versatility while batting a respectable .296. He was the regular left fielder playing next to his friend Tris Speaker and helping the Indians finish just two games behind his former team, the Red Sox.

In 1919, he lost his starting position, but he still got into 72 games, hitting .255. Speaker replaced Lee Fohl as manager and the Indians again finished a strong second, this time trailing the infamous Black Sox by only four games.

He stayed with the Indians the next spring, appearing in 61 games and finishing with a .270 batting average. He was in the World Series for the first time since his Red Sox had defeated Mathewson and the Giants in that memorable 1912 Series. In 1912, he was the star hurler; in 1920, he was a utility outfielder. Yet in the World Series, Wood started three games ahead of the regular right fielder, Elmer Smith. His friend, Tris Speaker, had not forgotten him. The Indians won the Series, five games to two. It was the following year that the last best-of-nine World Series was played.

Wood's final two seasons in major league baseball were impressive. Unlike many veterans who barely hang on in their final year, Joe Wood in 194 at-bats hit a team-leading .366 and batted in 60 base runners, a very high total for so few at-bats. The Indians again were contenders, but finished second to the Yankees. So Joe returned for one final season.

This time, remarkably, he returned to a starting role, playing 142 games and driving in a team-leading 92 runs. His final batting average was .297. This ended Smoky Joe's major league career, and he was not yet 33 years old.

Wood believed he could have played the outfield another "four or five years. But in those days, we'd come off a road trip of two or three weeks and my boys wouldn't know who I was."

When he was offered a job as baseball coach at Yale University, he accepted. It was the beginning of a long and successful second career that spanned two decades, from 1923 until 1943. His players at Yale included the famed Albie Booth, Larry Kelley, Bruce Caldwell, and his own son, Joe, Jr., who briefly appeared with the Red Sox in 1944. His other two sons, Stephen and Robert, both played college ball for Colgate University.

After 20 years of coaching at the collegiate level, Joe Wood retired. He moved to Los Angeles and managed a golf range for his brother. In 1950, he came back East and shared his time between New Haven, Connecticut, and Pikes County, Pennsylvania. He became an avid golfer, shooting regularly in the low seventies and even on occasion flirting with the sixties. He won a number of tournaments in Connecticut, New York and Pennsylvania.

Wood was a remarkable athlete. During his baseball years, he spent time playing pocket billiards and displayed unusual talent. Benny Allen, world's champion pocket billiards player in the early 1900s, encouraged Wood to go on the touring circuit. Charlie Peterson, famous trick shot artist, thought that Wood had the finest pool stroke he had ever seen. Wood was also a talented swimmer, rifleman, skater, horseman and fisherman.

But baseball was always Wood's game. In retirement, he helped with local baseball in Pennsylvania. He was coach of the Welcome Lake Honor Brand team of the Delaware Valley League, and he made guest appearances at numerous baseball sponsored events. To the end, he maintained his interest in baseball. He always attended Old Timers' games. His final appearance at a Yale baseball game was in 1981. He watched Ron Darling pitching for Yale lose a 1–0, 12-inning NCAA playoff game to St. John's University. Pitching for the Red Storm was Frank Viola. At that game, the venerable baseball writer for *The New Yorker Magazine*, Roger Angell, had the opportunity to interview the 91-year-old Wood. Angell said something admiringly about the watch Smoky Joe checked while waiting for the game to begin. Wood said, "I've had that watch for 68 years. I always carried it in my vest pocket, back when we wore vests." The watch had a faded inscription on the back. While worn and hard to read, it said:

Presented to Joe Wood
by his friend A.E. Smith in
appreciation of his splendid
pitching which brought the
WORLD CHAMPIONSHIP
to Boston in 1912.

Angell asked Smoky Joe who A.E. Smith was. Wood answered, "A manufacturer."

There have been attempts to persuade Baseball's Old Timers Committee to select Smoky Joe Wood for induction into the Hall of Fame. Frank Williams and Robert K. Wood have compiled statistics and facts about Wood's career, organized them and presented them to the committee. They worked out statistical comparisons and analyses with other players in the Hall. The most meaningful comparison is with Addie Joss, who died from tubercular meningitis in April 1911, after nine seasons in the majors. Joss finished with a 160–97 win-loss record. Joss was selected for the Hall in 1978. Dizzy Dean, at best, had nine productive years as a pitcher, winning 150 while losing 83. Wood, by comparison, spent seven years as a productive pitcher and closed his career with 116 wins and 57 losses, compiling a remarkable .623 winning percentage and a 2.03 career ERA. Walter Johnson's career earned run average, for example, was 2.17, for many more years of course. Christy Mathewson's career winning percentage was .665, similar to Joe Wood's .671.

Wood also played the field for Cleveland for five additional years, but as a relative journeyman. His stint in the outfield enabled him to become only the second person to play in the World Series both as a pitcher and outfielder. The first was George Herman Ruth.

Each time Wood's name has been proposed, the Hall of Fame Old-Timers' Committee has declined to name Wood. His career was too short, and his overall statistics were not impressive enough. Bob Lemon, infielder-outfielder turned pitcher, in a relatively short career won 90 more games than Wood. Lemon did make the Hall of Fame.

However, at age 95, recognition of another kind came to Smoky Joe Wood. On January 16, 1985, Yale President A. Bartlett Giamatti traveled to Wood's home in New Haven to confer upon the wheelchair-bound Wood an Honorary Yale Doctorate of Humane Letters. This gesture of respect moved Joe Wood to tears. His son Bob leaned over and said softly, "Just say thank you, Dad."

The one-time pitching great wiped away tears and said, "Thank you, sir." Then someone placed a Red Sox cap on his head. A few months later, on Saturday night, June 26, 1985, Joe Wood died at the Southview Convalescent Home. He was 95.

If the ghost of Tris Speaker, Wood's best baseball friend, and that of Walter Johnson, his great pitching rival, attended the small funeral, they undoubtedly recalled some of those great pitching duels of 1911 and 1912 between the Big Train and Smoky Joe, and perhaps they also replayed the finale of the great World Series of 1912. They probably felt the same as writer Lee Goodwin when he wrote that Smoky Joe Wood was "the best baseball player never to make the Hall of Fame."

JOE WOOD

Born Oct. 25, 1889, Kansas City, Mo.   Died July 25, 1985, West Haven, Conn.
Batted right, threw right.

Year	Team	W–L	Pct.	ERA	G	GS	CG	IP	H	BB	SO	ShO
1907	Hutch.	18–11	.621	N/A	29	N/A	N/A	196	N/A	97	224	N/A
West. Asso.												
1908	Bos AL	1–1	.500	2.38	6	2	1	22⅔	14	16	11	1
1909	Bos AL	11–7	.611	2.21	24	19	13	158⅔	121	43	88	4
1910	Bos AL	12–13	.480	1.68	35	17	14	197⅔	155	56	145	3
1911	Bos AL	23–17	.575	2.02	44	33	25	276⅔	226	76	231	5
1912	Bos AL	34–5	*.872	1.91	43	38	*35	344	267	82	258	*10
1913	Bos AL	11–5	.688	2.29	23	18	12	145⅔	120	61	123	1
1914	Bos AL	9–3	.750	2.62	18	14	11	131⅓	94	34	67	1
1915	Bos AL	15–5	*.750	*1.49	25	16	10	157⅓	120	44	63	3
1916	Did not play.											
1917	Cle AL	0–1	.000	3.45	5	1	0	15⅔	17	7	2	0
1919	Cle AL	0–0	.000	0.00	1	0	0	.2	0	0	0	0
1920	Cle AL	0–0	.000	22.50	1	0	0	2	4	2	1	0
Major League												
Totals		116–57	.671	2.03	225	158	121	1434.1	1138	421	989	28
11 yrs.												

*Indicates led league.

World Series Record

Year	Team	W–L	Pct.	ERA	G	GS	CG	IP	H	BB	SO	ShO
1912	Bos AL	3–1	.750	3.68	4	3	2	22	27	3	21	0

Record as Outfielder

Year	Team	G	AB	R	H	2B	3B	HR	RBI	BB	SB	Ave.	Slug.
1918	Cle AL	119	422	41	125	22	4	5	66	36	8	.296	.403
1919	Cle AL	72	192	30	49	10	5	1	27	32	3	.255	.375
1920	Cle AL	61	137	25	37	11	2	1	30	25	1	.270	.401
1921	Cle AL	66	194	32	71	16	5	4	60	25	2	.366	.562
1922	Cle AL	142	505	74	150	33	8	8	92	50	5	.297	.442
Major League													
Totals		460	1450	202	432	92	24	19	275	167	19	.298	.433
5 yrs.													

World Series Record as Outfielder

Year	Team	G	AB	R	H	2B	3B	HR	RBI	BB	SB	Ave.	Slug.
1920	Cle AL	4	10	2	2	1	0	0	0	1	0	.200	.300

2 HITTING THE WALL

PISTOL PETE REISER

> "He was one hell of a ballplayer. They talk
> about me getting into the Hall of Fame.
> If he didn't get hurt, he was a lock for that.
> He was as good a player as Musial."
> PEE WEE REESE

The talented Pistol Pete Reiser was the last piece of the puzzle needed to turn the Brooklyn Dodgers from a contender into a pennant winner. Dodgers President Larry MacPhail had begun rebuilding the perennial second-division "Bums" into heroes by acquiring slugging first baseman Dolph Camilli from the Philadelphia Phillies in 1938. The following year, MacPhail made starting shortstop Leo Durocher player-manager, and picked up hard-hitting outfielder Dixie Walker on waivers from the Detroit Tigers and pitcher Whitlow Wyatt from the Cleveland Indians.

The results were immediate. The Dodgers climbed from seventh to third place, finishing 12-and-a-half games behind the pennant-winning Cincinnati Reds. It was Brooklyn's first winning season since 1932.

Additional deals cemented what by 1940 was becoming an outstanding team. First, in a major move, MacPhail got 1937 Triple Crown winner Joe (Ducky) Medwick, who, in 1939, had hit .332 with 117 runs batted in, and Curt Davis, a 22-game winner in 1939, from the St. Louis Cardinals. In the trade, he gave up only outfielder Ernie Koy, three no-names (pitchers Carl Doyle and Sam Nahem and infielder-outfielder Bert Haas) and $125,000 in cash. The penny-pinching Cardinals were once more unloading high-priced players and hoping to replace them with cheaper and younger players from their vast farm system. The hard-hitting Medwick helped the Dodgers move up to second place in 1940.

Then, in November of that year, the Dodgers got Kirby Higbe from

Philadelphia. Higbe had toiled 283 innings for the Phillies in 1940, losing 19 games but leading the National League with 137 strikeouts.

Early in the 1941 season, MacPhail solidified the Dodger infield by acquiring Billy Herman, an All-Star second baseman, from the Chicago Cubs.

Yet, with all the dealing for veterans, the missing piece of the puzzle for Brooklyn was provided by Baseball Commissioner Kenesaw Mountain Landis. In 1938, Landis completed an investigation of illegally signed, assigned and covered-up players. As a result of the investigation, he declared 91 St. Louis Cardinal farmhands free agents.

One of them was Harold Patrick (Pete) Reiser, a St. Louis native and minor league shortstop. When the Dodgers learned that the 18-year-old Reiser was to be freed from the Cardinal chain, an old Dodger scout, Ted McGrew, offered Reiser $100 to sign. Having received nothing to sign with the Cardinals, $100 must have looked like a lot of money. Reiser jumped at the opportunity and signed on to be one of "dem Bums."

Reiser played at Superior in the Northern League in 1938 and hit .302. On the basis of that performance, the Dodgers brought him to spring training in 1939. Reiser's debut in a game situation came on March 21 against the team that originally signed him, the St. Louis Cardinals. He hit a home run his first time at bat with two men on base and then singled twice and walked. The home run he belted in his debut was off Curt Davis, the Cardinal who would win 22 games in 1939 before being traded to Brooklyn.

The next day against the Reds, young Pete was even better. He hit two home runs and two singles, batted in four runs and scored three. Pat McDonough wrote this glowing report of young Reiser in the *Sporting News*: "Fiction and movie writers wouldn't dare to put on paper the feats a young rookie in the Brooklyn Dodger camp has accomplished in his first two days in a major league line-up."

To continue his cannonade, Reiser walloped a home run in his first time up against the Detroit Tigers' ace curveballer, Tommy Bridges. The first time up against the New York Yankees, he hit a home run off Lefty Gomez. It was an incredible string.

Duly impressed, the cross-town Yankees offered $100,000 and five players for him. The Dodgers refused and sent Reiser to Elmira in the Eastern League to develop further. And develop he did. He batted .301 in 38 games and, despite arm injuries that kept him out of action for most of the season, seemed ready for Triple A baseball or even the majors. He was moved up to Montreal for three games in 1940, then went back to Elmira, where he was sensational. He scorched the ball at a .378 clip and stole 28 bases in just 67 games.

Durocher brought the 21-year-old Reiser to Brooklyn in the middle of the 1940 season and put him in the lineup on July 23. The starting Dodger outfield at the time consisted of Joe Vosmik, Dixie Walker and Ducky Medwick, a formidable trio with the bat, if not in the field. But the Dodgers were determined to find a place for young Reiser. Everything about him screamed superstar. He could run, throw, field and hit. He also had a tremendous desire to play the game and had great baseball instincts.

But where to play him? He had played mostly in the infield in the minors, primarily at shortstop, so there was talk of shortstop or second base. But the Dodgers already had promising rookie Pee Wee Reese, a future Hall of Famer, at shortstop.

Although basically positionless, Reiser became a regular within two weeks. Durocher used him in 30 games at third base, 17 in the outfield, and five at shortstop, as Reiser hit .293 in 58 games. Durocher knew that his new protégé belonged in center field. He planned to move Walker from center to right and remove Vosmik from the lineup to make room for young Pete in 1941.

The new Brooklyn Dodgers, the team of the Durocher era, peaked in 1941. Fans now spoke of "dem Bums" affectionately, instead of in disgust. The Dodgers were loaded with talent. On the mound, they had Wyatt, Higbe, Davis, Hugh Casey and Luke (Hot Potato) Hamlin, a 20-game winner in 1939. Camilli was at first, Herman at second, Pee Wee Reese at short and Cookie Lavagetto at third. Mickey Owen was behind the plate. In the outfield, they had Walker in right and Medwick in left. And playing his first full major league season was 22-year-old Pete Reiser in center. Brooklyn didn't breeze to the title in 1941 because the always tough Cardinals pursued them the entire season before finishing three games back. In fact, the Dodgers and Cardinals seesawed between first and second throughout the entire campaign before the Dodgers finally won. Brooklyn won 100 games for the first time in its history.

There were strong individual performances. Wyatt and Higbe each won 22 games, tying for the league lead. Walker hit .311. Medwick chipped in with .318. Camilli led the league with 34 circuit blasts and 120 RBI. Reese proved to be the glue of the infield.

But the key to the team was Pete Reiser. His 1941 season was sensational. He scored a league-leading 117 runs, won the batting title with a .343 average and led the league in doubles (39), triples (17), total bases (299) and slugging average (.558). Despite 50 fewer at-bats, Reiser was barely nosed out in the total hit category by Stan Hack of the Cubs, 186 to 184.

Yet Reiser missed several games due to injuries. On April 23, he was hit on the head with a pitch thrown by Ike Pearson of the Philadelphia Phillies and was sidelined for a week. Reiser was knocked unconscious in the third inning by a fastball that struck him on the right cheek. X-rays revealed no fracture, but the injury left a severe bruise, and the impact was so great that the seams of the ball were imprinted on Pete's cheek. Dr. D. A. McAteer, Jr. said that Reiser would have a "very sore face" and that he would be unable to play again for two weeks. The plastic protective plate covering his cap had saved Reiser from more serious injury, although he was carried off on a stretcher. He actually missed eight games, and returned as a pinch hitter on May 1 and started against Chicago on May 2, going 1-for-4.

Then on May 9 against the Cardinals in a game the Dodgers won 5–4, Reiser was again hurt when he leaped against an iron door exit in center field, 400 feet from the plate, to snare Enos Slaughter's line drive. Reiser suffered a cut on the back and was removed to the hospital for treatment. He left the field under his own power.

This time, Reiser missed five games and returned on Sunday, May 18, going 2-for-4, but the Dodgers lost 7–4 to the Cubs. On May 25, he faced Pearson again. This time he hit a grand slam inside-the-park home run that beat the Phillies. His drive hit the top of the outfield screen in deep center field and dropped to the ground, but not in time to head off the lightning-fast youngster from rounding the bases. This mighty wallop removed any doubt that Reiser would be "gun shy."

Reiser was appropriately selected as the center fielder for the National League All-Stars. While he played the entire game, Reiser was hitless in four at-bats and committed two errors. With victory in its grasp, National Leaguers were disappointed when Ted Williams of the Red Sox ended the contest with a dramatic three-run homer off Claude Passeau of the Cubs in the bottom of the ninth inning in Detroit's Briggs Stadium to win the game, 7–5.

Statistics alone, however, do not tell the story of the Dodgers' young star. He played baseball with such abandon that he was heralded as the new Ty Cobb. He had great speed, a strong and accurate arm, and was intensely aggressive. Few players have ever had a better first full season. American Leaguers in the summer of 1941 witnessed Ted Williams' sensational .406 batting average and Joe DiMaggio's 56-game hitting streak, but National Leaguers hailed a young phenom, romantically nicknamed Pistol Pete, a moniker Reiser had gotten as a youngster from his favorite movie serial, "Two Gun Pete." Reiser clearly was the league's most valuable player, but the award went to the veteran Camilli, who batted .285, 58 points under Reiser's .343, although Camilli hit with more power. At 22 years of age, Pete Reiser had become the youngest player to win a National League batting title. Fourteen years later, Al Kaline of the Tigers would win a batting crown before his 21st birthday to equal Ty Cobb's record as youngest to win a major-league batting crown.

The 1941 World Series against the Yankees was a letdown for the rampaging Dodgers. This Series will always be known as the one in which Hugh Casey's third strike on Tommy Henrich, with two outs in the ninth inning and the Dodgers leading 4–3, eluded catcher Mickey Owen in the fourth game on October 5. Henrich reached first safely on the passed ball. The play opened the gates to a Yankee 7–4 victory, and they won the Series in five games.

Reiser's contributions in the Series were modest. He got four hits in 20 at-bats for a .200 batting average, one hit being a home run.

In 1942, Pistol Pete was out to prove he was not a flash in the pan. He was leading the league in hitting with his average soaring to .374 on June 9. As the season progressed into July, Reiser's average dipped to .348 by July 2. It went up to .361 on July 9, just before the All-Star game.

He once more started the All-Star game, getting one hit in three at-bats. But the American League beat the senior circuit for the seventh time in ten tries, 3–1. Reiser's batting average of .361 was the best on either team.

Reiser was eager to get back to their regular season, since the Dodgers were involved in another run for their money against St. Louis. That July, Reiser was hot, and so were the Dodgers. By July 12, their lead over the Cardinals reached nine games.

Brooklyn moved to St. Louis for a critical three-game series with Reiser's average at a league-leading .359. On July 18, the series opened with a doubleheader. The Cardinals won the opener, 8–5, scoring in the bottom of the eighth. Reiser was hitless in five at-bats. In the second game, the Dodgers and Cardinals went into the eleventh inning tied 6–6 before Enos Slaughter blasted a long drive to center field. Reiser went after it full speed, but the chase ended with a dull thud as he crashed into the concrete wall.

Reiser recalled later, "I caught the ball just before I hit, and that's the last I remember until I woke up in the hospital. Pee Wee told me, though, that I dropped the ball, then picked it up and threw it to him before collapsing. Slaughter got an inside-the-park home run. I don't remember a thing until I woke up the next morning in the hospital, still wearing my uniform."

Roscoe McGowen, writing in the *New York Times*, described the scene: "As Slaughter crossed the plate, an extraordinary crowd of 34,443 went wild, and cushions came sailing from every section onto the field or among spectators in lower sections. The cushion-throwing continued for ten minutes despite frantic appeals over the public address system."

Reiser was taken to the hospital for an X-ray examination to determine the extent of his injuries. He remained in St. Louis until July 22. The report in the *New York Times* said simply that Reiser would "probably sit out the next few games." Cardinals team physician Dr. Bob Hyland saw the game and the crash into the wall. He cautioned Reiser about returning to the line-up early. But Reiser, eager to play, disregarded Hyland's advice and was back in uniform on July 23, just five days after hitting the wall.

He returned to the lineup on July 26 in a doubleheader against Pittsburgh. He went 1-for-3 in the first game, and 2-for-4 in the nightcap as the streaking Dodgers swept the Pirates. He continued to play and was still leading the league in hitting, batting .354 on July 27. Reiser played the next series against the Cardinals, going 2-for-10. He played another series against the Cubs on July 30, August 1 and 2. Reiser did not hit well against Chicago, and his average fell to .343 by August 6.

Trailing Pistol Pete was Ernie Lombardi of the Boston Braves, who eventually overtook Reiser and won the batting title. On July 31, the Dodgers were 70–29 and led the Cardinals by nine-and-a-half games. The prospects of a second pennant and perhaps another batting title for the Pistol were excellent.

Reiser, however, was not well. An August 6 *New York Times* story by McGowen reported, "The condition of Pete Reiser sidelined again is worrying the Dodgers. He's been idle three straight games." The following day, the story was more dire. Club secretary John McDonald advised that Reiser "who had been suffering from headaches and nausea has been placed under the care of Dr. Charles Weeth, Brooklyn physician, and probably will be out of uniform a few days."

While the Dodgers still held a big advantage over the second-place Cardinals, leading by 10 games on August 5, the Reiser injury put a real damper on the club. He did not play from August 3 until August 10, when he returned for a game against the Philadelphia Phillies, won 6–0 by the Dodgers. Reiser was hitless in three at-bats. Meanwhile, the Cardinals got hot. They began to whittle away at the Dodgers' huge lead. By August 20, the lead was down to six-and-a-half games, and Reiser's batting lead over Lombardi was only 13 points, .338 to .325. By August 27, Reiser had almost been overtaken by Enos Slaughter, who was hitting .323 to Reiser's .328.

On August 28, Reiser suffered a torn ligament in his left thigh, and physicians said he might be out for a week. In fact, he did not return until

September 5. On September 10, Lombardi overtook Reiser, and the Cardinals, led by rookie Stan Musial and Enos Slaughter on offense and Johnny Beazley and Mort Cooper on the mound, took over first place by a game and a half. St. Louis went on to win 43 of their final 51 games to win the pennant by two games.

Reiser's return to the diamond after hitting the wall became the source of many problems. He was prone to dizzy spells that affected his play. His batting average plummeted to .310 by season's end, fourth in the league, and he lost the batting crown to Lombardi, who finished with a .330 average. Slaughter, at .318, and Musial, at .315, also overtook him. The only category in which Reiser led the league was stolen bases with 20. What had started out to be a sensational year ended sadly, with the Dodgers, despite 104 victories, watching the World Series rather than playing in it. The victory total was the most ever by a second place finisher.

Since Reiser was only 23, there were high hopes that he would recover fully and lead the talent-laden Dodgers to another flag, but Uncle Sam intervened and drafted Reiser despite his recurring headaches and dizziness. His weight fell to an alarming 135 pounds. Four times he signed papers for a medical discharge, but each time the order was rescinded.

During his Army stay, Reiser played baseball. He played on three teams and paced every one of them to a championship, managing one and playing almost every position on the diamond for all. *New York Times* baseball writer Arthur Daley wrote that Reiser "chased a long fly ball through a hedge guarding the outfield edges and plummeted into a gully just beyond. He damaged his right shoulder badly. So he played the outfield left-handed because he could throw as well left-handed as right-handed."

Reiser returned from the war in 1946. The Dodgers again were a strong club and anticipated a run for the pennant. But sadly, Pete Reiser, who should have been the mainstay of the team, was not the same player. His problems started in spring training when he missed 20 games because he ripped apart some clavicle muscles.

As the injury record of Pistol Pete Reiser mounted, no one doubted that injuries had taken a cruel toll on an unusually talented performer who loved to play the game.

All the same, he batted .277, led the league in stolen bases with a career-high 34 and led his team with 11 home runs. He drove in 73 runners to trail only Dixie Walker's 116 on the Dodgers. Reiser set an all-time record in 1946 when he stole home seven times in eight tries. Rod Carew equaled the feat in 1969. Reiser's statistics for the year were respectable, but they were not up to his standards. His batting eye had been blunted by injuries to his head.

Pete Reiser set a major league record for stealing home in 1946 (Corbis-Bettman Archives, New York, New York).

The Dodgers tied the Cards for the pennant but lost the best-of-three playoff series in a two-game sweep, playing without Reiser, who was injured on September 25 in the first inning of a game against the Phillies. Sliding back into first base, Reiser caught his foot on the bag, and he suffered a fractured fibula in his left leg. Again Reiser was carried off the field on a stretcher.

Reiser played only two more seasons for the Dodgers. The 1947 season was his final decent year. While he played 110 games, he again showed his intensity and competitiveness. Reiser batted .309, tops on the Dodgers, but it was his last .300-plus season. Branch Rickey's great experiment came to pass with the shattering of the color line through the presence of Jack Roosevelt Robinson, who led the National League in stolen bases with 29. Reiser's total of 14 was good for second place in the league.

During the season, Reiser again rammed full tilt into the outfield wall. The accident occurred in Brooklyn at Ebbets Field. It was June 4 and the Dodgers were playing the Pirates. Culley Rikard of the Pirates hit a shot to deep center field, and Reiser arrived at the outfield wall at the same time as the ball. Pete's glove shot up, the ball banged into the pocket with a smack, and Pete's head banged into the concrete wall with a thud. He was carried off the field on a stretcher for the third time in his career.

Dick Young of the *New York Daily News* described the scene in the locker room: "I ran downstairs to the clubhouse and into the trainer's room where Doc Wendler, the team trainer, was examining Pete. Soon, the team doctor arrived, and then a priest. I don't suppose another ballplayer ever has received last rites in a ballpark, and that must be Reiser's distinction, instead of inclusion in Cooperstown."

Another report filed by *Times* writer McGowen indicated that Reiser was "stunned for several minutes and had no recollection later of having caught the ball. He suffered a V-shaped cut on the crown of his head but, according to Dr. Dominick Rossi, who made the initial examination in the clubhouse, had no fracture."

"I don't even remember making the catch," said Reiser in the dressing room, smoking a cigarette while waiting for the ambulance. While Dr. Rossi did not think there was a fracture, Reiser was also examined by Dr. Gerard Casper, a brain specialist, who reported that the patient's pulse was normal while he was sewing up the wound.

Reiser was replaced in center field by Edwin "Duke" Snider, a rookie from Fort Worth who was beginning a career that would not end until 1964. Eventually, Snider, rather than Pistol Pete, was inducted into the Hall of Fame.

The next day, the report from Swedish Hospital was good. Reiser had indeed not suffered any fracture. Instead the report indicated a brain concussion and lacerations.

A week later, Pete Reiser was in the clubhouse before the game, and trainer Harold Wendler asked about his condition. Pete grinned wanly and replied, "I'm just sore all over. My left side, my neck, and my left wrist — everywhere. Haven't had any headaches, but I've had a kind of groggy feeling. Anyway, I guess I'm better, and I hope I'll be all right soon."

Ten days later on June 15, Pete Reiser's bad luck dogged him. Having successfully begged off flying to Johns Hopkins to see a couple of doctors, Reiser was in uniform and standing in center field during practice when pitcher Clyde King, chasing a fungo fly, crashed into Pete and knocked him down. While there was no serious injury, Pete had a little grogginess added to what he already had.

Writers urged Branch Rickey to provide Reiser more protection. "A gravel path along the base of the stands will give Reiser warning that he is in danger by the feel of the gravel under his spikes," claimed one writer.

On that same day, general manager Branch Rickey revealed that the plan to install sponge rubber padding along the wall at Ebbets Field because of Reiser's crash had been abandoned because it could not be procured that season. The Mahatma said he favored an incline toward all outfield walls, which would warn the outfielder of his proximity to the barrier.

Reiser did not return to the lineup until July 15 in a doubleheader against the Pirates. Reiser went 1-for-4 in the first game and 1-for-3 in the nightcap. The teams split the twinbill. The report in *The Sporting News* said that the Dodgers "were heartened for the big drive ahead by the return of Pistol Pete Reiser to his outfield chores." However, on July 21 against Cincinnati, Reiser threw his left shoulder out of place attempting a shoe-string catch of Babe Young's line drive. He snapped it back but retired for several days' rest after taking one more turn at bat.

Reiser did return on July 25 and maintained a .300-plus hitting pace for most of August and well into September. He was batting .316 on August 21 when he crashed into Cincinnati Reds star hurler Ewell Blackwell at the plate, severely injuring his right knee. Reiser returned and raised his average to .317 by September 4, but finished at .309, eight points behind Bob Elliott of the Boston Braves, who was second to Harry Walker of the Cards who won the title with a .363 average. But the Dodgers won another pennant, beating their usual rivals, the Cardinals, by five games.

Reiser played in his second World Series, starting in center field. In the third game on October 2, Reiser walked in his first at-bat. Moments later, as he slid into second base, he felt his ankle give way. The injury was diagnosed as a fracture. The doctors wanted to put a cast on the ankle. Reiser pleaded with the doctors to tape the ankle rather than putting on the cast. They assented, and the next day Reiser was back in uniform, but unable to start. He was replaced by Carl Furillo.

A historic game was played Friday, October 3. New York writer Dick Young of the *Daily News* wrote the next day, "Out of the mockery and ridicule of the worst World Series in history, the greatest ballgame ever played was born yesterday." Going into the bottom of the ninth, New York Yankee pitcher Floyd "Bill" Bevens was making a bid for the first World Series no-hitter.

While Bevens was wild, walking a record 10 batters, the Yankees were leading 2–1 as the Dodgers came up in the bottom of the inning.

Dodgers catcher Bruce Edwards flew out. Furillo then drew a walk. Al Gionfriddo, who would make World Series history himself in game six with a spectacular catch of a long drive off the bat of Joe DiMaggio, was sent in to run for Furillo. Spider Jorgensen fouled out weakly to George McQuinn near the dugout at first base. Bevens was now just one out from pitching the first World Series no-hit game.

Manager Burt Shotton, who replaced Durocher for the year because Commissioner Happy Chandler had banned "The Lip" from baseball for a year for associating with gamblers, called on Reiser, broken ankle and all. The Yankees knew the ankle had been injured but were unaware it was fractured. Reiser hobbled to the plate. With Reiser at the plate, Gionfriddo stole second. Yankee manager Bucky Harris ordered Bevens to walk the left-handed-hitting Reiser, and Eddie Miksis was sent in to pinch run for him.

Cookie Lavagetto, batting for Eddie Stanky, on an 0-and-1 count then spoiled the no-hitter with a double off the right field screen that scored both pinch runners and gave the victory to the Dodgers. Reiser later commented, "Just think how much more they would have second-guessed poor Bucky Harris if they had known he intentionally walked a guy who had a broken ankle!"

Reiser played again for the Dodgers in 1948. But it was the end of the line for Reiser with Brooklyn. Injuries, most of them self-inflicted by overly aggressive play, had robbed him of his magnificent skills. The Dodgers, sporting players who would lead them to championships in the 1950s and eventually be dubbed "The Boys of Summer," slipped to third place.

Robbed of his considerable skills by injuries, Reiser played in only 29 games and batted 127 times. His average dropped to .236. If it had not been for his success as a pinch hitter (10-for-21), he would have hit only .189.

Prior to the start of Reiser's last season with Brooklyn, the Dodgers organization covered the outfield walls in Ebbets Field with foam rubber. Soon after that, warning tracks began to appear. Wrigley Field in Chicago was the first to have a warning track that encircles the outfield just inside the fence. The granular texture of the track makes outfielders aware that they are approaching the outfield wall as they go back for fly balls. Somewhat later, warning tracks were installed at Braves Field in Boston and Shibe Park in Philadelphia. Pete Reiser may be one big reason why all major league parks today have warning tracks.

After the 1948 season, Reiser was traded to the National League champions, the Boston Braves, for outfielder Mike McCormick on December 15, 1948. Manager Billy Southworth hoped that somehow the excitement and magic that Pistol Pete had shown in 1941 and 1942 would return, but it didn't. Although only 30, he was relegated to part-time duty. He played in 84 games, batted .271 and hit eight home runs. Reiser was clearly marking time. He returned for the 1950 season and appeared in only 53 games for the Braves, mostly as a pinch hitter, with his batting average falling to .205.

Released by the Braves, Reiser signed with the Pittsburgh Pirates on November 30 and spent the entire 1951 season with them. The Pirates also used him essentially as a pinch hitter. He batted .333 in that role, but his overall average was only .271 and he was released on November 13, 1951. After four poor seasons playing part-time, it appeared to be the end of the line, finally. However, Reiser was signed again, this time by an American League team, the Cleveland Indians, managed by Al Lopez. The Indians were an excellent team with outstanding pitching that had finished just two games behind the champion Yankees. In an interview on April 5, 1952, Lopez said of Reiser, "Ten years ago, Pete was a great player — and I mean a great one. Well, he slipped quite a bit after being hurt so many times, but I think now he's got his confidence back. I really think he's going to be a big help to us."

Reiser was thrilled. "I signed with the Indians, and I'm very happy I did. I think it's a great ball club, and I think it has a wonderful manager," said the Pistol. It was his final stop in the major leagues.

Reiser managed only six hits in 44 at-bats for a .136 batting average. Three of his hits were home runs. He ended his major league career with a lifetime batting average of .295. It was a sad, sorry ending to a career that 10 years before had seemed so great. Pete Reiser was out of organized baseball as a player at age 33.

While Reiser was finished as a player, his career in organized baseball was far from over. After two years out of the game, he began a minor league managing career with Thomasville in the Georgia-Florida League in 1955, leading the team to a fifth-place finish with a 66–72 record. The next year, his Kokomo team finished eighth in the Midwest League at 51–75, but he led the team to a pennant in 1957, going 77–50.

Reiser moved on to Green Bay in the I.I.I. League — also known as the Three I League, short for Illinois, Indiana and Iowa — in 1958, finishing third in the first half of a split season, 29–29, then tying for second in the second half at 36–35. Then in 1959, he managed Victoria to the Texas League pennant with an 86–60 record, for which the *The Sporting News* named him Minor League Manager of the Year. It was his second pennant in three years.

His minor league managing success brought Reiser back to the Dodgers in 1960 as a coach. He stayed on through 1964. In 1965, he was named to manage the Dodgers' Spokane farm club in the Pacific Coast League, but suffered a heart attack in spring training. He quit on May 20 with his team's record at 1–1.

But Reiser was not out of baseball for long. On April 30, 1966, he joined the Chicago Cubs as a scout. On May 18, he replaced Stan Hack as manager of the Cubs' Dallas-Fort Worth farm club in the Texas League. He led the team to a 20–26 record and sixth place before joining the Cubs' coaching staff on July 13. Lou Klein replaced him in this last managing job. In five full seasons and parts of two others, Reiser's overall managing record was 366–348.

As a Cubs coach, Reiser was reunited with his first big league manager, Leo Durocher. Reiser remained with the Cubs through 1969, when they blew a big September lead and lost the Eastern Division title to the amazing New York Mets. He joined the California Angels in 1970. After two seasons with the Angels, he returned to the Cubs in 1972, retiring from coaching after the 1973 season.

Reiser's numerous concussions, broken ankles and assorted injuries took a heavy toll. Twelve times he had rammed into outfield walls. He suffered five skull fractures and seven brain concussions. Two of the concussions and the skull fractures were the result of wall crashes.

Don Honig, author of *Baseball: When the Grass Was Real,* interviewed Reiser, who told him, "Actually, you know, I ran into the wall only twice that I really hurt myself—in 1942 and 1947. Hell, any player worth his salt has run into a wall more than once. I'm the guy who got hurt." In typical Reiser fashion, he minimized his misfortune.

Yet, no other player in the history of baseball suffered the frequency or severity of injury that Reiser did. Dave Anderson of *The New York Times* summarized Reiser's injuries in a story on February 1, 1976: "Of his seven collisions with outfield walls, he crumpled unconscious five times. The other two times, he dislocated his left shoulder and fractured his right collarbone. As a baserunner, he fractured both ankles, damaged the cartilage in his left knee and tore muscles in his left leg. He was beaned twice, a decade before batters wore helmets. In all he was carried off the field 11 times."

That injuries shortened a career destined for the Hall of Fame is virtual certainty. His first big league manager, Leo Durocher, said, "If he hadn't been hurt, you'd probably be talking about him the rest of your natural life. I think Willie Mays was the best I ever saw, but Pete might have been better. He hit from both sides like Mickey Mantle and had the same kind of power. He fairly flew down to first base."

In 1976, the New York baseball writers honored Pete Reiser, and 1,300 guests turned out to pay tribute to him and other players. Reiser received the Casey Stengel "You Could Look It Up" Award. The writers sang an eight-line mini-tribute to Reiser to the tune of "Battle Hymn of the Republic." It went like this:

> Mine eyes have seen the glory of the wall at Ebbets Field,
>   I kept battering with my head, but the damn thing wouldn't yield.
> I never got to Cooperstown, but that is not the worst,
>   'Cause my hair gave out first.
> Glory, glory to Pete Reiser,
>   The Hall of Fame was just a teaser,
>   Glory, glory to Pete Reiser,
> Oh, his hair gave out first.

Pete Reiser, who by that time had indeed lost his hair, sat on the dais with Hall of Famers Mickey Mantle and Joe Cronin, as well as Robin Roberts, who was to be inducted into the shrine that summer. Stan Musial and Charley Gehringer, both Hall of Famers, were in the audience as well.

Phil Pepe, writing about the banquet in the *New York Daily News*, noted that Reiser never made it to the Hall. "He never even came close ... well, that's not quite true because he did come close. He only got 14 votes, six in 1958 and eight in 1960, but he came close, as close as the difference between hitting that wall at old Ebbets Field and not hitting it."

Pepe observed that it was interesting that fate should have put Pete Reiser and Mickey Mantle on the same dais, because in 1941 Pete promised to be all that Mickey became, a slick-fielding hitter with enormous power and blazing speed.

Red Corriden, a Yankees coach, was once asked who was the greatest player he had ever seen. "Pete Reiser," said Corriden.

But even as a coach, Pete Reiser could not avoid injury. In his final year as coach with the Cubs in 1973, the Giants and the Cubs were involved in a beanball brawl on May 6. During the melee, the 53-year-old Reiser was knocked out and carried from the field on a stretcher. He was either kicked or hit in the head. Nine years earlier, on April 17, 1964, in Los Angeles while with the Dodgers, he had suffered a mild heart attack while batting fly balls to outfielders.

On October 28, 1981, Harold Patrick Reiser died at age 62 of a respiratory illness. Dick Young wrote that Reiser died 33 years after he had received the last rites of the Roman Catholic Church. "That's how tough Pete Reiser was," said Young. "If the Dodgers had kept Reiser at shortstop, who knows? If rubber padding and outfield warning tracks had been put into big league parks sooner, who knows?"

Had Reiser stayed in an infield position it is certain that his hitting and base stealing skills would have made him one of the dominant players of the 1940s and 1950s.

After all, he broke in at age 21, the same as Williams and Musial, and could have played through the decade of the 1950s had he stayed as healthy as they did.

Paul Olsen, in his book *The Future of Being Human*, captures the essence of Harold "Pistol Pete" Reiser: "If there was a hero soon to become the anti-hero, a man who epitomized the frustration and impotence of all of us, it was Pete Reiser, the wunderkind outfielder of the Brooklyn Dodgers. In 1942, he was destined to become perhaps the greatest baseball player in the history of the game."

But Reiser played so recklessly, and challenged the wall so often, that it produced disaster. "The wall won," writes Olsen, "and we could never again watch an outfielder tear hell-bent after a fly ball without feeling a bolt of panic, even terror. He could do it all — run, field, throw, but especially hit — with an authority that caught your breath short."

Byron Rosen of *The Washington Post* wrote of padding and warning tracks after Reiser's death in 1981, "If such protection had been provided in his day, Harold Patrick Reiser might be in baseball's Hall of Fame."

HAROLD PATRICK REISER

5'11", 185 lbs.   Born Mar. 17, 1919, St. Louis, Mo.   Died Oct. 28, 1981, Palm Springs, Calif.   Batted left, threw right, batted both 1948–51.

Year	Team	Pos.	G	AB	R	H	2B	3B	HR	RBI	BB	BA	SA	SB
1937	New Iberia Evang.	SS, OF	7	23	3	6	0	0	2	4	n/a	.261	.558	n/a
1937	Newport N.E. Ark.	SS	70	270	41	77	7	9	6	41	26	.285	.444	5
1938	Superior Northern	SS	95	387	78	117	27	10	18	59	26	.302	.563	21
1939	Elmira Eastern	SS-OF	38	123	33	37	7	5	3	21	26	.301	.512	6
1940	Montreal Int.	OF	3	16	2	4	1	0	0	1	n/a	.250	.313	n/a
1940	Elmira Eastern	OF	67	249	55	94	15	12	7	46	40	.378	.618	28
1940	Bkn NL	3B, OF, SS	58	225	34	66	11	4	3	20	15	.293	.418	2
1941	Bkn NL	OF	137	536	117	184	*39	*17	14	76	46	*.343	*.558	4
1942	Bkn NL	OF	125	480	89	149	33	5	10	64	48	.310	.463	*20
1943–1945	In Military Service													
1946	Bkn NL	OF, 3B	122	423	75	117	21	5	11	73	55	.277	.428	*34
1947	Bkn NL	OF	110	388	68	120	23	2	5	46	68	.309	.418	14
1948	Bkn NL	OF, 3B	64	127	17	30	8	2	1	19	29	.236	.354	4
1949	Bos NL	OF, 3B	84	221	32	60	8	3	8	40	33	.271	.443	3
1950	Bos NL	OF, 3B	53	78	12	16	2	0	1	10	18	.205	.269	1
1951	Pit NL	OF, 3B	74	140	22	38	9	3	2	13	27	.271	.421	4
1952	Cle AL	OF	34	44	7	6	1	0	3	7	4	.136	.364	1
1955	Thomasville, Ga.-Fla.	PH	1	0	0	0	0	0	0	0	0	.000	.000	0
Major League Totals 10 yrs.			861	2662	473	786	155	41	58	368	343	.295	.450	87

Asterisk indicates led league

World Series Record

Year	Team	Pos	G	AB	R	H	2B	3B	HR	RBI	BB	BA	SA	SB
1941	Bkn NL	OF	5	20	1	4	1	1	1	3	1	.200	.500	0
1947	Bkn NL	OF	5	8	1	2	0	0	0	0	3	.250	.250	0
World Series Totals			10	28	2	6	1	1	1	3	4	.214	.429	0

HERB SCORE

"The kid wound up and — zoom!
I never even saw that first pitch."
CATCHER BIRDIE TEBBETTS

The Cleveland Indians won their third pennant in 1954 by setting an American League record for games won, garnering 111. It was a team blessed with extraordinary pitching. Four members of the staff eventually made it to Cooperstown (Wynn, Feller, Lemon and Newhouser). Early Wynn, Bob Lemon, and Mike Garcia won 65 of the games. Art Houtteman added 15. Bob Feller, in the final years of a brilliant career, won 13 and lost only three. And the Indians possessed an excellent relief duo of Ray Narleski and Don Mossi who together saved 20 — quite a few under pitching customs and save rules of the day. Hal Newhouser, who had come over from the Tigers, saved another seven.

That the Tribe was swept in a World Series they were overwhelming favorites to win put a humbling endnote to the 1954 season. The New York Giants, led by their young batting champ Willie Mays and deluxe pinch-hitter Dusty Rhodes (4-for-6 with 7 RBIs) swept the Tribe, winning the fourth game, 7–4, in front of 78,102 disappointed Indians fans.

Despite that postseason humiliation, Manager Al Lopez was ecstatic about the prospects for 1955. He had his entire squad returning, and coming up from his top minor-league team, the Indianapolis Indians, was 21-year-old Herb Score, who had registered 22 victories while losing only five times in the American Association in 1964. He fanned 330, an American Association record, and posted an ERA of 2.62. The reports on Score were lavish. A surefire Hall of Famer. The greatest southpaw in history. A pitcher hyped to the extent of establishing unreasonable expectations. "Phenomenal" was the buzzword.

Score started the 1955 campaign with the big club, and he went on to rack up an excellent record, winning 16 and losing 10, fanning a league-leading 245 and winning Rookie-of-the-Year honors.

During the season, Birdie Tebbetts, longtime catcher and manager, told about his first meeting with the fireballing left-hander. "I'll never forget that day," Tebbetts recalled. "It was during batting practice before a night game in June of 1952, and Al Lopez, the manager, brought this skinny, long-legged kid over and said to me: 'Grab a mitt, Birdie, and catch this kid for a while, will you?'

"So I guided this boy over to the sidelines near the Indians' dugout, took my position in back of a makeshift home plate, and casually held out the mitt. The kid wound up and — zoom! I never even saw that first pitch. Lucky for me it was two feet over my head or I wouldn't be here to tell you about it. The balls bounced in front of me, behind me, shot over my head, to the left and to the right of me. But every one was a bullet. The few he did get over almost tore the glove right off my hand. I was 41 years old then, and I said to myself, 'Birdie, if you value your life, you'd better get out of here.'"

The Indians signed the 19-year-old Score the next day for a $60,000 bonus. The young fireballer (a name that would be used often to describe him over the next five years) was sent to the Indians' top minor-league farm in Indianapolis to finish the season. Score was wild, but he had a great fastball, averaging one walk and one strikeout per inning.

The following year, the Indians sent him to Reading in the Eastern League, where he pitched 98 innings, walking 124, winning seven and losing three.

But Score seemed injury-prone. While he always looked healthy, even robust, at six feet two inches and 185 pounds, he suffered a number of illnesses and injuries before pitching his first inning for Cleveland. Early in his career, he received dietary treatment for a spastic colon. At Reading in 1953, Score dislocated his left collarbone. The next year after winning 22 at Indianapolis, he had a serious bout with pneumonia during the last week of the season.

Despite his physical problems, Herb Score exploded on the major-league scene on April 15, 1955, beating the Tigers 7–3. He was almost two months shy of his 22nd birthday. He credited his pitching progress to ex–Cardinal pitcher Ted Wilks, who had coached him at Indianapolis. "Wilks taught me to throw a curve and control. If it hadn't been for him, I'd have gone right back to Reading," a grateful Score remarked.

About a month into the 1955 campaign, the Indians were in first place

Herb Score was often referred to as a left-handed Bob Feller (NATIONAL BASEBALL HALL OF FAME LIBRARY, COOPERSTOWN, NY).

after sweeping a doubleheader from the Red Sox. The two pitchers responsible for the sweep were 36-year-old Bob Feller, who pitched six-and-one-third innings of no-hit baseball and recorded the twelfth one-hitter of his career, and rookie Herb Score, who fanned 16 to win the nightcap, 2–1. Score fanned nine in the first three innings and finished the game two shy of Feller's record of 18 — not bad for a rookie in his first month.

The flame-throwing lefty went on to fan 245 that year, the highest total ever achieved by a freshman. Score's record stood nearly 30 years, until New York Mets hurler Dwight Gooden broke it in 1984. *New York Times* writer Arthur Daley noted in his famous "Sports of the Times" column that Hall of Fame pitchers Grover Cleveland Alexander (227), Christie Mathewson (215), Dizzy Dean (191), and Rube Waddell (186) had fallen far short of Score's mark in their rookie seasons. Even the man to whom Score was being compared, Rapid Robert Feller, recorded 76 and 150 strikeouts in his first two seasons with the Indians before fanning 240 in his third season in 1938, the year he set the strikeout record of 18 in one game.

There is a strong parallel between Feller and the man they called the "left-handed" Bob Feller. Each was discovered by Cy Slapnicka, long-time Cleveland scout, each had a blazing fast ball, and each had problems with control. On the other hand, Feller had no minor-league experience, having been brought up to Cleveland at age 17, while Score spent three seasons in the minors and came up as a 21-year-old rookie.

Score was deeply religious and often prayed while he pitched. In an article in which Score addressed and thanked his mother for what she had done for him, he said, "You also showed me that praying when things were going well is just as vital as seeking God in a pinch. So it became natural for me to pray when I was pitching. Just quiet prayers to myself, to calm my temper and use my head." Arthur Daley predicted greatness for Score after his rookie season. He wrote, "Prayer and a strong left arm may make this youngster one of the great men in baseball history. He certainly is off to a rousing start."

Score's second season was sensational. Without even a hint of the "sophomore jinx," Score, despite being out 12 days with an intestinal disorder, became a 20-game winner. His winning percentage of .690 was tied for second in the league to Whitey Ford's .760. He led the league with 263 strikeouts, an average of 9.49 per nine innings, while lowering his walk total to 129. He pitched 249 innings and recorded the lowest ERA of the great Indians' mound crew, finishing with 2.53, second in the league to Ford's 2.47.

New York had again regained first place, finishing nine games ahead of Cleveland, but the Indians' pitching was again the class of the league. Score was now 23 years old, and the Tribe, going into the 1957 season, was a strong contender for the American League flag.

The Sporting News, in an article on April 10, 1957, asked in a headline, "Will Herb Score Be the Greatest Left-hander?" The author of the article, Ed Bang, went on to celebrate Score's record to date and to compare him to

Hall of Fame lefthanders. Wrote Bang, "In my book Grove stands out as the greatest of all left-handed pitchers." Bang also mentioned Hubbell, Plank and Lefty Gomez. Associating a 23-year-old pitcher, in only his third major league season, with greats of the past is a measure of the regard Score commanded as the 1957 season approached. The Indians were again optimistic about unseating the Yankees. With their wealth in the pitching department and two young emerging sluggers, Rocky Colavito and Roger Maris, the Tribe looked to be strong contenders for the pennant. To an already strong team they had added veteran outfielder Gene Woodling from New York and shortstop Chico Carresquel from Chicago.

Early that year, Joe Cronin, the Boston Red Sox general manager, had startled the baseball world during the Grapefruit League by offering the Indians $1 million for Score. Cronin, like others, believed that the Tribe was overloaded with pitching and might be willing to part with some of it, but he couldn't get anywhere with Hank Greenberg, the Indians' GM. Finally, in desperation, Cronin asked Greenberg whether he would take $1 million for his prize pitcher. Greenberg's mouth shot open wide, and then he said, "Joe, I could not let you have Score." Another writer explained that Cronin knew if Greenberg had grabbed the million for Score, the Cleveland club would have had to padlock its park and transfer the franchise to California.

All reports leading into the 1957 season predicted greatness for Score. Yankee slugger Mickey Mantle, who had won the Triple Crown in 1956, admitted that Score had given him the most trouble of any American League pitcher that year. Asked why Score was so tough for him, Mantle said, "I don't know. I just can't hit him good. Everybody knows he's fast, but he's also got a good curve ball, and when Herb learns a little more control, brother, he's going to be even tougher to hit."

Score was selected by new Indians manager Kerby Farrell to be his 1957 opening-day pitcher against the White Sox and their new manager, former Cleveland boss Al Lopez. In the six seasons he had managed Cleveland, Lopez guided his team to one pennant and five second-place finishes. So it was an interesting meeting of the successful Lopez and his former rookie phenom. Billy Pierce, a left-handed fastballer for the White Sox, beat Score in extra innings. The Cleveland lefthander gave up seven hits and two earned runs. He fanned 10 and walked 11.

Score came back one week later to shut out the White Sox with a four-hitter. That time, he walked only two. On April 27, Score's record went to 2 and 1 as he beat the Tigers, 2–1. He fanned ten, giving up only three hits. Score also pitched on May 1, but did not get a decision. He fanned 12 in five-and-one-third innings. Score seemed on his way to a great season, already leading the league in strikeouts.

On May 7, he started against the world champion New York Yankees. The writers had picked New York, Cleveland and Chicago to battle it out for the flag. The Yanks' first three batters were Hank Bauer, Gil McDougald and Mickey Mantle. Score retired Bauer on a grounder. The second batter, McDougald, was the typical Yankee of the 1950s — steady, dependable, and effective. He had been part of the Yankee infield since 1951, alternating between second and third, until 1956, when he moved to shortstop. In his years with New York, only once — 1954 — did the Yankees fail to win the world championship.

The count went to 2 and 2 against the right-handed hitting McDougald. With Mantle up next, catcher Jim Hegan, not wanting to risk having Score miss the strike zone and run the count to 3 and 2 with a curve or slider, called for a fastball inside and over the knees, and that is what Score threw.

Score recalled months later, "After I released the ball, I didn't see it again until it was three feet away from me. I heard the crack of the bat when my head was down in my follow-through. All I ever saw as my head came up was this white blur bulleting at me. I snapped up my glove, but the white blur blasted through the finger tips and smashed into my right eye." The ball deflected to Smith at third, who threw McDougald out at first. Ironically, Score received an assist on the play.

As soon as Score went down, the field announcer asked, "If there is a doctor in the stands, will he please report to the playing field?" Within 20 seconds, six physicians, including Dr. Don Kelly, the club doctor, went to the pitcher's mound. Score's eye was closed, and he was bleeding from his nose and mouth as he was placed on a stretcher and carried to the clubhouse. He never lost consciousness. While waiting for the ambulance, he joked, "I wonder if Gene Fullmer felt this way" — referring to boxer Fullmer's knockout by Ray Robinson in a title bout. The ambulance took him to Lakeside Hospital for treatment.

New York	AB	R	H	PO	A	Cleveland	AB	R	H	PO	A
Bauer, rf	3	0	1	2	0	Strickland, 2b	4	0	0	2	1
McDougald, ss	4	0	0	0	0	Woodling, lf	4	1	2	2	0
Mantle, cf	4	0	0	2	0	Smith, 3b	4	0	0	2	2
Berra, c	4	0	1	10	0	Wertz, 1b	3	1	2	9	1
Skowron, 1b	4	0	1	6	0	Raines, ss	0	0	0	0	1
Martin, 2b	4	0	0	2	0	Maris, cf	3	0	1	3	0
Howard, lf	3	1	1	1	0	Colavito, rf	2	0	0	4	0

	AB	R	H	PO	A		AB	R	H	PO	A
a-Slaughter	1	0	0	0	0	Carresquel, ss	3	0	0	0	3
Carey, 3b	2	0	1	1	4	d-Altobelli, 1b	1	0	0	1	0
b-Collins	1	0	0	0	0	Hegan, c	2	0	0	2	0
Sturdivant, p	2	0	1	0	0	c-Ward	1	0	0	0	0
						Nixon, c	0	0	0	1	0
TOTALS	32	1	6	24	4	Score, p	0	0	0	0	1
						Lemon, p	3	0	0	1	3
						TOTALS	30	2	5	27	12

a-Flied out for Howard in 9th. b-Struck out for Carey in 9th. c-Struck out for Hegan in 7th. d-Flied out for Carresquel in 8th.

New York	0	0	0	0	0	0	1	0	0 — 1
Cleveland	0	0	0	0	0	0	1	1	x — 2

Errors — Smith 2, Carey, Martin, Bauer. RBI — Bauer, Colavito. 2b — Skowron. S — Sturdivant, Carey, Colavito. DP — Cleveland 1, New York 1. LOB — New York 7, Cleveland 8. HBP — Sturdivant (Maris). W — Lemon (2-3). L — Sturdivant (1-2). U — Rice, Rommel, Stevens, Napp. T — 2:29. A — 18,586.

	IP	H	R	ER	BB	SO
Sturdivant	8	5	2	2	2	9
Score	⅓	0	0	0	0	0
Lemon	8⅔	6	1	1	1	2

The baseball world was stunned. It was the Ray Chapman/Carl Mays incident reversed. McDougald was in a state of shock. After the game, a wet-eyed, shaken McDougald said, "If anything happens to Score's eye, I'm through with baseball." McDougald, Yogi Berra, and Hank Bauer called on Score at Lakeside Hospital after the accident. Talking to Bauer, McDougald again threatened to quit baseball if anything happened to Score. "If he loses his sight — and you hear me, Bauer — I'm going to quit this game. It is not that important when it gets to this." Score sent word to McDougald by way of a nurse, "Don't worry. It's not your fault."

The specialist who attended Score, Dr. C. W. Powers, issued the following medical report:

> Herb has a broken nose, a cut right eyelid, a contusion of the right cheek bone. There is considerable swelling with hemorrhage in the right eye ball. The hemorrhage is being absorbed and gradually is disappearing. It will be two days, possibly a week, before any accurate diagnosis can be made. X-rays will be taken tomorrow. Score needs rest and quiet and is to have no visitors. His condition showed considerable improvement this morning over what it was last night, although he did spend a very uncomfortable night.

The baseball world watched the Score situation anxiously. Three weeks after the accident, Score was still in the hospital. He told a reporter standing three feet away that with his injured right eye, "I can tell you are there, but I can't recognize you." The left-handed fireballer, who had been considered the ace despite the veteran pitchers on the staff, was cheerful and optimistic. He was able to see light and motion with his damaged eye, and it was improving every day.

Asked when he might resume pitching, Score said, "It is up to the doctor. He's managing me."

Score bantered with the reporters permitted to see him since "The Line Drive." He took off the glasses he normally wore for reading. The right lens was covered with a black disk, which had a pinprick hole in the center. The left lens was clear. He took the glasses off momentarily, revealing that almost all external evidence of the line shot that had felled him had healed. There seemed to be slight swelling on the cheekbone and on his nose.

An eye specialist said that Score's first vision tests showed satisfactory response to treatment. He predicted that Score would be released from the hospital before his birthday, June 7. The specialist said that an examination had shown the remaining injury was a swollen retina, the thin membrane at the back of the eyeball that receives light and transmits impressions to the brain. He explained that this was a normal result of a jarring blow and that the swelling often disappeared with medical treatment. No surgery was going to be necessary.

Through all of this, Herb Score remained optimistic and confident that with time he would regain his form and again be the feared lefthander of the Indians' staff. Score planned to recuperate in Hagerstown, Maryland, where his uncle, A.F. Flood, lived. He knew that it would be several weeks before he could work out, exercise or throw. But responding to questions about his return, Score told reporters, "I can't hide behind the mound. What I wonder is how this will affect my hitting." Apparently, the accident had not affected Score's sense of humor. He was batting .091 at the time of the injury.

A year later, Score was back with the Indians. The reports on him were excellent. Daley, writing in the *New York Times*, said on May 7, 1958, "A year ago this month a line drive off the bat of Gil McDougald struck the handsome 24-year-old wonder in the right eye and almost ended a career that seems destined to reach completion some day in the Hall of Fame. Yet his career did not end because he's back as good as ever."

Another report came out of spring training. Veteran writer Dan Daniel wrote, glowingly, "A fully recovered, resurgent Herb Score is going to bring plenty of woe to the Yankees, over whom he holds an edge. However, the Bombers are highly gratified that the Cleveland southpaw's first 1958 test was a complete success."

Score pitched three innings and fanned six. The happiest Yankee of all was Gil McDougald, whose line drive had felled Score in 1957. McDougald commented about how terrible he felt after the accident and said, "Now I am able to forget it."

Those reports and many like them were premature. Score was able to pitch only 41 innings in 12 games in 1958. He did fan 48, averaging more than a strikeout per inning, but he had trouble with his vision and with his arm.

In 1959, he won 9 and lost 11 games, and his earned run average zoomed to 4.71. Equally alarming, he walked 115 batters in 160 innings, although his hits allowed per inning pitched remained good, 123 hits in 160 innings.

On April 18, 1960, Indians general manager Frank Lane traded Score to the Chicago White Sox and to Score's former manager and mentor, Al Lopez. What the lefthander brought in return was 23-year-old righthander Barry Latman, who had won eight and lost five for the White Sox. Just five years earlier, Joe Cronin and the Red Sox had offered a record $1 million for Score. The deal followed by one day the heralded Colavito for Kuenn deal in which the home run champ of 1959 went to the Tigers in exchange for batting champ, Harvey Kuenn.

Score's departure from Cleveland was not pleasant. He had been close to Rocky Colavito and asked Lane to trade him after Colavito had been dealt. Chicago, however, was thrilled to get Score. Manager Al Lopez said, "I am very fond of Score and have wanted him on our side for some time. He pitched exceptionally well for me when I was in Cleveland. He was injured after I had gone to the Sox. I think he is still a fine pitcher and we plan to work with him with the hope that he will return to the form he had when I was his manager in Cleveland."

Frank Lane said, "Herb's trouble was more psychological than physical. He was always complaining of aches and pains but he did that when he was winning 20 games and striking out fourteen a game. I think he still hasn't gotten over the accident that nearly robbed him of his sight three years ago."

Score did not get along with Joe Gordon, the Cleveland manager. "Joe Gordon doesn't like me," he told Lane. "He gives me no sympathy."

So after five seasons with the Cleveland Indians, Score became reunited with Al Lopez and donned a White Sox uniform. While his record for 1959 was unimpressive, he did have flashes at brilliance. After pitching a total of 77 innings in 1957 and 1958, Score pitched 161 innings in 30 games in 1959, striking out 147. His ERA was 4.70. He was a part of the starting rotation, starting 25 games, nine of them complete. Only Cal McLish and Gary Bell started more. Score won all nine games prior to the All-Star game, but from then to the end of the season, he failed to win another game.

The Indians gave the White Sox a real battle for the pennant in 1959, finishing five games back. After that, the Indians never finished higher than third until 1995, when they won the American League East championship but lost to Atlanta in the World Series. Score's exit, of course, cannot account for all that happened, but it did mark the beginning of the club's decline. They became perennial doormats for the American League in the 1960s, '70s and '80s, consistently finishing near the bottom of the standings.

As for Score, in 1960 he started 22 games for Lopez, and he had five complete games. He pitched 113 innings with an ERA of 3.72. He fanned only 78, winning 5 and losing 10. As late as July 22, writers were still wondering about Score. He pitched a complete game in late July, leading Joe Williams to speculate, "Only recently turned 27, the New York–born left-hander still has the calendar on his side and if he has finally shaken off the psychological albatross, or whatever it was that imprisoned his fastball, he can still make it back to the top." Williams went on to note that but for the accident, "Score would certainly be the most celebrated pitcher in the game today, as well as the highest salaried in history."

The 1960 season ended with the Yankees again victorious and the White Sox finishing third. Score's former team, the Indians, finished fourth, 21 games behind, and, for the first time since 1946, finished below .500.

After the start of the 1961 season, Herb Score was optioned to San Diego of the Pacific Coast League. Al Lopez reported that Score was sent down to work on his control, and said that Score would be recalled later. "We had a long talk with Herb and he was agreeable to the move," Lopez said. "There's nothing wrong with his arm. He can throw hard on the sidelines for 45 minutes solid. If there was anything wrong with his arm, he couldn't do that. What he needs most is control."

Score was optioned two weeks before his twenty-eighth birthday. His San Diego stint was unimpressive. While he won seven and lost six, he walked 136 in 134 innings. His ERA was 5.10. In this long, painful ordeal, Score continuously insisted that he would come back. Perhaps his relatively youthful age played a part, and the support and belief expressed by Lopez also prolonged the fight.

In 1962, Lopez tried again to restore his lefthander, but after four brief appearances, he once more was optioned, this time to Indianapolis, the scene of his great 1954 season. He had reached the end of the line in the major leagues. He almost quit when the prospect of returning to the minors was brought up, but then Score said, "It's no great tragedy. I feel real good about my throwing this year and my arm feels fine." He reported to Indianapolis and won ten and lost seven in the American Association.

Herb Score quit baseball on April 8, 1963. It was one month short of six years from the time the line drive off Gil McDougald's bat shattered his eye and destroyed a career destined for greatness. His tenacity was remarkable; his spirit was impressive. Although Score has maintained that it was a sore arm, not the eye injury, that hurt his career, clearly the injury headed the one-time Cleveland fireballer toward mediocrity.

As for Gil McDougald, he retired at the young age of 32 after the 1960 season. McDougald finished his career with a .281 batting average. But in his three seasons after the accident, he batted only .250, .251, and .258. It would appear that the "line drive" affected McDougald's career as well.

Score gives few interviews these days. He lives in Rocky River, Ohio. He does the commentary for Indians' radio broadcasts and harbors no bitterness or regret. "Now I never think what my career might have been," Score said. "I think I'm very fortunate ... everything I have I owe to baseball."

The irony comes from some of the new Indians players who will ask Score, "Hey, did you used to play?"

If a pitcher like Herb Score, who won 20 games and struck out 263 as a 23-year-old, had enjoyed a full career, he would today be in the Hall of Fame.

HERBERT JUDE SCORE
Born June 7, 1933, Rosedale, N.Y.   Batted left, threw left.

Year	Team	W–L	Pct.	ERA	G	GS	CG	IP	H	BB	SO	ShO
1952	Indian.											
	A.A.	2–5	.286	5.23	12	10	3	62	37	62	61	0
1953	Read.											
	Eastern	7–3	.700	4.68	23	17	6	98	64	126	104	2
1954	Indian.											
	A.A.	*22–5	*.815	*2.62	33	32	21	251	140	140	330	5
1955	Cle AL	16–10	.615	2.85	33	32	11	227⅓	158	154	245	2
1956	Cle AL	20–9	.690	2.53	35	33	16	249⅓	162	129	263	5
1957	Cle AL	2–1	.667	2.00	5	5	3	36	18	26	39	1
1958	Cle AL	2–3	.400	3.95	12	5	2	41	29	34	48	1
1959	Cle AL	9–11	.450	4.71	30	25	9	160⅔	123	115	147	1
1960	Chi AL	5–10	.333	3.72	23	22	5	113⅔	91	87	78	1
1961	Chi AL	1–2	.333	6.66	8	5	1	24⅓	22	24	14	0
1962	Chi AL	0–0	.000	4.50	4	0	0	6	6	4	3	0
Major League Totals 8 yrs.		55–46	.545	3.36	150	127	47	858⅓	609	573	837	11

4   BLURRED VISION

KIRBY PUCKETT

> "You know what's sad ... that there
> are not more Kirby Pucketts, so when you
> lose one, you don't notice it as much."
> WILLIE RANDOLPH, YANKEE COACH

Kirby Puckett's brilliant career ended with an eye injury that will keep him from reaching 3,000 hits or winning another batting title. One of his 1995 teammates, who will make the Hall of Fame despite numerous injuries and eight trips to the disabled list, is Paul Molitor. Molitor, who is still active as this book is written, reached 3,000 hits late in the 1996 season. Kirby Puckett, whose 12-year statistics are much more impressive, will not achieve the marks that longevity allows. He may eventually win election to the Hall of Fame because he was a strong impact player over a significant time frame, but his eye problem has put his election in jeopardy.

In order to understand the impact a player like Kirby Puckett can have on a franchise, we will briefly trace the history of the Minnesota team.

The franchise began as the Washington Senators in 1901 when the American League was established. In the 60 years the team represented the capital city, from 1901–1960, the Senators won only three pennants, the last one in 1933. After that, the Senators finished in the second division every year except for three; second in the war years of 1943 and 1945, and fourth in 1946. They finished seventh or eighth 13 times. Also, in those 60 years, only once did they draw more than one million fans — in 1946, when the boys came back from the war and the Senators drew 1,027,216. In the same period, for example, the Detroit Tigers drew over one million 19 times, and the Boston Red Sox topped the million mark 13 times.

In Washington's entire history, only once did they win a World Series, and that was back in 1924, when the Walter Johnson–led team managed by

Bucky Harris beat the Giants in seven games. Hence, while there were threats from Congress and even a plea from President Dwight D. Eisenhower not to move the franchise, the Senators moved to Minnesota in 1961. The Twins became the first team to adopt the name of a state instead of a city. None of the previously relocated teams had state names. The St. Louis Browns became the Baltimore Orioles. The Boston Braves became the Milwaukee Braves. The Brooklyn Dodgers and the New York Giants assumed the names of the new cities that adopted them, as did the A's who moved from Philadelphia to Kansas City.

Four new clubs were formed when the first expansion of major league baseball occurred in 1961, and they all adopted the names of their cities: the Houston Colt 45s, which later became the Astros; the New York Mets; the new Washington Senators; and the Los Angeles Angels, which changed to the California Angels in 1965. (They reverted to the name of their city in 1997 when they became the Anaheim Angels.)

The original Senators, now the Twins, had much greater success in their new location, and their attendance was better. They have typically reached the million mark in attendance and have topped the two-million mark several times and even reached three million once. But in 1983, prior to the arrival of Kirby Puckett, the Twins finished sixth, 29 games behind Chicago. They finished near the bottom in team batting average, and their pitching staff had the highest ERA. The first 10 years in Minnesota had brought memories of three first-place finishes and one pennant, but no World Series championship.

After the 1970 season, the Minnesota Twins did not win another division title until Kirby Puckett joined the team. It was not that they lacked good players; they boasted stars like Tony Oliva and Rod Carew, who captured all the batting titles from 1971 to 1978 except for the 1976 season when George Brett narrowly edged Carew and his Kansas City teammate, Hal McRae. The team was essentially a .500 ball club finishing third or fourth every season from 1972 through 1980.

The early 1980s saw a new crop of ballplayers come into the majors. From 1982, with the debuts of Wade Boggs, Ryne Sandberg, Darryl Strawberry, Willie McGee and Cal Ripken, to 1983, a year that introduced Tony Gwynn, Don Mattingly, Brett Butler and Tony Fernandez, to 1984, the year that Joe Carter, Tony Pendleton, Chili Davis and Kirby Puckett came up as regulars, baseball was rich with players who had the ability and promise to compete statistically with the greats of the past. Certainly, Boggs and Gwynn are among baseball's greatest hitters, and Mattingly seemed assured of a place in the Hall of Fame until his career started to go up and down, like McGee's.

The one player who came up in that period who maintained a Hall of Fame consistency after his first two years was Kirby Puckett.

Puckett was discovered by accident, and his career ended with an injury. He played almost 12 full seasons brilliantly, and his presence in this book is a result of the affliction that suddenly brought his career to an end.

The Minnesota Twins' signing of Puckett was like the guy who went fishing and found a diamond in a bass's mouth. The "fisherman" was Jim Rantz, Twins assistant farm director. Because of the 1981 players' strike, he had time to travel to Peoria, Illinois, to watch his son Mike play in an Illinois Collegiate League game. However, Rantz couldn't take his eyes off a player for opposing Quincy, Illinois, who was built like a manhole cover with legs and banged baseballs into the street. If Puckett had come up in the thirties or forties, some writer would have dubbed him with a nickname. But throughout his major league career he has been Kirby Puckett — no nickname, no middle name — just Kirby Puckett.

"I wasn't on assignment, but I guess when you're at a ball game, you're working," Rantz said. "They had this guy playing for Quincy. At that time, he was playing in the outfield. And he had a bad day. He went three for four, hit a home run, threw someone out at the plate and stole a couple of bases. I didn't know it at the time, but he was leading the league in hitting, too."

The player Rantz described, Kirby Puckett, grew up on Chicago's South Side, graduating from Calumet High School in 1980. When he graduated, he was 5'8" and weighed 165. By the time he retired in 1996, he had filled out to a solid 215 pounds.

Puckett enrolled at Bradley University in Peoria, just outside Chicago, and he hit .378. Puckett's father died unexpectedly in 1981, so Kirby transferred to Triton Junior College in River Grove, and he became eligible for the 1982 draft. The Minnesota Twins, solely on Rantz's recommendation, made Puckett their first choice and the third pick overall. The Twins offered Puckett $6,000, not enough to sign him. Instead, Puckett stayed at the junior college for the 1982 season. It was a good decision because it allowed the 21-year-old to showcase his talents and induced the Twins to more than triple their offer, upping it to $20,000. Puckett took his junior college team to a berth in the Junior College World Series, hitting .472 for the season, with 28 doubles, eight triples, 16 home runs, and 42 stolen bases.

Rantz said after the series, "Thank God we had the rights to him."

Puckett accepted the Twins' offer and reported immediately to their Elizabethtown team in the Appalachian League, a rookie league that started its season in the middle of June. He played the full season, which ran through August, and in 65 games, he hit a league leading .382. Puckett, however, showed none of the power or speed for which he would later be known. He hit only three home runs and stole no bases. Nevertheless, he was promoted to the Twins' team in the California League, the Visalia Oaks, where he hit .314 with 97 RBI. In 1984, after a brief stint in Toledo where in 21 games he hit .262 with five home runs and eight stolen bases, Puckett came to Minnesota to play and stay. His first game was on May 8, 1984.

The addition of Kirby Puckett, who in his first year hit a modest but solid .296, spurred the Twins to a tie for second place in the American League West, only three games behind Kansas City. He was the one significant change in the team, and although he played in only 128 of the team's 162 games, Puckett was among the leaders in at-bats and hits. It was a good rookie season, good enough so that Puckett's $50,000 salary was increased to $130,000 in 1985.

Puckett's second season, 1985, saw the Twins floundering again. After Manager Billy Gardner was fired in early June, Ray Miller took over, and the Twins played .500 ball but finished in a fourth place tie, 14 games behind the Kansas City Royals. Puckett was a mainstay, playing in 161 games and collecting 199 hits, but his average of .288 was not close to the leaders. After two seasons, Puckett had become an important player for the Twins, but he was overshadowed by players like Boggs, Mattingly, and Strawberry, who hit 29 home runs to go with 26 stolen bases in 1985. Puckett's first two years did not suggest the greatness that was ahead. Indeed, Kirby Puckett seemed to be good but not great.

The career of Kirby Puckett veered toward greatness in 1986. While his team endured its fifth managerial change since 1980 with the hiring of Tom Kelly, Puckett had his first big year. In 161 games, he batted .328 with 223 hits, 119 runs scored, 31 homes runs and 96 RBI. Puckett had come of age. But could he keep it up?

In 1987, the Twins raised Puckett's salary to $437,000, modest by league standards, and Puckett led a strong Twins team to the American League West Championship, two games ahead of the Royals. His season was spectacular. He led his team in hitting and the league in hits with 207. The Twins beat the heavily favored Detroit Tigers in five games to win their first pennant since 1965 and only the fifth in the 87 years of the franchise.

In the World Series, they faced the St. Louis Cardinals and beat them in a tough seven-game series. Whitey Herzog, the highly regarded manager of the Redbirds who had brought his team into the World Series for the third time in six years, said of the Twins, "They'd probably finish fourth in either the National League East or the American League East." But the Twins, led by Puckett, beat the Cardinals and accomplished what they had not been able to accomplish before: a world's championship. Puckett's importance cannot be understated. He was the anchor of the team and among the leaders in several offensive categories. He batted .332 to finish among the top five and, along with Kevin Seitzer of the Royals, led the league in hits. In 1987, Puckett was 26 years old. In the World Series, after a slow start, he sparked the Twins to victories in games six and seven with six hits in his last eight at-bats. He finished the series with a .357 average, and his 10 hits tied Willie McGee for most hits in the series.

The following season, 1988, Puckett took his skills to another level. He finished second to Wade Boggs with a .356 batting average while leading the league in hits for the second straight year with 234, and he finished second to Jose Canseco in RBI with 121. Kirby Puckett had boarded the fast train to Cooperstown, and in 1989, he again proved his legitimacy. He led the league in hitting, replacing Wade Boggs, who had won the previous four titles. Puckett's average of .339 was almost 20 points lower than his 1988 figure, and his RBI dropped from 121 to 85. Yet, he led the league in hits with 215, becoming only the fourth player in this century to have 200 or more hits for four consecutive seasons. Also, Puckett became only the third player to lead the league in hits for three straight seasons, joining Ty Cobb and Tony Oliva. Paul Waner and Ty Cobb were the others with four consecutive 200-hit seasons while Charlie Gehringer had five, and Boggs holds the record with seven. Puckett was certainly in Hall of Fame company. He concluded four superior seasons from 1986 through 1989. In November 1989, Puckett became a $3 million player faster than any other player in history. And no one questioned whether he was worth it. His career batting average was .323, and his .356 batting average in 1988 was the best for a righthander since Joe DiMaggio in 1941.

Just six days after Puckett signed the big contract, Rickey Henderson signed a four-year, $12 million deal. Later, free agent pitcher Mark Langston got $16 million from California for five years. But the first was Kirby Puckett. He was 28 years old as he and his Twins teammates prepared for the 1990s. Would the franchise have to wait another 63 years to win another championship?

Puckett basked in the limelight. He even signed a contract to get paid for autographing baseballs at card shows, but that was not his style, and he felt extraordinarily awkward. He reported how he felt: "At the first card show, I felt bad seeing those little kids paying to get my autograph. It didn't hit me right. I felt it in my heart. I made a vow that once the contract is over, I'm done. I'll still sign, but not for money. I wouldn't do it for a million dollars."

No, the big money he was beginning to earn did not change the man. He was still the good guy from the South Side of Chicago. He never forgot his roots.

The Twins tumbled into last place in the A.L. West in 1990, and Puckett recorded his lowest average since 1985. He batted .298, the best on the Twins' roster, but he slipped to 164 hits, falling shy of the 200-hit level for the first time since 1985 when he had 199. The Twins appeared ready for rebuilding as they lost key players to free agency, notably their slugging third baseman Gary Gaetti, who signed with California. The Twins signed free agent Chili Davis and called up a fine rookie prospect to play second base. His name was Chuck Knoblauch, a great fielding 23-year-old who could score runs and steal bases. Puckett had another great year in 1991, sparking the Twins from last to the division championship by eight games over the Chicago White Sox.

In the championship series, the Twins, behind Puckett, beat the Toronto Blue Jays in five games to go to the World Series for the second time in four years. In the ALCS, Puckett batted .429, starring in the fourth and fifth games. In the fourth game, he went 3-for-4, including a home run that sparked a four-run rally in the fourth inning, and he singled home the tie-breaking run in the eighth inning. He was named MVP of the series. In the World Series, against a tough Atlanta team, Puckett was extraordinary. Minnesota returned home down three games to two. In that sixth game, Puckett had a single and a triple in a game that was tied and going into extra innings. In the tenth, he saved the game with a leaping catch; then he hit a homer off Charlie Leibrant in the eleventh that took the Twins to the seventh game, which Jack Morris won with a masterful shutout. The Twins had their second world's championship in just four years.

In 1992, Puckett had an excellent season, hitting .329, with 210 hits and 110 RBI. In 1993, he fell under .300 for only the fourth time in his decade in the majors, but rebounded in 1994 and 1995 with .317 and .314. Hence, Puckett's career never experienced a decline. Throughout his 12-year career, he was a model of consistency and inspired play.

It is interesting to note that in his 12-year major league career, Puckett never once was on the disabled list. His sole injury occurred on Friday, September 29, 1995, when a Dennis Martinez fastball shattered Kirby's jaw in the first inning of a game against the pennant-bound Cleveland Indians. Martinez, with a reputation for throwing inside, hit Puckett on a 1-2 count square in the jaw just above the left corner of his mouth. Puckett bled quite a bit and was taken to a hospital, where an oral surgeon stitched cuts inside his mouth.

Kirby Puckett's outstanding career was unexpectedly ended by glaucoma (NATIONAL BASEBALL HALL OF FAME LIBRARY, COOPERSTOWN, NY).

Comparing Puckett to Don Mattingly, Paul Molitor or even the durable Robin Yount is interesting. Mattingly, in 14 seasons with New York, was on the DL five separate times. Yount in his 20 seasons with Milwaukee went on the DL three times. Molitor, in 19 seasons plus with several teams, was on the DL eight times. Even George Brett, in a distinguished career with Kansas City, visited the DL eight times. Kirby Puckett was not only an extra-ordinarily high achiever but a durable one.

In the spring of 1996, Puckett showed no trace of the beaning and was having an excellent spring until glaucoma afflicted him. On March 29, 1996, a career headed for Cooperstown went on hold. The day before, Kirby Puckett, eager to launch the thirteenth year of a career studded with accomplishments and records, had two hits off Greg Maddux, the brilliant Braves righthander who in 1995 became the first pitcher in history to win three straight Cy Young Awards. The next morning, Puckett could barely see out of his right eye. The ailment occurred just that quickly.

Initially, Dr. Bert Glaser of the Retina Institute of Maryland believed that it might be possible for Puckett to play later. "The jury's still out," he told the press, "but it can happen that fast. One day you're fine. The next, your vision is drastically reduced."

Puckett was diagnosed as having suffered an occlusion of the central retinal vein, blocking blood flow to the retina. On April 19, *Boston Globe* writer Peter Gammons wrote, "The fact there is a good chance that Kirby Puckett will never play baseball is the biggest story in sports right now." Gammons, writing as though Puckett's career was over, praised Puckett as a great player, "arguably the most consistent great player over the decade 1986–1995."

Some of his accomplishments include six Gold Gloves, 10 All-Star teams, and the best lifetime average of any right-handed hitter with 3,000 at-bats who began his career after World War II. Puckett's .318 lifetime average for a right-handed hitter is the highest since Joe DiMaggio.

Two days later, Claire Smith, writing in the *New York Times*, quoted Boggs, "You feel for the guy. He's one of the ambassadors of the game. He's physically OK. He just couldn't see. But in order to hit the little white rat, you've got to be able to see."

The prospect of his great career ending suddenly did not daunt Puckett. Actually, he downplayed it. He said his left eye had 20-20 vision to see his wife and children. That his kids were healthy was significant to Puckett after he had served as a pallbearer at Michelle Carew's funeral three weeks before his eye ailment occurred. Puckett said simply, "I loved this game when I was 5, and I love it more now that I'm 35. I owe this game much more than I could ever give back. I would never misuse it or disrespect it. Any time I put my spikes on, it was to play like I was supposed to. That's what I have pride in."

During the first months of the 1996 season, Puckett had four surgeries. His vision improved slightly but not enough to warrant a return to the diamond.

On July 12, 1996, Puckett announced his retirement from the game he loved. The official reason was "the irreversible glaucoma condition in the right eye." After his announcement, the accolades for Puckett poured in from across the country. Writers in all the baseball markets heaped praise on the charismatic Minnesota outfielder. Many indicated that despite a shortened career the Hall of Fame should be on Puckett's horizon. Baseball statistician Bill James, in his book *The Politics of Glory*, had Puckett slated for the Hall of Fame in 2008. This prediction was predicated on Puckett having an uninterrupted career and retiring in the early part of the next century, perhaps in 2001 or 2002. If he played until age 40 or 41, as did so many of his contemporaries like George Brett, Paul Molitor, Robin Yount and Dave Winfield, Puckett would indeed have played to 2001. In his book, James offers two methods of rating Hall of Fame candidates, using 11 standards to judge retired players. His first method is primarily a measure of offensive achievement, and in James's design, the average Hall of Famer would score exactly 50. Puckett scored 48, which indicated his legitimacy as a candidate for Cooperstown before his retirement.

James's second standard incorporates the team's performance, Gold Glove awards, All-Star appearances, World Series appearances, batting championships and leading the league in other categories. James says, "If he [the player] has 100 points or more, he is likely to get in the Hall of Fame. Above 130, he is almost certain to be in."

Kirby Puckett scored 185, in just 12 seasons. He ranks among the greatest of the players with shortened careers. Kirby Puckett had more than a taste of glory; he had generous drafts of the limelight.

Perhaps Puckett's measure will be his two World Series appearances. As mentioned earlier, in 1987 against the Cardinals, Puckett carried the old Washington franchise to its first world championship in 63 years! In 1991, Puckett was even more impressive. He again took charge with his fielding and his hitting, leading the Twins to a second championship.

Cal Ripken, baseball's real iron man, said of Kirby Puckett, "He's a rock of a man mentally. To me, he just seemed to be invincible." This from a man whose consecutive game streak has already spanned 16 seasons.

In his final year, 1995, Puckett was strong in all offensive categories. But for his affliction, he would have played several more seasons. His lifetime average of .318 is higher than that of several Hall of Fame inductees, including players with glittering reputations such as Carl Yastrzemski, Al Kaline, Mickey Mantle and Roberto Clemente.

Of the players elected to baseball's Hall of Fame with shortened careers, none has the stats of Kirby Puckett. Jackie Robinson was a pioneer; Ralph Kiner was a home-run machine; and Roy Campanella was a dominant catcher who appeared in five World Series in his 10 years. Dizzy Dean and

Sandy Koufax were uncommonly dominant pitchers during their shortened careers. Of the players memorialized in this book, Kirby Puckett probably has the best chance of making it to Cooperstown.

Kirby Puckett, with no middle name and no nickname, played in baseball's most troubled and confused time with an aura of class. Mike Kinsley, a senior writer for *The Sporting News*, wrote three days after Puckett announced his retirement, "Every day was a beautiful day for a Kirby Puckett ballgame or two. And I wonder if the days are going to be as nice from now on."

KIRBY PUCKETT
Born Chicago, Illinois, March 14, 1961.   Batted right, threw right.

Year	Team	Pos.	G	AB	R	H	2B	3B	HR	RBI	BB	SB	BA	SA
1982	Eliza-bethton, Appal.	OF	65	*275	*65	*105	15	3	3	35	25	0	*.382	.491
1983	Visalia, Calif.	OF	138	*548	195	172	29	7	9	97	46	0	.314	.407
1984	Toledo, Int.	OF	21	80	9	21	2	0	1	5	4	8	.263	.325
1984	Minn., AL	OF	128	557	63	165	12	5	0	31	16	14	.296	.336
1985	Minn., AL	OF	161	691	80	199	29	13	4	74	41	21	.288	.385
1986	Minn., AL	OF	161	680	119	223	37	6	31	96	34	20	.328	.537
1987	Minn., AL	OF	157	624	96	*207	32	5	28	99	32	12	.332	.534
1988	Minn., AL	OF	158	*657	109	*234	42	5	24	121	23	6	.356	.574
1989	Minn., AL	OF	159	635	75	*215	45	4	9	85	41	11	*.339	.465
1990	Minn., AL	OF, 2B,3B,SS	146	551	82	164	40	3	12	80	57	5	.298	.446
1991	Minn., AL	OF	152	611	92	195	29	6	15	89	31	11	.319	.460
1992	Minn., AL	OF, 2B,3B,SS	160	639	104	*210	38	4	19	110	44	17	.329	.490
1993	Minn., AL	OF	156	622	89	184	39	3	22	89	47	8	.296	.474
1994	Minn., AL	OF	108	439	79	139	32	3	20	*112	28	6	.317	.540
1995	Minn., AL	OF	137	538	83	169	39	0	23	99	56	3	.314	.515
Major League Totals, 12 yrs.			1783	7244	1071	2304	414	57	207	1085	450	134	.318	.477

League Championship Series Record

Year	Team	Pos.	G	AB	R	H	2B	3B	HR	RBI	BB	SB	BA	SA
1987	Minn., AL	OF	5	24	3	5	1	0	1	3	0	1	.208	.375
1991	Minn., AL	OF	5	21	4	9	1	0	2	6	1	0	.429	.762
Totals			10	45	7	14	2	0	3	9	1	1	.311	.556

World Series Record

Year	Team	Pos.	G	AB	R	H	2B	3B	HR	RBI	BB	SB	BA	SA
1987	Minn., AL	OF	7	28	5	10	1	1	0	3	2	1	.357	.464
1991	Minn., AL	OF	7	24	4	6	0	1	2	4	5	1	.250	.583
Totals			14	52	9	16	1	2	2	7	7	2	.308	.519

5 THE OTHER IOWA FARM BOY

HAL TROSKY

> "I have no doubt that in time he [Trosky] will stand out as the greatest first sacker of the majors and the hitter of this league."
>
> ED BARROW, BUSINESS MANAGER, NEW YORK YANKEES

It was 1933. The nation was paralyzed by a great depression. Franklin D. Roosevelt was inaugurated president for the first time, and Jimmie Foxx won the Triple Crown. The great Bambino was in his last full year as a New York Yankee, and at age 38 hit .301 and finished with 34 home runs, second behind Foxx. The Cleveland team finished third behind New York and Philadelphia, and the baseball world was looking for a hero to replace George Herman Ruth.

The preeminent first basemen in the American League were Lou Gehrig and Jimmie Foxx, both candidates to supplant the Babe as the league's foremost slugger. The Tigers had a big, new, first baseman named Hank Greenberg who showed promise in 1933. Then, on September 11, 1933, Hal Trosky debuted with the Indians.

He was born Harold Arthur Troyavesky, but conveniently shortened his name by four letters to become Hal Trosky. The 20-year-old rookie played 11 games in 1933, finishing with a .295 batting average in 44 at-bats.

Trosky replaced Harley Boss at first base for Cleveland. Boss, an obscure player, was released by the Indians after the season. He was an excellent fielder, but he had been under observation for pains in his head caused by having been hit by a ball. Once Trosky took over first base, Boss, despite being only 24 years old, never played again in the big leagues.

In 1934, the 21-year-old Trosky surprised the baseball world by batting .330, blasting 35 home runs—the most ever hit by a rookie—and driving in 142 runs. Trosky's 35 home runs was a club record for the Indians that would stand until Al Rosen belted 43 in 1953. Albert Belle recently set a new record in 1995 with 51.

The reports on Trosky were extravagant. The venerable Grantland Rice commented upon Babe Ruth's departure from the league after the 1934 season that "the dull roar of the home run remains one of the game's leading features and it is about time nominations were in order for the Babe's successor. The two leading entries at this point are Lou Gehrig and Jimmy Foxx. This pair has put on a keen rivalry for the last two or three years, ever since the Babe started skidding a trifle. But there is another young challenger on the way by the name of Trosky."

The Tribe's spring camp in 1935 was oozing with optimism. The team, with Earl Averill, Joe Vosmik, "Bad News" Hale, and Billy Knickerbocker, was strong in hitting and fielding. Pitching was good with Mel Harder, Monte Pearson, and Willis Hudlin. And there was the brilliant young slugger, Hal Trosky.

A report released to the press on January 27, 1935, was effusive in praising Trosky. It began, "Cleveland baseball fans nominate Hal Trosky as Babe Ruth's successor for the major league slugging honors, and they have mighty good reasons for so doing as the 22-year-old boy from Iowa accomplished more in his first year as a regular big leaguer than did Lou Gehrig or Jimmy Foxx, two of the great home run hitters in the history of the game."

The report also explained how Trosky had been signed by the Indians' veteran scout, Cyril Slapnicka. "Slap," as he was known, loved to visit the sandlots in smaller towns. He saw Trosky while visiting a county fair in Iowa in October 1930. Trosky was pitching for one of the teams. Slap liked him, but not as a pitcher. He loved the way the 17-year-old stood at the plate and hit the ball. But he did not attempt to sign him. In fact, he felt the boy was so awkward that it would be a while before anyone might be interested in him. Slapnicka filed away the Trosky name.

Young Trosky, in the meantime, read in his hometown weekly that Bing Miller of the Athletics was visiting relatives in Vinton, Iowa, a short distance from Norway just outside Cedar Rapids. Trosky, in his youthful exuberance, borrowed his father's flivver and drove to Vinton to ask the Athletics star to recommend him to Connie Mack for a tryout as a pitcher. Trosky impressed Miller, and so Miller told him that he would. To Trosky's surprise, on his return home, he found Cy Slapnicka waiting for him with a contract. The young Iowan signed it quickly. A few days later, Trosky also received a letter from Connie Mack advising him to report for a tryout.

After signing Trosky at age 17, Cleveland sent him to Cedar Rapids, which was not far from his Norway, Iowa, home. There, in 102 at bats, he hit .302. He quit pitching. In 1932, Trosky played in the outfield for Quincy in the Three I League, batting .331 in 68 games. He next moved to Burlington in the Missouri Valley League. There he hit .307 and was switched from the outfield to first base. In 1933, Trosky played for Triple A Toledo, for whom he batted .323, hit 33 home runs and played first base.

A report published on September 19, 1933, said, "What Trosky did to the American Association pitching was criminal. Every time an opposing pitcher saw him coming to the plate, he looked to the bench hoping the manager would wig-wag to pass him."

Trosky was not a gifted first baseman, but his manager, Walter Johnson, liked the way he took his swings. In one Sunday doubleheader in Yankee Stadium in September 1933, Hal faced two pretty good southpaws: Russ Van Atta, who won 12 games that year, and Lefty Gomez, a 16-game winner. Trosky did not fare well against either of them, but Johnson liked the way he kept swinging. Johnson consoled him by saying that he would not be facing pitchers like them every day of the week. Trosky sheepishly replied, "It's just as well I don't, or it would be back to the cows and chickens for me."

He would not go back to being an Iowa farmer tending cows and chickens. Hal Trosky was on his way to becoming the Indians' first sacker, and, according to many observers, he was starting the journey to the Hall of Fame. In the midst of his rookie year, umpire Bill McGowan commented, "They'll have a tough time getting that big boy out next year."

After that big 1934 season, writers began comparing him to Babe Ruth, touting him as the next dominant slugger. Trosky was a big strapping fellow, standing six feet, two inches and weighing 205 pounds. Players and managers talked about Trosky holding his own against the great first basemen of the day, such as Foxx, Gehrig and Greenberg.

In 1935, the predictions continued. Dan Daniel, the renowned baseball writer for the *New York Times*, quoted Ed Barrow, the business manager of the New York Yankees: "Hal Trosky, first baseman of the Indians, has the best chance to succeed Lou Gehrig as the powerhouse of the American League. It is really too bad that our scouts did not like Trosky when he was in the minors. Trosky will go far in his profession, and I have no doubt that in time he will stand out as the greatest first sacker of the majors."

Barrow went on to laud Trosky as being better than Hank Greenberg of the Tigers and far superior to Chicago's Zeke Bonura. Barrow rated the 23-year-old Trosky the absolute class of the rookies of 1934, ahead of such names as Cecil Travis of the Washington Senators, Harlond Clift of the St. Louis Browns, and even Red Rolfe of his own team.

However, the 1935 season saw Hal Trosky afflicted by the sophomore jinx. His average slumped to .271. While he finished in the top five in both home runs with 26 and RBIs with 113, he failed to equal his rave reviews, and it may have cost his manager, Walter Johnson, his job. With the Indians struggling to reach .500, Johnson was fired after 94 games in favor of Steve O'Neill, who led the team to a strong, third place finish, 11 games behind the champion Detroit Tigers.

The Indians were a talented team, but each year one star or another would have an off year. In 1935, it was Trosky and star outfielder Earl Averill who slumped. Averill had his first sub-.300 season. While pitchers Mel Harder and Willis Hudlin matched their 1934 stats, Monte Pearson went from 18 wins to eight. With more consistency, the Indians might have mounted a challenge.

Trosky returned for the 1936 season determined to erase the previous year from the minds of fans and writers, and he did. It was a career year for the 23-year-old slugger. He got off to a great start and he never wavered. In the end, he led the league in total bases and in RBI. He was in the top five in three additional categories: slugging average, home runs, and total hits. His slugging average of .644 was second to Lou Gehrig's .696, and he finished second to Gehrig in home runs with 42.

It is interesting to note that while Trosky's league leading RBI total was ten better than Gehrig's 152, it was still the lowest total to lead the league since 1929. Yet, since 1936, only three players have topped Trosky's total of 162: Hank Greenberg and Joe DiMaggio in 1937 with 183 and 167, respectively, and Jimmie Foxx with 175 in 1938.

Trosky batted .343 in 1936, and since he was only 24 years old, his prospects for a brilliant, productive career were outstanding.

Despite Trosky's slugging, the Indians finished fifth in 1936, 22 games behind the champion Yankees. Again, one of the Indians' regulars slumped. Joe Vosmik tumbled from .348 in 1935 to .278 in 1936, the lowest on the club. The Indians led the American League in hitting with a .304 team average.

But they had strong prospects in their farm system. Bob Feller would debut in 1937 to win nine while losing seven. The 1937 season, however, was disappointing for the Indians and Trosky: he hit 32 home runs and drove in 128 runs, but his average slumped to .298; Cleveland finished 19 games behind New York as the Yankees won a second straight world's championship.

Trosky was a veteran of four seasons at age 24. Yet, he was the youngest of the top first sackers in the league, and only two years older than the league's new sensation, Joe DiMaggio, who came up in 1936 and batted .323. With Feller highly touted and with Jeff Heath and youngsters Ray Mack and Kenny Keltner arriving, the Indians again made a managerial move, firing O'Neill and bringing in Ossie Vitt to manage the team for the 1938 campaign. Vitt, a former major-league infielder with the Tigers and Red Sox, was 48 years old. It was his first managing assignment in the majors. It would also be his last.

The team, behind 19-year-old Feller, who won 17 games, and Trosky, who lifted his average to .334, gained on the Yankees but still finished third, 13 games behind. Jeff Heath in his first full season batted .343.

During the year, Trosky began having severe migraine headaches, but he did not tell anyone. With the Indians becoming stronger every year, Trosky was hoping to play for a pennant winner. Cleveland, a young team, approached the 1939 season with confidence. Their key players were returning, and they strengthened themselves by acquiring veteran outfielder Ben Chapman, who had hit .340 in 1938 for the Boston Red Sox.

Despite Bob Feller winning a league-leading 24 games in his second full season, the Tribe finished third for the fourth time since Trosky had become a regular. The Yankees won 106 games in 1939. It was at that point their third highest total. Only the fabled 1927 and the 1932 teams won more games. The Indians finished a disappointing 20-and-one-half games behind the champion Yankees to finish third in the league.

Trosky played in only 122 games, his lowest total since arriving in Cleveland. The headaches became a constant handicap. Trosky finished 1939 with respectable statistics: he batted .335 with 25 home runs and 104 RBIs.

The 1940 season was the most frustrating of Trosky's career, and perhaps the most bitter campaign for the Tribe. It was the year the Cleveland Indians appeared ready to challenge the Yankees after the New Yorkers had won an unprecedented four straight world championships. Cleveland had excellent pitching with Feller, Milnar, Smith, and Harder. Lou Boudreau won Rookie-of-the-Year honors after batting .295 and driving in 101 runs. Ray Mack, Keltner and Trosky were the rest of an excellent infield. In the outfield, they had Stormy Weatherly in center, Chapman in left, with Beau Bell and a slumping Jeff Heath in right.

But a rebellion was brewing. The team and Manager Ossie Vitt were incompatible. Trosky continued to experience excruciating headaches that affected his play. The big first baseman became frustrated with Vitt, who was not a communicator, and Trosky became the leader of the forces vying against the manager.

The players presented a petition to the owners for the release of Manager

Vitt. It was signed by all the players — rookies and veterans alike — but as one would expect, the Indians' management rejected the demand. The rebellion began early in the season and blossomed before the Fourth of July. When word of the petition got out, the press labeled the Indians "Cry Babies." The term preceded them wherever they went. Instead of the Cleveland Indians, they were now the Cleveland Cry Babies.

Despite the morale problems and the continued tension, the team stayed in contention as they battled the Tigers and the Yankees for the lead. The players spoke to Vitt only when it was absolutely necessary. In one exchange, when the team was in New York and the weather was cold and wet, Hal Trosky said he wished the game were called off. Playing, he added, would be risking pneumonia. Manager Vitt retorted, "Well, for all the good you are doing us, you might as well have pneumonia." Trosky was livid. After that event, Trosky battled Vitt through the end of the year.

Another time, Mel Harder, a 13-year veteran, was pitching and gave up two hits and a walk. Vitt became incensed and turned to Trosky and said, "Why doesn't that guy quit baseball? He's through." Trosky mentioned the remark to Harder, and the pitcher became another hardened Vitt foe.

The Indians, riddled by dissension and saddled with a manager they refused to talk to, lost the pennant to the Tigers in the last series of the season. Thirty-year-old rookie Floyd Giebell, who won a total of three games in his major league career, beat Feller on September 27, 1940, to clinch the pennant for Detroit. It was a good Detroit team, but it was a pennant Cleveland should have won. Although the Tigers got a career year from Buck Newsom, their pitching was not as strong as the Indians'.

Again, key Cleveland players had bad years. The worst was Jeff Heath, who had hit .292 in 1939 but dropped to .219 in 1940. Kenny Keltner slumped from .325 to .254. Trosky and the Indians, with an opportunity to win a pennant for the first time in 20 years, let it slip away. It was hard for the team to accept this result. For Hal Trosky, it was the end of the line. While his average in 1940 was .295 with 25 home runs, his RBI total fell below 100 for the first time in his major league career.

The Indians fired Vitt and brought in Roger Peckinpaugh to manage the team in 1941. For Trosky, 1941 was torture. His headaches worsened. On July 12, he finally told Peckinpaugh and the baseball world about his problem. He disclosed that a "thumping headache" had bothered him at least half the time during the last three baseball seasons. Trosky declared emphatically that he had no intention of retiring, but said, "Gosh, a fellow can't go on like this forever. If I can't find some relief, I'll simply have to give up and spend the rest of my days on my farm in Iowa." He then added, "It was so

Although overshadowed by Foxx, Gehrig and Greenberg in the 1930s, Hal Trosky was a powerful hitter before migraine headaches shortened his career (NATIONAL BASE-BALL HALL OF FAME LIBRARY, COOPERSTOWN, NY).

bad one day last summer that I walked out to Mel Harder, who was pitching, and asked him not to try to pick the runner off first base. I knew if Mel threw me a fast ball, I wouldn't even see it."

Peckinpaugh said that he knew for several seasons that Trosky had been bothered by headaches but that he was surprised that they were so serious and so frequent. He replaced Trosky on July 12 with Oscar Grimes. Trosky said he seldom had headaches in the off season, leading him to think that they stemmed from baseball activity. "The thing that aggravates them is my inclination to worry about my work on the field," he said. "I can't take bad days in stride. I have trouble getting my sleep and become nervous and irritable. I find myself barking at the kids about nothing at all."

Trosky played 89 games in the 1941 season. He batted .294, but he hit only 11 home runs and drove in 51. His career was in jeopardy at age 28. Trosky's migraine headaches curtailed what could have been a long and productive career and prevented entry into the Hall of Fame. While sluggers like Greenberg, Williams, and DiMaggio entered the military and returned from the war to enjoy some productive seasons, Trosky's career was shortened by migraine headaches.

He announced prior to the 1942 baseball season that it was "for the best interest of the Cleveland club and for myself that I stay out of baseball this year. I have asked the Cleveland club to place me on the voluntarily retired list." Trosky predicted that if his problem continued, his major league career would be over. He explained that he had visited doctors but that none had helped him. "If, after resting this year, I find that I am better, perhaps I'll try to be reinstated," Trosky said.

Yet, since baseball was being decimated by players leaving for the war, interest in Trosky was great. Several teams inquired concerning his availability. Dan Daniel wrote, "Having signed Billy Knickerbocker, utility infielder, as a free agent, the Yankees today began to pay new attention to the prospect of landing Hal Trosky from the Indians to play first base. Trosky was only 30 on November 11. Unless again hampered by the migraine headaches to which he attributed his 1940 and 1941 slumps, Hal could be quite a ball player for Joe McCarthy."

Daniel was wrong. Trosky did not return to baseball in 1942. In fact, he stayed out in 1943 as well. Daniel wrote in early 1943 that the Yankees had abandoned the effort to sign Trosky and instead acquired Nick Etten from the Philadelphia Phillies. It appeared that the Indians were demanding too much for Trosky. Ed Barrow of the Yankees explained that the "exorbitant demands of the Cleveland club" stood in the way. A contributing factor involved medical examinations concerning Trosky's headaches.

"We could not possibly give up the men Alva Bradley [the Indian's owner] wanted. Not for a player who might turn out physically unfit," Barrow said.

Further, Trosky expressed an interest in going to either Chicago or Detroit, if he continued to play, so that he could be closer to his Norway, Iowa, farm.

In June 1943 Trosky expressed an interest in returning to baseball. He was no longer suffering from the migraine headaches that had forced him out. The Indians urged Trosky to consider returning for the 1944 season but sold Trosky on November 6, 1943, to the Chicago White Sox for an undisclosed amount of cash. Trosky's nine-year Cleveland career, eight as a regular, was over.

He came to Chicago from his home in Iowa 20 pounds lighter, down to 185 pounds. He told reporters, "I'm not suffering from the migraine headaches like I formerly did. My troubles seemed to have disappeared. I am happy because of it. I'm eager to return to baseball." He quickly signed with Chicago and reported to spring training.

The White Sox were elated at the prospect of Hal Trosky at first base for the 1944 campaign. The Sox had finished in the first division in 1943 and felt a healthy Trosky would help them move up in the standings. Reports in early 1944 were positive. Trosky was taking vitamin B-1 shots to curb his migraines and appeared enthusiastic about returning to baseball.

"Look at the power, the stance, the cut," explained Manager Jimmie Dykes. "Trosky is going to have a good season, maybe a great one. He's the power this club has needed ever since I quit playing."

"I'm already hitting better than when I quit in 1941," Trosky added modestly. To back that up, he hit for an even .500 the first five exhibition games against major league pitching.

Sadly, it was not to be. Trosky did take over the first base position, but the two-year absence from the game had an impact on his batting eye. Trosky's average slumped to .241. Although he appeared in 135 games, his once great home run power was diminished, and he was able to hit only ten. The White Sox finished seventh. Trosky again quit the game.

He returned one final time after the war in 1946. Perhaps it was nostalgia that made him do it, as all the players he had formerly played with and against were returning from the military to major league baseball. Trosky appeared in 88 games with the White Sox, batting .254 with only two home runs.

What seemed apparent in 1941 became reality in 1946. The migraine headache problem had cost Trosky his major league career. He quit baseball after his dismal showing in 1946. While he scouted for the White Sox in 1947 and 1948, his playing career was over.

What had begun in 1933 with power and drama ended quietly 13 years later. Despite his outstanding record in the thirties, Trosky never appeared in an All-Star game. Lou Gehrig, Jimmie Foxx and Hank Grenberg dominated the early years of Trosky's career. Despite Trosky's impressiveness early in his career, he never received a single vote for the Hall of Fame. Before his illness, Hal Trosky could hit with the best of them, but the migraines made him just another player.

Bob Feller, from Van Meter, Iowa, is remembered as the Iowa Farm Boy. But there was another great player from rural Iowa who played for Cleveland at the same time. "The other Iowa farm boy," Hal Trosky, was inducted not in Cooperstown but in the Iowa Hall of Fame in recognition of his talents.

On June 18, 1979, Hal Trosky died in Cedar Rapids, Iowa. The one-time slugger was 66. His major-league career fell far short of Ed Barrow's early prediction because of recurring migraine headaches, not because Hal Trosky couldn't hit!

HAROLD ARTHUR TROSKY
Born Nov. 11, 1912, Norway, Iowa.   Died June 18, 1979.   Batted left, threw right.

Year	Team	Pos.	G	AB	R	H	2B	3B	HR	RBI	BB	SB	BA	SA
1931	Cedar-Rap.–Dubuque, M.V.L.	P OF	52	162	11	49	8	2	3	n/a	11	n/a	.302	.432
1932	Toledo A.A. No record													
1932	Quincy, I.I.I.	OF	68	260	55	86	14	6	15	n/a	n/a	1	.331	.604
1932	Burling-ton, M.V.L.	1B, OF	56	218	41	67	15	9	4	n/a	n/a	6	.307	.514
1933	Toledo, A.A.	1B	132	461	86	149	25	5	33	92	58	2	.323	.620
1933	Clev AL	1B	11	44	6	13	1	2	1	8	2	0	.295	.477
1934	Clev AL	1B	154	625	117	206	45	9	35	142	58	2	.330	.598
1935	Clev AL	1B	154	632	84	171	33	7	26	113	46	1	.271	.468
1936	Clev AL	1B	151	629	124	216	45	9	42	162	36	6	.343	.644
1937	Clev AL	1B	153	601	104	179	36	9	32	128	65	3	.298	.547
1938	Clev AL	1B	150	554	106	185	40	9	19	110	67	5	.334	.542
1939	Clev AL	1B	122	448	89	150	31	4	25	104	52	2.	.335	.589
1940	Clev AL	1B	140	522	85	154	39	4	25	93	79	1	.295	.529
1941	Clev AL	1B	89	310	43	91	17	0	11	51	44	1	.294	.455
1942	Temporarily retired.													
1943	Temporarily retired.													
1944	Chi AL	1B	135	497	55	120	32	2	10	70	62	3	.241	.374
1945	Temporarily retired.													
1946	Chi AL	1B	88	299	22	76	12	3	2	31	34	4	.254	.334
Major League Totals 11 yrs.			1347	5161	835	1561	331	58	228	1012	545	28	.302	.522

6   THE CUBAN CRUNCHER

TONY OLIVA

"The best pure hitter I've ever faced or seen."
DAVE MCNALLY

He won three batting championships, the first two during his first two full-time major league seasons. Five times he led the league in total base hits, and three times he was first in doubles. Eight times he was chosen to the American League All-Star team. Tony Oliva was plainly a premier performer during the latter half of the 1960s and early 1970s. But for multiple knee injuries, he might today be in the Hall of Fame with contemporaries Carl Yastrzemski, Willie McCovey and Lou Brock.

Pedro Oliva was born July 20, 1940, one of ten children in a family living on a farm at Pinar del Río, Cuba. Like many Cuban boys of the time, Pedro developed an early love for baseball. However, the Oliva family was so poor that the boys had to make their own equipment. Like many other farm kids, the Olivas often used the butt end of a corn cob for a ball, and they fashioned a bat from a piece of wood taken from a tree. At other times they used a plastic ball. When they finally obtained an old baseball, they played with it until the cover came off; then, just like boys have often done in rural and lower-class America, they taped it with friction tape and continued to play with it.

Pedro was the best player in the Oliva family. When he came of age, the Minnesota Twins in 1961 scouted and signed him. Pedro, not possessing a visa himself, used brother Tony's visa to get into the United States to play baseball. That is how he came to be known as Tony.

Oliva's first stop was at Wytheville in the Appalachian League, where his bat absolutely sizzled. In his first minor-league season at age 21, he led the league in four categories: batting average, .410; hits, 102; total bases, 159; and slugging, .639. The Cuban's talents were not restricted to hitting. He was a fine fielder and a smart and speedy baserunner. He used his powerful arm to throw out a league-leading 12 base runners, including three for double plays. With such a sensational record, Oliva was named Appalachian League Rookie of the Year in 1961.

The Twins, aware that they had an unusually talented line-drive hitter and great all-around player, moved Oliva to Charlotte of the South Atlantic League in 1962. Young Tony responded with a .350 average. He lost the batting championship to Asheville's Elmo Plaskett by a mere fraction, .3497 to .3498.

The Twins brought Oliva to Minnesota at the end of the year, sent him up to bat nine times, and four times Oliva hit safely for a .444 average.

The Twins, who had moved from Washington, D.C., to the Twin Cities in 1961, won 91 games and finished just five games behind the Yankees. They were a strong team that featured an outfield of Harmon Killebrew, Lenny Green and Bob Allison. The Twins decided that the Cuban Cruncher needed more seasoning, so they sent him to Dallas-Fort Worth of the Pacific Coast League for the 1963 season. His average dropped to .304 at the Triple A level, but he showed power with 30 doubles and 23 homers. At the end of the season, Oliva again came to Minnesota and responded with three hits in seven at-bats.

Not being able to return to Cuba because of Fidel Castro's rule, and having no family himself, Tony gladly played winter baseball in Puerto Rico and the Dominican Republic because it kept him busy. He hit .350 in the Puerto Rican League and .340 in the Dominican League. He was beset with loneliness between seasons when he was not playing baseball, and he called his parents in Cuba. He told them that he would come home if they wanted him to, but his mother instructed him to stay in America where he had an opportunity to play baseball. Many times he sent his parents gifts, but they were always confiscated by government agents.

After completing his stint in the Dominican Republic, Oliva took 15 days off to relax before reporting to the Minnesota spring camp for the 1964 season. When he reported to the Twins, they determined that he was ready to take his place in the Minnesota outfield. But the Twins' outfield was strong with Jimmie Hall and Bob Allison joining Harmon Killebrew. Determined to get their new prodigy into the lineup, Manager Sam Mele moved Allison from right field to first base and assigned Oliva to right.

Allison responded well to the move and even helped Tony to play the wall in the rightfield corner of Metropolitan Stadium. He warned him of the problem of picking up fly balls against the background of the shirt-sleeved crowd in a triple-decked stadium.

"If you don't pick up the ball quickly, you're in trouble," Allison said. "I can help Tony some. But like learning to play the hitters, this he'll have to learn for himself." Oliva was a quick study. "It's a good field, and the lights are good," the affable Tony said. "I think I'm going to like it here fine."

Indeed, he liked it there just fine, and his teammates and much of baseball warmed to him quickly. Tony had a cheerful disposition, and he approached both life and baseball with a positive attitude. "You never see Tony brooding," Clark Griffith, the club owner, observed. "In fact, I can't recall that I have ever seen him without a smile on his face."

At the start of the season, Oliva began hitting the ball. By June 16, Minnesota writer Max Nichols said, "If the Twins have improved enough to battle the Yankees for the American League pennant, it's because of Tony Oliva."

Minnesota teammates also sang praises of him. "Oliva makes our whole batting line-up better," Jimmie Hall said. "With Oliva following a .300 hitter like Rich Rollins, we've got two men getting on base all the time. The pitchers have to pitch to Bob Allison and then to me and then to Harmon Killebrew and so on down the line with men on base."

After only 13 games, Griffith, the notoriously conservative Minnesota owner, said with conviction, "Oliva could become another Mickey Mantle or another Al Kaline."

After two weeks, Tony was hitting for a .345 average, had hit safely at least once in 11 of his first 13 games, and had hit every kind of pitch, although he was more adept at hitting the curve than the fastball. What's more, he proved he could hit to all fields, especially to left. He stood bent over, deep in the box, and much like a golf swing, swung inside out, driving the fast ball to left and the curve to right. As the pitch approached, he stepped into it. If the pitch was outside, he stepped toward the plate; if inside, he stepped straight forward, or slightly toward right. Clark Griffith thought that Oliva swung "like the old hitters used to swing."

Manager Mele also offered praise: "It's getting to be a big joke in our dugout when Tony goes to bat. The players are laughing and yelling about where Tony will hit this time, not *if* he will hit."

With the addition of Tony Oliva and good new pitchers, Mudcat Grant and Jim Perry, hopes were high for a strong finish in 1964. But the club stumbled and tumbled to seventh place, winning 79 while losing 83. The disappointing finish, however, was not due to Oliva's performance, but rather to the resurgence of the Orioles and White Sox. The Yankees with first-year manager Yogi Berra won the pennant.

Oliva was sensational throughout. He was selected to the American League All-Star team as a rookie, the first of eight consecutive selections (he was selected but did not play in 1969 and 1971), breaking a record held by Joe DiMaggio of the New York Yankees. Oliva finished the season leading the league in five categories. Most importantly, he was the first rookie to win the batting title, which he did with a .323 average. He also led the league in runs scored, 109; in hits, 217; in total bases, 374; and in doubles, 43. Also of note, Oliva hit 32 homers and nine triples. Not surprisingly, Oliva was named Rookie of the Year by both the Baseball Writers Association and by *The Sporting News.* Despite their disappointment in 1964, the Twins were optimistic about their chances in 1965. The mound corps was strong. Jim Kaat was on top of his game; Mudcat Grant was coming into his own, and Jim Perry was a rising star. Camilio Pascual could still pitch, and the club had added Al Worthington, a journeyman but someone who had been deceptively effective the year before, finishing with a 2.16 ERA. Slugger Harmon Killebrew was only 30, and the rest of the lineup was made up primarily of veterans. Oliva, of course, was the centerpiece.

The team did not disappoint. They won 102 games and finished ahead of second-place Chicago by seven games. Oliva provided the offensive leadership the Twins had hoped for. He won a second batting title with a .321 average, thereby becoming the only player to ever win batting titles his first two full-time seasons in the league. Not even the great Ty Cobb had done that. Oliva led the league in base hits, 185, and in sacrifice flies, 10. He hit 40 doubles, 16 homers and batted in 98. In Minneapolis-St. Paul, they were ready for their first World Series. They would face the Los Angeles Dodgers, who had defeated the San Francisco Giants for the National League pennant.

The Dodgers were tough. They had speed and a good fielding infield, but their offense was suspect, hitting for a .245 team average, the lowest of the top six teams. What they had was outstanding pitching and speed. Sandy Koufax was 26–8 with a league-leading 2.04 ERA. Don Drysdale finished 23–12 with a 2.77 ERA, and Claude Osteen, a tough lefthander, finished 15–15. Maury Wills, the best base stealer since Ty Cobb, stole 94 bases.

The Series opened in Minnesota. Mudcat Grant was matched against Don Drysdale because the game fell on the Jewish holiday Yom Kippur and Koufax sat it out. Minnesota jumped on Drysdale for six runs in the third inning and went on to win, 8–2. Jim Kaat opposed Koufax in the second game. This time, the game remained scoreless until the sixth when Minnesota broke through with two runs. The Twins went on to score three more and won the game, 5–1. Harmon Killebrew and Tony Oliva provided the batting punch. Bob Allison provided a spark in the field when he made a diving catch of Lefebvre's wicked drive to help Jim Kaat pitch a complete game win. Oliva reported after the game that he was glad Koufax was in the other league because he had seen enough of his fastball: "I hit a changeup off him, and after that he threw me five fastballs in a row. I swung at all of them and didn't touch one."

The Twins were in the driver's seat as the Series moved to Los Angeles. The West Coast, however, was unkind to Minnesota. Osteen shut them out 4–0 in the third game and Drysdale beat Grant 7–2 in the fourth, a game in which Oliva homered. Koufax completed the sweep in Dodger Stadium with a 7–0 shutout. What had looked so certain for Minnesota when they flew to the coast now was riddled with doubt and anxiety.

The Twins, however, came back to their own park to take the sixth game, 5–1. Game seven saw Koufax come back to pitch with only three days' rest. He was brilliant, holding the Twins to three hits and no runs, beating Jim Kaat, 2–0.

The Twins had come so very close, but their hitters failed. Minnesota's team batting average was .195. Oliva was disappointed. In five of the seven games, he had been up against two of the toughest left-handed pitchers in baseball, Sandy Koufax and Claude Osteen. The Twins' young left-handed batter managed only five hits in 26 at-bats in the Series, including one double and one homer, for a .192 average.

In his third season in 1966, Oliva's average dropped to .307, but it was good enough for second best in the league. It was an era of great pitching and low batting averages. The league batting average was only .240 in 1966. Frank Robinson won the batting championship with a .316 mark that year, which until then was the third lowest average to win a title. Only Elmer Flick's .306 in 1905 and George Stirnweiss's .309 in 1945 were lower. Oliva led the league in total hits with 191. He scored 99 runs, hit 32 doubles and 25 homers. *The Sporting News* awarded Oliva a "Gold Glove" as an outfielder on their "All-Star Fielding Team." The Twins finished second to the miracle Red Sox with 89 wins, eight games back.

In 1967 and 1968, Oliva's average dipped below .300 to .289. On September 8, 1967, Oliva got eight consecutive hits off Baltimore pitching in a doubleheader, which became nine in a row when he singled in his first at-bat the next day. In 1968, his .289 average was third best in the league; Yastrzemski won the championship with the all-time low average of .301.

In 1968, the injury jinx began to visit Oliva. He missed 34 games due to a pulled leg muscle in July and a separated shoulder in August. Despite the missed time, Oliva led the league with 16 intentional walks, indicating the respect opposing clubs had for his bat.

In 1969, Oliva brought his average back up to .309, which tied him for

Tony Oliva won three batting titles (Corbis-Bettman Archives).

second best with Reggie Smith of Boston. He led the league in hits with 197 and in doubles with 39. He batted in 101 runs. His best day came against Kansas City. In a doubleheader played on June 29, he got eight hits, two of which were for the circuit in the second game. He missed tying the record for most hits in a doubleheader by one.

The Twins won the American League West by nine games over Oakland. While Baltimore swept Minnesota three straight in the championship series, Oliva had a great series. He got five hits in the three games, good for a .385 average, including a double and a home run.

The early seventies produced two of Oliva's best years. In 1970, he hit .325, four points below Alex Johnson's and Carl Yastrzemski's .329. Oliva was leading the league until the last week, but a 1-for-25 slump cost him the championship. Oliva led the league in hits with 204 and tied in doubles with 36. He batted in 107 runs, a personal high. His 323 total bases were two fewer than Yastrzemski's league-leading 325. He batted an even .500 in the ALCS against Baltimore, which the Orioles won in three games. Oliva homered in the second game. His slugging average for the series was an astonishing .917. In 1971, the Twins fell to fifth place in the six-team American League West, but it was an outstanding year for Oliva. He won his third batting title with his personal-high average of .337. He also led the league in slugging with a .546 average.

The season had quite a downside for Oliva. He had to miss action due to surgery on his right knee, the first of five operations he underwent. The injury occurred in the 64th game of the year when he dived for a Joe Rudi line-drive in Oakland, hitting a wet patch of grass. Oliva's batting average was soaring at .390 on 106 hits at the time of the injury. He returned after surgery to play 126 games, officially batting 487 times. At the end of the season, he was named American League Player of the Year by *The Sporting News*.

Oliva missed most of the 1972 season due to extensive knee surgery. Nearly 100 fragments of bone and cartilage were removed from his right knee. He participated in only ten games, stepping up to the plate 30 times, for a .321 average.

He even played six games in the outfield. He could still hit when his knee held up. He found being on the sidelines difficult. He said, "The ball club would be losing by one run, there'd be a man on third, but he'd stay there, and I'd be thinking that if I was playing, I would get him home. I would hit the ball some place."

The Twins lost many one-run games without their Cuban Cruncher.

The 1973 season saw the American League inaugurate the designated hitter rule. This rule allowed an individual hitter to bat for the pitcher without fielding a position. Oliva extended his career by becoming a designated hitter. He played in 146 games and batted .291, good enough to rank him among the top dozen hitters in the league. On July 3, he hit for the circuit three times in one game. He found being the DH better than nothing, but he preferred to play. "Playing puts me more in the game. When you go to hit, you are ready," Oliva said. "I go in the runway behind the dugout to keep me loose, to keep ready to hit. As an outfielder, my blood's more warmer, I'm more ready to hit." Yet he was glad that he was helping the ball club in some way.

Oliva continued as Minnesota's designated hitter in 1974 and 1975, hitting .285 and .270, respectable averages for someone standing in the batter's box on gimpy legs and for someone who was unable to leg out any infield hits. In 1975, he led the league in one category: he was hit the most times by a pitched ball, 13.

Oliva's active career ended in 1976. He participated in 67 games that year, but his once golden batting stroke was gone, and his average slipped all the way down to .211.

When Oliva retired, he held two major-league records: (1) Most at bats in a season for a rookie with 672 in a 162-game schedule; and (2) most total bases for a rookie in 162-game schedule, 374. He had set the following American League records:

* Consecutive years leading league in hits — three.

* Most years, ten or more intentional bases on balls — nine.

* Most hits in a season for a rookie — 217.

Oliva felt that, but for the knee injury, he could have played another five or six years and had a chance for 3,000 hits, a certain ticket to the Hall of Fame. But the injury was even worse than most people knew. "There was nothing left of the knee, just bone on bone," Oliva revealed. Rod Carew, who roomed with Oliva, reported in his book, *Carew*, written with Ira Berkow: "I'd be asleep and sometimes I'd hear Tony moaning and groaning. Or he'd get up and be in agony from the pain in his leg ... wandering all over the hotel trying to find ice to put on his knee." Oliva fell 83 hits shy of 2,000. For that nine-year period, from 1964–1972, Tony Oliva was a better hitter than most of his contemporaries, including Hall of Famers Brooks Robinson, Carl Yastrzemski and Lou Brock.

Upon his retirement as an active player, Oliva stayed with the Twins in various capacities. Minnesota had made him a player-coach in 1976, and in the next two years, he coached first base and offered batting tips around the cage. In 1979, the Twins asked him to be their minor league hitting instructor, a job for which he seemed well suited. He, however, found the life of a minor league hitting instructor a lonely one, and he longed to get back to the big leagues.

In 1981, when the Twins hired a new hitting instructor, they chose Jim Lemon instead of Oliva. President Calvin Griffith explained it this way: "The only natural hitter who was a good instructor was Ted Williams. Jim Lemon had to struggle to become a good hitter." Lemon hit .262 as a major league player. Besides, the Twins thought that Oliva did not speak English well enough to communicate the fine art of hitting. Oliva found this hard to understand because the young minor leaguers he was coaching seemed to understand him well enough.

In 1991, he had replacement surgery for his right knee and had the left one scoped. Baseball had been his life, and he hoped to spend the rest of his time serving in some capacity, as coach, hitting instructor or, preferably, manager.

Painted on the outfield wall at the Metrodome in Minneapolis are three uniform numbers the Twins have retired. They belonged to Hall of Famers Harmon Killebrew and Rod Carew, and Tony Oliva. The Twins obviously thought of Oliva in the same category as Killebrew and Carew. Oliva was inducted into the Minnesota Sports Hall of Fame in 1988. Michael Katz, writing in the *The Daily Sports News*, May 10, 1987, argued that Oliva should be in baseball's Hall of Fame. "Oliva shouldn't have to die to get into the

Hall of Fame," Katz lamented. "If it hadn't been for those operations, Tony Oliva would have had no problem getting into the Hall of Fame." Katz went on to argue that Oliva was among the best of his peers.

Comparing players with their peers makes for an interesting projection of Oliva's talents. Using the 11 years in which Oliva was a regular, his batting average was .306. The league batting average for the same time frame was .246, a plus .060 margin for Oliva. Comparing that, for example, with Hall of Famer Ross Youngs, who hit only .036 better than the league average in a career that spanned only nine years, makes a strong argument for Oliva's case. Moreover, the average ERA during Youngs' nine years was 3.78, whereas for Oliva's 11 years, it was 3.53. Again, the statistics point to Oliva as the stronger performer while playing in a pitcher's era that virtually spanned his career.

Oliva also won three batting championships; Youngs won none. Oliva never was designated the A.L. MVP but was a serious candidate five seasons. Perhaps Youngs does not belong in the Hall of Fame. Yet, the comparison establishes the star status of Tony Oliva who will be remembered as one of the premier hitters and all-around performers of his day.

PEDRO LOPEZ OLIVA
Born July 20, 1940, Pinar del Río, Cuba.　　Batted left, threw right.

Year	Team	League	G	AB	R	H	2B	3B	HR	RBI	BB	SB	BA	SA
1961	Wytheville	Appal.	64	249	55	*102	15	6	10	*81	18	4	*.410	*.639
1962	Charlotte	So. Atlantic	127	469	71	164	35	6	17	93	43	1	.350	.559
1962	Minn.	AL	9	9	3	4	1	0	0	3	3	0	.444	.556
1963	Dal.–Ft. Wor.	PCL	146	536	79	163	30	8	23	74	31	9	.304	.519
1963	Minn.	AL	7	7	0	3	0	0	0	1	0	0	.429	.429
1964	Minn.	AL	161	672	*109	*217	*43	9	32	94	34	12	*.323	.557
1965	Minn.	AL	149	576	107	*185	40	5	16	98	55	19	*.321	.491
1966	Minn.	AL	159	622	99	*191	32	7	25	87	42	13	.307	.502
1967	Minn.	AL	146	557	76	161	*34	6	17	83	44	11	.289	.463
1968	Minn.	AL	128	470	54	136	24	5	18	68	45	10	.289	.477
1969	Minn.	AL	153	637	97	*197	*39	4	24	101	45	10	.309	.496
1970	Minn.	AL	157	628	96	*204	*36	7	23	107	38	5	.325	.514
1971	Minn.	AL	126	487	73	164	30	3	22	81	25	4	*.337	*.546
1972	Minn.	AL	10	28	1	9	1	0	0	1	2	0	.321	.357
1973	Minn.	AL	146	571	63	166	20	0	16	92	45	2	.291	.410
1974	Minn.	AL	127	459	43	131	16	2	13	57	27	0	.285	.414
1975	Minn.	AL	131	455	46	123	10	0	13	58	41	0	.270	.378
1976	Minn.	AL	67	123	3	26	3	0	1	16	2	0	.211	.260

Year	Team	League	G	AB	R	H	2B	3B	HR	RBI	BB	SB	BA	SA
Major League Totals 15 yrs.			1676	6301	870	1917	329	48	220	947	448	86	.304	.476

Asterisk indicates led league.

League Championship Series Record

Year	Team	League	G	AB	R	H	2B	3B	HR	RBI	BB	SB	BA	SA
1969	Minn.	AL	3	13	3	5	2	0	1	2	1	1	.385	.769
1970	Minn.	AL	3	12	2	6	2	0	1	1	0	0	.500	.917
Totals			6	25	5	11	4	0	2	3	1	1	.440	.840

World Series Record

Year	Team	League	G	AB	R	H	2B	3B	HR	RBI	BB	SB	BA	SA
1965	Minn.	AL	7	26	2	5	1	0	1	2	1	0	.192	.346

7   A REAL GAMER

THURMAN MUNSON

"He was a gamer."
JAY JOHNSTONE

Major league baseball has a crisis plan in case a team plane crashes. Fortunately, this plan has never been used. Yet, plane crashes have taken the lives of major league players. The most famous ballplayer to be killed in an airplane accident was Pittsburgh's Roberto Clemente, who, on a mission of mercy to help starving people in Central America, was killed when his cargo plane disappeared on New Year's Eve of 1972. Clemente, an 18-year veteran, had amassed an even 3,000 hits. A brilliant fielder with a powerful arm and enough power to hit 240 home runs, Clemente was a certain choice for the Hall of Fame, and was elected in 1973. The usual five-year waiting rule was waived. Only once before had the waiting period been waived: In 1939, Lou Gehrig was voted in immediately after his retirement.

Small, individually owned planes have also crashed and taken the lives of major league players. On February 15, 1964, a skinny-looking, six-foot, 22-year-old brilliant fielding infielder for the Chicago Cubs crashed on an ice-crusted lake near Provo, Utah, killing both Ken Hubbs and the plane's other occupant, Dennis Doyle. In 1962, at age 20, Hubbs broke two major league fielding records for second basemen previously held by Bobby Doerr of the Red Sox. He played 78 consecutive games without an error and handled 481 chances. Whether or not Hubbs would have improved enough as a hitter to reach genuine stardom is not known. Sportswriters thought enough of his rookie season to name him Rookie of the Year in 1962.

On August 2, 1978, another private plane crashed, taking the life of an established star well on his way to Cooperstown. The accident happened at approximately 3 P.M., when a small Cessna Citation 1 jet aircraft was preparing to land at the Akron-Canton airport. The pilot had been cleared for landing. The plane was slightly off center in its descent, but was carrying plenty of fuel to reach the runway. The plane was approaching the landing strip from the north, and the weather was no factor. The plane's landing gear was locked into the normal landing position. The pilot of the plane was Thurman Munson; the plane bore the number 15NY, the famous Yankee catcher's number.

Munson lived in the Canton, Ohio, area. He had taken up flying a few years earlier and found it both exhilarating and practical. He got tired of the old Beechcraft Duke he had been flying and purchased a faster Cessna Citation jet. It cost him almost $1 million to buy it, but he liked the 350-knot cruising speed which could take him from New York to the Akron-Canton area in just over an hour.

Changing from flying the old propeller-driven plane to the jet was a challenge. He had only about 30 hours of flight time with the new Cessna. The Wichita-based Cessna Aircraft Company had awarded Munson his Citation rating in July 1978, certifying him as qualified to fly it without special training.

Munson was a strong family man, and he sorely missed being home during the baseball season. He told a writer, "Home is what it is all about. Places like Las Vegas, Los Angeles and New York are great, but it's home that is important." Home, to Munson, was Canton, Ohio. "My three children are in school here, they have their friends and my wife and I have our friends here. This is where I grew up. I'd like to be here as much as possible," Munson said. In May 1979, Munson was honored as "the baseball father of the year" in advance of Father's Day. "It was a nice honor for the man with the grumpy, grouchy reputation," Munson wryly observed in his autobiography, *Thurman Munson: An Autobiography.*

Before the 1978 season, Munson had strongly promoted his being traded from New York to Cleveland so that he could spend more time at home. In a cross-country flight back to New York after the Yankees had won the divisional championship, Munson was heard proposing various trades with Cleveland to George Steinbrenner — Dennis Eckersley and Fred Kendall for Munson, for example.

"No," Steinbrenner responded. "They wouldn't give Eckersley for you. I can get Frank Duffy and John Lowenstein. If they throw in Tom Buskey, I'll make the deal."

Not succeeding in his trade proposals, Munson was tempted to quit baseball. He wrote in his autobiography, "I hadn't been able to move to the Indians. There was no doubt in my mind that I wanted to go with them. My confusion was over whether to quit or play for the Yankees again."

After a personal meeting with George Steinbrenner, Munson signed a contract to return to New York for the 1978 season for $420,000, with two additional years guaranteed. "When it came time to make the decision," Munson wrote, "my continuing love for playing baseball made me realize what I should do."

The contract had no restrictive clause concerning the flying of a plane, as most guaranteed contracts do. Munson saw his ability to fly as a means of spending more time at home. Owning his own plane, he seized every opportunity to fly back to Ohio and be with his family.

The Yankees had Thursday, August 2, off, and Munson flew to Canton to spend time with his wife and children. Still a novice pilot, the All-Star catcher was practicing landings. He was accompanied by David Hall, who was Munson's copilot, and Jerry D. Anderson, a friend who was kneeling between Munson and Hall during the descent.

The safe landing speed was 104 knots, or 120 mph, but Munson's aircraft was coming in at only 94 knots, or 108 mph, for his third touch down. The plane was coming in too low for the landing field, and suddenly it began shearing treetops. Munson tried to pull the plane up, but it lost power, began to roll and crashed. The plane hit a tree stump, spun around, and overturned, coming to rest on a two-lane highway, about 1,000 feet short of the runway. The landing strip was 20 feet above the highway and over a small hill some 30 yards south of the road. It was 3:02 P.M.

When the plane stopped, Hall and Anderson alertly escaped the aircraft. But Munson had been knocked unconscious by the accident. Hall and Anderson kicked open the emergency door in an effort to rescue the Yankee catcher, but when the door came open, fuel, stored in the wing, ignited. They tried to pull the unconscious Munson from the craft, but they were driven back by the fire.

Both men suffered burns. They had about 30 seconds from the time the plane crashed to when it burst into flames. Three minutes after the crash, Munson died from asphyxiation when flames used up the cabin's oxygen. Tragically, a great Yankee catcher was dead.

Great teams in baseball history have usually had outstanding catchers. From the Yankee dynasties of the 1920s through the 1960s to Cincinnati's Big Red Machine of the 1970s, catchers like Dickey, Cochrane, Hartnett, Campanella, Berra, and Bench took good teams and made them great. It is hard to visualize a championship-caliber team without strength behind the plate.

It was such a team that New York was building in the 1970s. After they had plummeted to the cellar in 1966, their lowest finish since 1912, the Yankees tried to rebuild. Finding a catcher out of the Dickey, Berra, and Howard mold was their number-one goal. The Yankee brass heard of a squat-bodied catcher tearing up the Cape Cod League who had picked three runners off base in one game. They started to follow him closely. In the spring, they sent their Ohio scout, Gene Woodling, to Kent State University to watch Munson. Despite Munson's "odd shape," Woodling couldn't "get over the way Munson could run for a guy built like that. And his quickness behind the plate. He had the quickest release throwing the ball of any catcher I've ever seen." Woodling signed Munson to a contract, and the Yankees' search for a catcher was over.

Munson's professional baseball career began with Binghamton of the Eastern League in 1968. He hit .301 in 71 games and was promoted to Syracuse the next year. Munson ripped International League pitching, hitting .363 in the first 28 games. His performance got the Yankees' attention, and they called him up to New York.

He broke into the major leagues in 1969, at age 22, and caught 26 games his rookie year, hitting .256. He suffered no sophomore jinx, for in his second year, he hit .302 and slugged .415. From then until that fateful day in 1979, he was the regular Yankee receiver. He was remarkably durable, catching most of his team's games. Small wonder that George Steinbrenner said of Thurman, "Hurt is in direct relation to character. I can remember Thurman Munson playing with all of his body black and blue."

Munson played hurt a lot. Once the doctor said that he should be out a week, but Munson told Billy Martin that he could be designated hitter the next day. A day later, he was catching again. Munson threw sidearm much of the time because of shoulder problems, but with a quick release he was able to keep baserunners in check. Munson, with a dour personality, failed to ingratiate himself with a lot of teammates, but he did have their respect as he played through one physical ailment after another. Despite badly aching knees in his final season, he continued to catch. Had he lived, he would have become the Yankee DH or first baseman.

Five times Munson hit over .300, and in 1977 he narrowly missed that hitters' benchmark with .297. His 11-year career average was .292. He hit 113 home runs and 229 doubles.

He achieved the distinction of being designated Rookie of the Year, the Most Valuable Player, and the Yankees' first captain since Lou Gehrig. Not even Joe DiMaggio had had that designation. Added to that list of honors, Munson received three Gold Gloves.

If Munson was good in the regular season, he was downright sensational in the postseason. He stung Kansas City in the 1976 ALCS with a .435 average, and for an encore, he hit .529 in the World Series against Cincinnati. The Yankees lost four straight to the Big Red Machine, but Munson got four hits in the final game and tied a World Series record by getting six straight hits.

In 1977, he dropped to .286 against the Royals in the league playoffs, but he hit Dodger pitching hard in the World Series with a .320 average.

In the 1978 ALCS, he only hit .278, but he had the one hit that doomed Kansas City. The two teams had split the first two games, and the Royals, largely on George Brett's three home runs, were leading in the third game going into the eighth inning. Roy White reached base, and Royals' manager, Whitey Herzog, brought Doug Bird out of the bullpen to relieve a tiring Paul Splittorff, the "Yankee Killer," as Howard Cosell dubbed him. Munson greeted Bird by driving a ball 440 feet over the left center field fence to win the game for the Yankees. It was probably the longest home run of his career.

Guidry then outdueled Leonard in the fourth game for the championship.

Munson hit .320 against Los Angeles in a winning effort as the Yankees won back-to-back championships for the first time since 1961 and 1962.

Munson's career ALCS batting average in 14 games was .339, and in 16 World Series games he hit .373, the third highest World Series average in history. Thurman Munson was as deserving of the title "Mr. October" as was Reggie Jackson.

Not only was Munson effective with the bat, but he also was a good handler of pitchers. Ed Figueroa said at Munson's funeral, "When I came from California, he made me a pitcher. He taught me how to pitch to the hitter." Ron Guidry also praised Munson's handling ability, saying, "He had so much to do with my success."

Throughout his career, Munson suffered from a bad-guy image. He tended to speak bluntly and often with some color. But behind that tough exterior was a sensitive man. For example, after a speaking engagement at Morristown, Pennsylvania, where he addressed 250 Little Leaguers, Munson stayed behind to sign autographs for two hours. Because of such actions, Lou Piniella thought that Thurman was all marshmallow inside. "He really had compassion," Piniella said. "He didn't want everyone in the world to know it, but he had compassion and tenderness."

In an era that belonged to Carlton Fisk, Johnny Bench, and Ted Simmons, Munson fought for recognition as an All-Star catcher. "I'm little. I'm pudgy. I don't look good doing things," Munson said. "Those big tall guys (like Fisk) look super. But nobody plays harder than me."

When the Yankees lost the 1976 World Series in four straight to Cincinnati, Sparky Anderson, Redleg manager, after the fourth game compared Munson and Bench. "Munson is one of the finest hitters I've seen," Anderson acknowledged. And then he added a double negative, "Don't compare no one to Bench. That would be embarrassing to the player."

Munson reached for the microphone and took exception. "For me to be belittled after the season I had and after the game I played tonight is not something I enjoy. I never compared myself to Johnny Bench." Munson added, "But, I'll tell you one thing, if I played in the National League on Astroturf, I'd be a heck of a player."

When Reggie Jackson joined the Yankees in 1977 as a free agent, a rivalry developed between Jackson and Munson. Munson felt that Steinbrenner had assured him when he signed his 1977 contract that no Yankee other than Catfish Hunter would earn more than he did. When Jackson signed as a free agent for a figure in excess of Munson's, Thurman was incensed. He engaged in a bitter financial battle with the Yankee owner that lasted until the end of spring training.

Ill will between Munson and Jackson got worse when Jackson, in a magazine article, talked of the dominant role he expected to play wearing pinstripes and that he expected to be "the straw that stirs the drink." Of that, Munson said, "He can only stir it bad."

Despite this rocky start, the two eventually learned to get along well enough to lead New York to two consecutive world championships over the Los Angeles Dodgers. "We talked about it over a beer a few times," Jackson said of the situation. "We got it settled. And hitting in front and behind each other, hitting when it counted, we grew to respect each other." The truce, however, remained an uneasy one.

The evening after Thurman died, eight Yankees took the field at Yankee Stadium in an early evening drizzle. They stood silently with bowed heads, facing the scoreboard. Jerry Narron, who was supposed to catch that day, remained on the top dugout step. Home plate was vacant. Archbishop Terence Cardinal Cooke delivered a brief eulogy, and Robert Merrill sang "America the Beautiful." Players from both teams shed tears and bowed their heads. Munson's image was flashed on the scoreboard, and the stony silence was broken with a respectful applause by fans that built into a crescendo until it was a thunderous ovation. For nine minutes, 51,151 fans chanted "Thurman ... Thurman ... Thurman" as they paid final tribute to number 15, Thurman Munson.

On August 6, 1979, in Canton, Ohio, hundreds of people lined the five-mile route between the Canton Civic Center where the funeral services for Thurman Munson were to be held and the Sunset Hills Cemetery where he was to be buried. About 1,000 people waited outside the center to pay their last respects. More than 500 mourners jammed the center. When the Yankee buses arrived, six pallbearers, hometown friends of Munson, carried the coffin inside the Civic Center where the funeral service was held.

A hymn was sung, Lou Piniella read from the Old Testament, and then four telegrams the family had received were read. They were from Anita and Lou Piniella, Muhammad Ali, Eleanor Gehrig and Reggie Jackson. The Rev. J. Robert Coleman, pastor of St. Paul's Roman Catholic Church, delivered the eulogy. At the close of the service, the Yankee catcher was laid to rest in the cemetery.

Munson's career, consisting of 11 seasons, may have been too short for election to baseball's Hall of Fame. The fatal accident cut at least five years off his career. Munson's biggest vote total for the Hall of Fame was in 1981, his first year of eligibility. He received 62 votes, which was far below the required 75 percent needed for election. After that, the votes decreased to an average of 28 over the next six ballotings.

A case for Munson's election was made by writer Phil Pepe. In his column "Baseball Spotlight," he argued that Munson played in more games than did Roy Campanella, Roger Bresnahan and Buck Ewing, and only 59 fewer than Mickey Cochrane. He had more hits than Bresnahan, Campanella, and Schalk. He had more .300 seasons than Berra, Bresnahan, Bench, Campanella, Ferrell, Fisk and Schalk, and more 100-RBI seasons than Bresnahan, Cochrane, Ewing, Ferrell, Fisk, Hartnett, Lombardi, and Schalk, all, except Fisk, in the Hall of Fame. Among his peers, Munson's batting average was 25 points higher than Johnny Bench's, and 21 points better than Carlton Fisk's. Carlton Fisk is often regarded as the American League's best catcher of the 1970s. He had more power than Munson. But Munson himself always resented the comparison. He believed that he was the better catcher. Fisk's most productive years came his first nine seasons when he played in Boston's Fenway Park. "Let's change ballparks," Munson pointed out, "and we'd see who hits more home runs." The left field home run alley in Yankee Stadium is much deeper than the Green Monster in Fenway Park.

Munson was an excellent catcher. In 1971, he set a fielding record, making only one error all season. His error occurred when he was knocked unconscious in a tag play at home plate. He was a three-time Gold Glove winner.

Munson was durable. As the Yankees' regular catcher, he averaged 144 games a season. Seldom has a catcher performed in such a high percentage

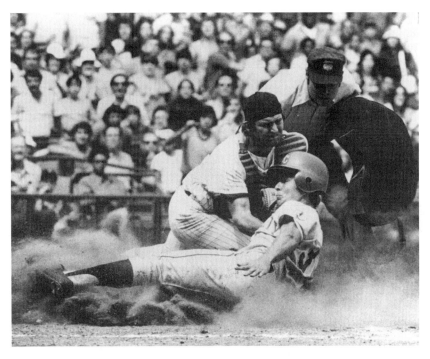

Thurmon Munson was a hard-hitting, tough-minded catcher on the New York Yankees' championship teams of the late seventies (ROCHESTER DEMOCRAT AND CHRONICLE).

of his team's games. Bill Dickey, Yankee great from an earlier era, as the regular catcher, averaged approximately 120 games per season.

Munson was the captain of three pennant-winning and two world championship teams. His .529 batting average in the 1976 World Series was the highest ever by a player on the losing team, and he had a record-tying six consecutive hits. More than one manager called him the toughest clutch hitter in baseball.

Don Honig, in his 1991 book *The Greatest Catchers of All Time*, included Thurman Munson among the 15 top catchers of all time. Of those, all eligible for the Hall of Fame have been elected except Munson. Three of the 15, Bob Boone, Gary Carter, and Carlton Fisk, will soon be eligible. Honig quotes another writer who said of the 1979 Yankees, "They were a team of stars, but when Thurman died, they were like a team without a heart."

Jay Johnstone, who played with Munson in 1978, summed up Munson's career succinctly. "He was a gamer."

THURMAN LEE MUNSON

Born June 7, 1947, Akron, Ohio.   Died Aug. 2, 1979, Akron, Ohio.   Batted right, threw right.

Year	Team	Pos.	G	AB	R	H	2B	3B	HR	RBI	BB	SB	BA	SA
1968	Bing--hamton, Eastern	C	71	226	28	68	2	3	6	37	36	4	.301	.460
1969	Syra-cuse, International	C, 2B, 3B	28	102	13	37	9	1	2	17	13	1	.363	.529
1969	NY, AL I.I.I.	C	26	86	6	22	1	2	1	9	10	0	.256	.349
1970	NY, AL	C	132	453	59	137	25	4	6	53	57	5	.302	.415
1971	NY, AL	C-117, OF-1	125	451	71	113	15	4	10	42	52	6	.251	.368
1972	NY, AL	C-132	140	511	54	135	16	3	7	46	47	6	.280	.364
1973	NY, AL	C-142	147	519	80	156	29	4	20	74	48	4	.301	.487
1974	NY, AL	C-137, DH-4	144	517	64	135	19	2	13	60	44	2	.261	.381
1975	NY, AL	C-130 DH-22, OF-2, 1B-2, 3B-1	157	597	83	190	24	3	12	102	45	3	.318	.429
1976	NY, AL	C-121, DH-21, OF-12	152	616	79	186	27	1	17	105	29	14	.302	.432
1977	NY, AL	C-136, DH-10	149	595	85	183	28	5	18	100	39	5	.308	.462
1978	NY, AL	C-125, DH-14, OF-13	154	617	73	183	27	1	6	71	35	2	.297	.373
1979	NY, AL	C-88, DH-5, 1B-3	97	382	42	110	18	3	3	39	32	1	.288	.374
Major League Totals 11 yrs.			1423	5344	696	1558	229	32	113	701	438	48	.292	.410

League Championship Series Record

Year	Team	Pos.	G	AB	R	H	2B	3B	HR	RBI	BB	SB	BA	SA
1976	NY, AL	C	5	23	3	10	2	0	0	3	0	0	.435	.522
1977	NY, AL	C	5	21	3	6	1	0	1	5	0	0	.286	.476
1978	NY, AL	C	4	18	2	5	1	0	1	2	0	0	.278	.500
Totals			14	62	8	21	4	0	2	10	0	0	.339	.500

World Series Record

Year	Team	Pos.	G	AB	R	H	2B	3B	HR	RBI	BB	SB	BA	SA
1976	NY, AL	C	4	17	2	9	0	0	0	2	0	0	.529	.529
1977	NY, AL	C	6	25	4	8	2	0	1	3	2	0	.320	.520
1978	NY, AL	C	6	25	5	8	3	0	0	7	3	0	.320	.440
Totals			16	67	11	25	5	0	1	12	5	0	.373	.493

8 THE WHIP

EWELL BLACKWELL

"I think the best pitcher who
ever lived was Ewell Blackwell."
JOE FALLS, *DETROIT NEWS*

They called him "The Whip." Red Smith described him as "a fly rod with ears." In the 1947 season, right-handed batters feared hitting against him as much as any pitcher who ever toed the rubber. Hitters instinctively wanted to keep one foot in the dugout when facing Ewell Blackwell. The six-foot-six-inch beanpole stepped toward third base, and whipped the ball sidearm across his body toward home plate, the pitch approaching 100 miles an hour. Blackwell's fastball seemed to come from third base and then it tailed back so that it fooled many a hitter. It took courage for a right-handed batter to keep his front foot from bailing out of the batter's box. Blackwell's number two pitch was a wide sweeping curve ball that came right at the batter and then swept across the plate in a magnificent arc.

Left-handed batters found it easier, for they could see the ball better. Yet, Blackwell's pitch was so alive with a sinking movement and came at such high velocity that hitting against him was no piece of cake for lefties either. The Whip's control was good enough to nip the outside corner with his breaking pitch, which he threw overhanded to batters working from the first base side of the plate.

Pee Wee Reese compared hitting against Blackwell with going up against one "of those softball phenoms." "The ball is on top of you before you're set for it," the Dodger shortstop related. "Blackwell has that ball behind his back one second, and the next second it's by you."

Pittsburgh Pirates manager Danny Murtaugh years later recalled, "If you were a right-handed hitter and you came out on the bench and saw Blackwell warming up for the game whipping those sidearm fast balls with that long right arm, you felt like crying. Or you started thinking up reasons why you shouldn't play that day." Ralph Kiner simply stated, "Your legs shook when you tried to dig in on him."

The Whip from Cincinnati led the National League in 1947 with 22 wins. He also had the most complete games, 23, and had a league high strikeout total of 193, almost as many as the strikeout king of the day, Rapid Robert Feller of the Cleveland Indians, whose 196 led the American League.

Blackwell won 16 straight games that year, second only to the 19 consecutive games won by Rube Marquard for the Giants in 1912 (April 11–July 3). Tim Keefe, also of New York, won 19 straight in 1888, but Keefe worked from a pitcher's box which was five and a half feet by four feet, and the distance to the plate was only 50 feet compared to the 60 feet, six inches of today.

Others who had won 16 in a row in one season were Walter Johnson of the Washington Senators in 1912 (July 3–August 23), Smoky Joe Wood with the Boston Red Sox, also in 1912 (July 8–September 15), Lefty Grove with the Philadelphia Athletics in 1931 (June 8–August 19), Schoolboy Rowe with the Detroit Tigers in 1934 (June 15–August 25), and Carl Hubbell with the 1936 Giants (July 17 to the end of the season). Hubbell began the next season by winning eight straight, thereby giving him the all-time record for consecutive games won over more than one season, 24.

Ewell Blackwell was born in Fresno, California, but his family moved to the Los Angeles suburb of San Dimas when he was 4. His father, Flugin Ewell Blackwell, who played semipro baseball around Fresno, encouraged his young son's budding interest in the game. At every opportunity, he played catch with him on a vacant lot across from the home and freely gave tips to the boy about throwing the ball.

Blackwell's father, always partial to baseball, insisted that Ewell try out for the Bonita High baseball team. The coach took one look at the tall, spindly kid, put him at first base and kept him there for three years. From the first base position, Blackwell whipped the ball around the bases so smartly that the coach decided to try him as a pitcher. From that day on, Blackwell wore a toe plate.

He became such a standout in high school and in local semipro circles that nearby La Verne Teachers College enticed him with a scholarship. Blackie's stay at La Verne was short-lived. He became convinced that he wanted to try professional baseball and left La Verne before the end of the 1941 school year.

In the summer of 1941 after he left La Verne, Blackwell worked as a riveter at Vultee Aircraft in the Los Angeles area and pitched twice a week for the company team. Major league scouts swarmed around young Blackie, and many began to visit his father.

The elder Blackwell told each scout that his son wanted a contract calling for the major league club to take him to spring training. This ultimatum caused several clubs to back off. For example, Ted McGrew, the Dodgers' master scout, pleaded with club president Larry MacPhail to sign the lad, but MacPhail scoffed at the thought of having a "busher" in his major league camp. The St. Louis Cardinals backed away for the same reason.

Pat Patterson, the Cincinnati Reds' West Coast scout, saw Blackie lose a 2–1 game in Anaheim, and promptly wrote general manager Warren Giles, "He's so good I'm afraid to tell you how good he is." He went to the Blackwell home and spoke with the boy's father. He quickly discovered that the Blackwells were not as interested in a big bonus as in an opportunity for quick advancement to the major leagues.

On January 9, 1942, Patterson called Giles and told him that Blackwell was ready to sign if the Reds promised to take him to spring training. Giles agreed. This enabled Patterson to sign the young phenom to a contract with the Ogden, Utah, Pioneer League Club for a $750 signing bonus and $125 a month. He was to receive an additional $250 if he was still around by the first of July.

When the Reds saw Blackwell's fastball at spring training, the club ripped up the Pioneer League contract and signed him to a major league agreement. Manager Bill McKechnie realized that Blackwell was a rare talent. He told the sportswriters "the boy has everything," and gave Blackwell a chance to prove himself in an exhibition game against the Boston Red Sox.

With a 6–4 lead in the ninth inning, double no-hit Johnny Vander Meer had filled the bases with Boston runners with no one out. McKechnie handed the ball to Blackwell and told him, "Get the ball over, son, and we'll win the game." Blackie got Lou Finney out on a slow grounder that scored the runner from third, but then the nervous youngster walked the next batter to reload the bases. He breathed deeply, regained his composure and got Johnny Pesky to ground into a game-ending double play. While he had manager McKechnie's confidence, the youthful phenom admitted to being plenty scared.

The Reds not only honored their signing promise of having Blackwell train with the major league club, they also opened the season with him on the Cincinnati bench. He pitched in two games.

McKechnie realized that Blackwell needed to pitch regularly and that he could profit from seasoning in the minor leagues. Wisely, he dispatched the young pitcher to Syracuse, the Reds' Triple A affiliate.

Blackie's sidearm slants terrorized International League hitters. He worked 227 innings, won 15 and lost 10 and posted an outstanding 2.02 ERA. He allowed only 168 hits, or 6.66 per nine innings.

In the postseason playoffs, he posted three shutouts and won a fourth game with three shutout innings, compiling a string of 30 consecutive scoreless frames. Syracuse, which had finished third during the regular season, defeated Montreal four games to one in the Governor's Cup Series, and then swept Jersey City four straight in the league finals. For Ewell Blackwell, the phenom label belonged.

It looked as if Blackwell would pitch Syracuse to the Junior World Series championship, but he contracted pneumonia during the playoffs and Columbus of the American Association won the series four games to one while Blackwell was hospitalized.

Before Blackwell had a chance to don a red-and-white Reds' uniform in 1943, Uncle Sam outfitted him with khaki green. He was drafted into the Army in December 1942, and sent to Camp Howze, Texas, near Dallas, for his basic training. By July 1943, he was transferred to Fort Benning, Georgia. The Whip pitched for the post baseball team at Benning, and his 71st Division beat Boston Braves second baseman Bama Rowell's 76th Division in the Third Army Finals.

In January 1945, Blackwell was sent to Europe with the 71st Division. The outfit saw considerable action against Hitler's forces. On V-E Day, he was in Austria. While waiting for demobilization in the summer of 1945, Blackwell pitched his division to the European Theater of Operations championship. He won 16 games, while losing only four. He matched his loss total with an equal number of no-hitters.

Blackwell was discharged on March 19, 1946. He reported to the Reds at Tampa on March 31, the day before Cincinnati broke spring camp. When the club headed north on an exhibition tour before the start of the season, Blackwell was left behind in Florida to train with Syracuse in nearby Plant City. He was so glad to be back in baseball that he bore down too hard on the Syracuse players. They refused to hit against him. Thereafter, Blackwell did most of his spring training throwing on the sidelines.

He rejoined Cincinnati in mid–April and pitched in a couple of games. By mid–May, the stiffness seemed to leave his arm and he was ready to take his turn in the starting rotation. He caught everyone's attention by beating St. Louis, 5–1, on a three-hitter on May 12 in the second game of a Sunday doubleheader, striking out 10. Bill McKechnie exuberantly declared that Blackwell "walked right out of Germany into my starting mound staff."

Blackie pitched well in his rookie season but found it difficult to win games. The Cincinnati scoreboard operator must have felt there was a run on goose eggs that year. Blackwell whitewashed the opposition in six of his nine victories, and the Reds were shut out in six of Blackie's 13 losses. He led the league in shutouts. His 7.41 hits allowed per nine-inning game placed him third in the National League behind Monte Kennedy of New York and Johnny Schmitz of the Chicago Cubs. His 2.45 ERA was fourth best in the league, and he was third in strikeouts per nine innings at 4.63.

At the close of the season, in which the Reds finished sixth with a 67–87 record, the new pitching sensation wanted to go on a barnstorming tour despite battling tonsillitis. At that time, star players commonly enhanced their income by touring and playing before audiences who often had never seen major league players perform. Giles intervened for the Reds. He persuaded Blackwell to pass up barnstorming by giving him $3,000, with the stipulation that the star pitcher submit to a tonsillectomy. Giles later reminisced, "Better money I have never spent. Blackie gained 18 pounds after that operation. He needed every pound of it."

Despite his increase in size and his better health, Blackwell opened the 1947 season slowly for new manager Johnny Neun. He won his first two starts, beating St. Louis, 3–1, on opening day, April 15, and Pittsburgh, 13–5, on April 21. On April 26, he held those same Pirates to two hits in seven innings, but he allowed six walks and received no decision in a game the Reds won, 3–2, for reliever Harry Gumbert by scoring twice in the bottom of the eighth inning. Next, on April 30, he worked against the Boston Braves, but they knocked him out of the box, nailing him for 10 hits in three innings. The Braves won the game, 10–3. The Phillies also kayoed him in seven innings four days later, beating the Reds 5–3.

Then, with a 2–2 record, the willowy righthander went to work. Well rested because of a series of rainouts, he beat Chicago 5–1, on May 10, beginning a 16-game winning streak that stretched to July 25. He went the route in all 16 victories. It was an amazing string. On May 14, he shut out the Brooklyn Dodgers, 2–0. On May 18, he beat Boston, 2–1, on nine hits. He stifled the Pittsburgh Pirates, 6–1, on May 27. On June 1 against the New York Giants, Blackwell was removed from the game for a pinch hitter in the seventh inning and received no decision. The Reds went on to win the game, 5–3. Then he bounced back to baffle the Philadelphia Phillies, 5–0, on June 5. He defeated Brooklyn, 3–1, on June 10 and edged New York, 4–3 on June 14.

On June 18, he pitched the first night game of his career. It proved to be his best effort. In front of 18,000 fans, he no-hit the Braves, 6–0, giving up four walks and allowing only one runner past first base. In the eighth inning, he walked Phil Masi and Sibby Sisti in succession, but he got Connie Ryan and Mike McCormick to end the inning.

Boston	AB	R	H	PO	A	Cincinnati	AB	R	H	PO	A
Holmes, rf	3	0	0	3	0	Baumholtz, rf	5	2	4	3	0
Hopp, cf	2	0	0	3	0	Zientara, 2b	3	0	1	2	2
Rowell, lf	4	0	0	0	0	Hatton, 3b	1	2	1	1	4
R. Elliott, 3b	3	0	0	1	1	Young, 1b	5	2	2	9	1
Torgeson, 1b	3	0	0	8	3	Haas, cf	4	0	0	3	0
Masi, c	2	0	0	2	1	Galan, lf	5	0	2	4	0
Sisti, ss	2	0	0	3	4	Miller, ss	5	0	0	2	1
Ryan, 2b	3	0	0	4	1	Lamanno, c	3	0	1	3	1
Wright, p	0	0	0	0	0	Blackwell, p	4	0	1	0	2
Lanfranconi, p	2	0	0	0	1	TOTALS	35	6	12	27	11
McCormick, ph	1	0	0	0	0						
TOTALS	25	0	0	24	11						

McCormick batted for Lanfranconi in eighth.

Boston	0	0	0	0	0	0	0	0	0—0
Cincinnati	3	0	0	0	0	0	0	3	x—6

Errors-Sisti 2. Runs batted in — Young 6. Home runs — Young 2. Sacrifices — Hopp, Zientara 2. Double plays — Miller to Zientara, Ryan to Sisti to Torgeson. Left on bases — Boston 3, Cincinnati 13. Hit by pitcher — Wright (Haas). Losing pitcher — Wright. Umpires — Barlick, Gore and Pinelli. Time —1:51. Attendance —18,137.

	IP	H	R	ER	BB	SO
Blackwell (10-2)	9	0	0	0	4	3
Wright (1-2)	1⅓	3	3	3	3	1
Lanfranconi	5⅔	6	0	0	1	0
Karl	1	3	3	3	1	0

Blackwell's feat gained additional luster because it was against the hardest hitting club in the league. In their last four games before Blackwell's gem, the Braves had scored 42 runs on 52 hits. All of Cincinnati's runs scored on two three-run home runs by first baseman Babe Young. It was the first nighttime no-hitter in the majors since Vander Meer no-hit the Brooklyn Dodgers under the lights in 1938.

On June 22, the slender righthander came close to providing even bigger drama. With 31,204 in the stands and double no-hit pitcher Johnny Vander Meer, who was still in the Reds starting rotation, sitting on the Cincinnati bench, Blackwell took the Dodgers into the ninth inning without allowing a base hit.

Gene Hermanski opened the final frame by lofting an easy fly to Augie

Galan for the first out. Eddie Stanky took the first pitch, and then lashed the second one back at the mound. Blackie stabbed at the ball with his glove, but it went between his legs into center field for a base hit, depriving Blackwell of two consecutive no-hit games. Stanky's smash was the first hit off the side-wheeling righthander in 19 consecutive innings of pitching. With the pressure off, Al Gionfriddo flied out to Galan, and then Jackie Robinson looped a bleeder to right field for the second single. Blackie then retired Carl Furillo and won on a two-hitter.

Brooklyn						Cincinnati					
	AB	R	H	PO	A		AB	R	H	PO	A
Stanky, 2b	4	0	1	0	3	Baumholtz, rf	2	0	0	3	0
Gionfriddo, lf	4	0	0	0	0	Zientara, 2b	4	0	0	1	5
Robinson, 1b	4	0	1	8	1	Hatton, 3b	4	2	1	0	1
Furillo, cf	3	0	0	4	0	Haas, cf	3	1	1	2	0
Walker, rf	1	0	0	3	0	Young, 1b	4	0	0	9	1
Jorgensen, 3b	3	0	0	2	0	Galan, lf	2	1	0	4	0
Reese, ss	2	0	0	3	3	Miller, ss	4	0	2	2	1
Vaughn, ph	1	0	0	0	0	Lamanno, c	2	0	0	4	0
Rojek, ss	0	0	0	0	0	Blackwell, p	4	0	0	0	0
Hodges, c	3	0	0	3	1	TOTALS	27	4	4	27	8
Snider, ph	1	0	0	0	0						
Bragan, c	0	0	0	1	0						
Hatten, p	2	0	0	0	0						
Behrman, p	0	0	0	0	0						
Hermanski, ph	1	0	0	0	0						
TOTALS	28	0	2	24	8						

Vaughn forced Walker at second for Reese in 8th. Snider struck out for Hodges in 8th. Hermanski flied out for Behrman in 9th.

Brooklyn	0	0	0		0	0	0		0	0	0	—	0 2 0
Cincinnati	0	0	0		0	0	1		0	3	x	—	4 4 0

RBI — Miller 3, Galan 1. Two base hits — Miller 2. DP — Miller, Zientara, to Young. Left on base — Brooklyn 4. Cincinnati 8. Umpires — Goetz, Conlan and Reardon. Time — 2:13. Attendance — 31,204.

	IP	H	R	ER	BB	SO
Blackwell (11-2)	9	2	0	1	6	2
Hatten (7-5)	5⅔	1	1	1	6	2
Behrman	2⅓	3	3	3	1	1

Through the years, Blackwell replayed that inning in his mind, always asking if he should have gotten down quicker and stopped Stanky's ball. More than two decades later, he reminisced that "it was awful tough to lose the second no-hitter that way."

The winning streak had reached nine games, with 10 runs allowed. On June 26, Blackwell made it ten in a row by turning back St. Louis, 6–3, on eight hits, but he allowed three runs. On June 30, he beat Chicago, 6–4, and on July 4, he shut out Pittsburgh, 8–0.

At the All-Star break, Blackwell was 14–2 with five shutouts and a sparkling 1.12 earned run average. He started the All-Star Game and pitched three innings, striking out four and giving up one hit to Joe DiMaggio. The National League lost the game for the tenth time in 14 tries, 2–1.

Blackwell's All-Star performance won him acclaim. "Right now, Blackwell is as good a pitcher as Bobby Feller," proclaimed Cleveland Indians player-manager Lou Boudreau, who struck out against the Cincinnati phenom in the All-Star Game. "Blackwell's speed is terrific. He is around the plate all the time, his curve is deadly and that sidearm sinker spectacular."

Jackie Robinson, who debuted that year as the first black player in the majors since 1884, was asked who were the three toughest pitchers in the league. He replied, "Blackwell. Blackwell. Blackwell."

Blackwell was compared favorably to Feller by most of the baseball people at the game. Bucky Harris of the Yankees, who contended that Feller was faster, and coach Chuck Dressen of the Dodgers, who claimed that Feller's curve was bigger, were lone exceptions.

After the All-Star game, Blackwell resumed his winning streak. On July 11, he beat Boston, 10–6; on July 15, he downed Philadelphia, 5–4, in 10 innings; on July 20 he defeated New York, 4–1; and on July 25, he again beat Philadelphia, 5–4, yielding 13 hits. He now had won 16 straight games, equaling the records of Johnson, Wood, Grove, Rowe, and Hubbell. He needed three more to tie Marquard's all-time record. (Since Blackwell, Jack Sanford of San Francisco won 16 in a row in 1962, and Pittsburgh's Elroy Face, a reliever, won 17 games without a loss in 1959.)

On July 30, he no-hit New York into the fifth inning, when Walker Cooper homered for the Giants. Although somewhat shaky, Blackie entered the ninth inning leading, 4–3. He was two outs away from winning his seventeenth straight when Willard Marshall, a left-handed hitter, tied the score with a home run into the right-field bleachers. In the top of the tenth, the light-hitting Buddy Blattner walked, and relief pitcher Monte Kennedy sacrificed him to second. Rigney grounded out. But moments later, Blattner scored on a single by Buddy Kerr. The Reds were unable to retaliate in the bottom of the inning, and Blackwell's streak ended with the 5–4 loss.

After the Giant loss, Blackwell suffered a letdown. He dropped a 4–2 decision August 3 to the Braves and on August 8 suffered a third consecutive, heartbreaking defeat at the hands of the Cubs, 2–1.

Ewell Blackwell, a lanky, side-arming righthander, won 16 consecutive games in 1947 (National Baseball Hall of Fame Library, Cooperstown, NY).

The defeat was peculiarly painful. Blackwell's parents had traveled to Chicago from California as guests of the team to see their son pitch for the first time since he left home in 1942. It looked as if the Reds would pull it out in the seventh, but the Cubs reeled off a dramatic triple play to preserve a 1–1 tie. Then, in the eleventh inning, Bill Nicholson unloaded a blast over Wrigley Field's ivy-covered wall in right field for a Cub victory. The

California couple sat stunned as riotous Cub fans swarmed out on the field. On the mound, their famous son felt crushed that he had let his parents down.

Tough luck prevented Blackwell from achieving his goal of 25 victories. In a play at the plate on August 21 in a game won by the Brooklyn Dodgers, 8–1, the reckless Pete Reiser stormed in from third in the fifth inning and collided with Blackwell, who was covering the plate. Blackie suffered a wrenched knee that sidelined him until August 28 when he notched win number 20 by beating the Boston Braves, 4–2.

After winning his twenty-first game against Pittsburgh on September 3, the lanky pitcher was struck by more bad luck. He pulled a muscle under his shoulder, and it looked as though his season might be over.

Blackwell, however, was able to come back to increase his total to a league-leading 22 victories against eight setbacks. He compiled a 2.47 earned run average, second to Warren Spahn's 2.33; he led the league in strikeouts with 193; he pitched the most complete games, 23; struck out a league-leading 6.36 batters per nine innings; and he was second in fewest hits per nine innings, allowing 7.48 to Harry Taylor's 7.22. Blackwell was tied for second in shutouts with six, and he was third in winning percentage at .733, outstanding for a pitcher on a fifth-place club that finished 73–81. Remarkably, the frail-looking right-hander showed real durability by finishing third in the league with 273 innings pitched.

Despite Blackwell's remarkable year, he surprisingly finished second by 30 points to Bob Elliott of Boston in the voting for the league's Most Valuable Player award. Blackwell responded by establishing the goal of a 30-victory season for 1948. He wanted to be the best pitcher in baseball.

He credited Bucky Walters with teaching him how to pitch, especially how to throw the curveball and hold runners on base. Walters called Blackwell an apt pupil. "He instinctively does the right thing. I've been working on a knuckler for quite a while. Damned if Blackwell can't throw it better than I can without even trying." Associated Press writers placed Blackwell on their all–major league team for the year as the best right-handed pitcher in baseball.

In the waning days of the 1947 season, Blackwell underwent a physical. Although doctors found no maladies, little did Blackwell realize the problems that lay ahead.

When Blackwell reported to the Reds at Tampa in March 1948, he seemed to be in excellent condition. The first day in camp, he threw about 10 minutes for batting practice and whipped in several fast ones that had the batters blinking. On the grapefruit circuit, he was touted as the hottest pitcher on a pitching-rich and ever-improving Cincinnati team. He held major league hitters scoreless for 16 straight innings that spring. On March 21, he shut out the New York Yankees for five innings. The Bombers praised Blackwell afterward and wondered how The Thin Man could "crack the whip so hard and not break an arm."

On April 2, he shut out the pennant-contending St. Louis Cardinals for five innings and drew praise from St. Louis players. But on April 7, Blackwell did not warm up sufficiently, and was rocked for three runs in the first inning by the Syracuse Chiefs.

Blackwell was the chief topic of the Cincinnati entourage. Johnny Neun became excited about the team's chances because of his club's pitching. "I like the looks of Johnny Vander Meer. I've confidence in the ability of Bucky Walters to do better than the 8–8 record he turned in last season. I don't have to tell you about Blackwell," he told reporters.

The Reds opened the season on April 19 against Pittsburgh with Blackwell on the mound. The tall righthander went the distance, winning 4–1 on a seven-hitter. Four days later on April 23, with relief help from Gumbert, he beat the Pirates again, 5–3. It promised to be another good year for the Whip.

However, on April 27, Chicago greeted him with a three-run outburst in the first inning, and Blackie was yanked after five innings as the Cubs went on to win, 7–2. Manager Neun dismissed the showing as just "one of those bad days."

But then he lost to Pittsburgh, 6–4, on May 2 when Ralph Kiner homered in the ninth inning. On May 7, Boston's Bob Elliott and Jeff Heath hit for the circuit off Blackie and led the Braves to a 4–3 victory. In the fifth inning, while pitching against Bill Voiselle, Blackwell injured his right shoulder and was forced to leave the game. He was expected to be out for ten days, but it turned out to be three weeks.

He returned for a relief stint on May 29 against the Chicago Cubs, and he helped Vander Meer win 4–3 by pitching two strong innings. On the basis of this showing, Neun started Blackie against the hard-hitting New York Giants on June 3. He responded by holding them to two hits over seven innings, winning 6–4. In his next outing on June 9, he lost to Philadelphia, 3–2, but he allowed only five hits in seven innings of work. Perhaps Blackie was all the way back.

But the Boston Braves shelled him with 11 hits in eight innings in the second game of a doubleheader on June 13, the Reds losing 10–5. His next start was a no-decision game on June 22 when he went seven innings against Philadelphia, allowing six hits and two runs in an 11-inning game won by Cincinnati, 6–4.

He won three straight prior to the All-Star game. On June 27, he beat New York, 4–3, with relief from Gumbert, and on July 4, he defeated St. Louis, 8–6, with relief help from Peterson and Gumbert. Then on July 8, he looked like the Blackwell of 1947 when he shut out the Chicago Cubs, 4–0. By the time of the All-Star Game, Blackwell's record stood at 6–5. Reds' manager Neun hoped that Blackie could build on that in the second half of the season. Both, however, experienced disappointment. Neun lost his job before the season ended, and the lanky righthander achieved only moderate success at best.

He lost his first two starts after the midseason break. On July 16, he lost to Brooklyn, 4–2, and on July 21, to Boston, 6–2. When Blackwell defeated Philadelphia, 9–2, on July 25, it would be his last win of the season. On July 30, he had to leave the game after two innings against the Phillies in a game the Reds won 8–5, and then, on August 13, he lost to the Chicago Cubs, 10–4, pitching into the sixth inning before being relieved. On August 17, he went the route against Pittsburgh but lost 4–3, as he allowed the Pirates 14 hits.

Then, on August 23, he started against the Philadelphia Phillies but had to leave the game in the eighth inning because he reinjured his shoulder. It was small consolation to Gumbert and the Reds that they won the game in 10 innings, 3–2, because their outstanding young hurler once more was disabled.

Blackwell made his final appearance of the year on August 27, pitching one inning in relief against the Brooklyn Dodgers and allowing two hits, the Dodgers winning 3–2. He was sidelined for the rest of the season with a sore shoulder.

For the year, Blackie compiled a 7–9 win-loss record and a disappointing 4.54 ERA in 138 innings of work. His pitches in 1948 never had the snap that they had the year before.

Clearly, Blackwell was ailing. It was revealed that not only had he suffered from arm woes in 1948, but that his kidney had been infected.

On January 20, 1949, doctors surgically removed Blackwell's right kidney, and he began a long convalescence. Prospects for the season looked grim. He pitched only 76 innings and split 10 decisions with a 4.23 ERA. He started four games and pitched 26 times in relief.

During the offseason, Blackwell regained his strength. He wrote Luke Sewell, the new Reds manager, that he was up to 200 pounds. Sewell thought that was "very good news." But Sewell added, "I can't help wishing his left instead of right kidney was removed, because a right-hander must put tremendous strain on the muscles of his throwing side."

Medical authorities assured Blackwell that having only one kidney would not handicap his comeback effort. So he worked to get his arm in shape and looked forward to another 20-win season. The Reds were optimistic about moving up in the standings. Grantland Rice wrote that with the return of the "Human Eucalyptus Tree" to the mound corps, Cincinnati would have a "pretty fair ball club."

Blackwell did his part to move the Reds up in the standings in 1950. The big pitcher bounced back strong, going 17–15 for a sixth-place club that finished 66–87. National League hitters were again calling him their toughest pitching opponent. "He's not as fast as he was," said the Giants' Tom Sheehan. "But he's still a vicious son-of-a-gun with that motion."

To Hal Newhouser, himself an outstanding pitcher, Blackwell was a marvel. "He is the only pitcher I know who hides the ball four times and shows you the ball four times," Newhouser said. "That is, you see the ball, the ball disappears, then you see it again. No wonder the batter gets cock-eyed trying to follow that ball. Then suddenly Blackwell turns the ball loose, and it's on you before you can move a bat."

Blackwell compiled a 2.97 earned run average, third best in the National League. Normally, a pitcher with an ERA that low does not lose 15 games, especially when the league average is 4.14. Unfortunately, the Reds wound up 21 games below .500, and scored few runs for their pitching ace. Blackwell pitched 18 complete games in 32 starts, being removed a number of times for a pinch hitter because the club was behind. He pitched 261 innings and allowed only 203 hits, seven per nine innings, second in the league. Blackwell was second in strikeouts, 188, and led the league in strikeouts per nine innings, 6.48, statistics that showed that Blackwell was back. He was easily the comeback story of the year.

On September 25, at about 2 A.M., Blackwell was stricken by acute appendicitis on a train ride to St. Louis. He was removed from the train at Indianapolis and taken back to Cincinnati for an emergency appendectomy, ending his season.

He pitched at almost the same level in 1951 as he did the year before. His win-loss total was 16–15, and he compiled a 3.45 ERA, a half a run below the league average of 3.96. Again, the hapless Reds finished well below .500 at 68–86. Late in the season, Blackwell began to experience shoulder pains.

In the spring of 1952, Blackwell's arm looked strong and he appeared sharp. Manager Sewell opined that Blackie might return to spearhead the Reds' staff, and that with better hitting behind him, he would return to the select 20-game-winners' circle. Sewell was wrong. The season was a disaster for Blackwell, and the Reds sold him to the pennant bound Yankees on

August 28. The Yanks habitually picked up veteran National Leaguers for the pennant chase and they outbid Cleveland and Chicago for Blackwell.

The Yanks were pleased when Blackwell in his Yankee Stadium debut pitched five strong innings on September 2 against Boston in a 4–0 triumph. He fanned four men in those five innings and showed occasional bursts of speed that reminded people of the old flame-throwing Whip. Blackwell was glad to be in New York, and said that he wished he could have gotten there earlier.

In his second appearance, on September 6, the Washington Senators rocked him for four hits in one inning. Altogether, he appeared in five games for the Yankees, going 1–0.

But Blackwell finally had a chance to pitch in a World Series, starting the fifth game on October 5. He struck out four, walked three and allowed four runs on four hits in five innings. That game was his only series action. What had been suspected much of the season was fact. Blackwell's right arm, that once magnificent whip, was giving him trouble again, and forced him to the bench.

"My arm has started to hurt me all over again," said Blackwell. "I have a sharp pain all the way from elbow to shoulder. I'm awfully sorry."

He reported to the Yankees the next spring at St. Petersburg weighing 209 pounds. He told reporters, "I am confident that I will justify the excitement which broke out when I came to New York last summer." He hoped to work his way into Casey Stengel's starting corps. Blackwell was optimistic in the spring of 1953, but performed unimpressively. On March 25, he pitched against the Cardinals, yielding five runs in the closing three innings of the game. Throughout, Yankee catcher Charley Silvera exhorted Blackwell to throw hard, but Blackie couldn't.

Stengel remained optimistic. Speaking in grammatically correct sentences, he said, "Professor Jim Turner [pitching coach] and I feel there is no reason to weaken on Blackwell. It's true Ewell has not been as impressive as we'd hoped. But there is nothing wrong with his arm or physical condition."

Stengel was not prophetic. Blackwell made eight pitching appearances in 1953, starting four games, pitching 19 innings. On July 6 he was placed on the disabled list because of a sore arm, and he returned home to Tampa for the rest of the season, missing the World Series.

Blackwell's name did not appear on the Yankees' roster in 1954, but he began to work out in February. Early in the exhibition schedule, Stengel named Blackwell to hurl the first three frames in a game with the Cardinals, but that morning Blackie notified Turner that he was giving up.

"For a time everything felt fine, and I thought I could make it," Blackwell said. "But as soon as I started putting pressure on the arm, the soreness which put me out last summer began coming back. When it extended from the elbow to the shoulder, I knew it was the same thing all over again." He thanked Stengel for giving him a chance and went home.

In the spring of 1955, Blackwell claimed that his arm was in good shape and criticized the Yankees for not giving him a contract. Stengel explained that the Yankees had invested a lot of money in Blackwell and that they had gotten little in return. "Now he makes a nasty crack about us not letting him make a living," Stengel rejoined. "I don't like people who distribute such trash." Yankees general manager George Weiss said that New York could not send Blackwell a contract because he was on the voluntary retired list.

On March 30, the Yankees sold Blackwell to the Kansas City Athletics. Blackwell pitched two games for Kansas City, before he was unconditionally released.

Blackwell's dreams were unfulfilled. He announced, "I know I can still pitch" and headed to the Pacific Coast for a tryout with the San Francisco Seals, but they did not sign him. But he caught on with the Seattle Raniers and appeared in 20 games with them. It was difficult for Blackwell to acknowledge that the end had come.

Blackwell and his wife settled in Tampa, Florida, where he was successful in the liquor business. From there they moved to Columbia, South Carolina, where by 1969 his business was sufficiently successful that he and Dottie contemplated another move, this time to North Carolina where he lived in retirement.

No one may ever have pitched better than Ewell Blackwell did from early May through July in 1947. Blackwell convincingly displayed Hall-of-Fame qualities throughout that season before physical infirmities removed him from the box. The Whip was so awesome that Joe Falls, a sports columnist for the *Detroit News*, wrote in 1971, "I think the best pitcher who ever lived was Ewell Blackwell."

EWELL BLACKWELL

Born Oct. 23, 1922, Fresno, Cal.   Died Oct. 29, 1996, Hendersonville, N.C.   Batted right, threw right.

Year	Team	W–L	Pct.	ERA	G	GS	CG	IP	H	BB	SO	ShO
1942	Cin NL	0–0	.000	6.00	2	0	0	3	3	3	1	0
1942	Syracuse IL	15–10	.600	2.02	29	27	20	227	168	79	87	4

1943–1945   In military service.

Year	Team	W–L	Pct.	ERA	G	GS	CG	IP	H	BB	SO	ShO
1946	Cin NL	9–13	.409	2.45	33	25	10	194⅓	160	79	100	6
1947	Cin NL	*22–8	.733	2.47	33	33	*23	273	227	95	*193	*6
1948	Cin NL	7–9	.438	4.54	22	20	4	138⅔	134	52	114	1
1949	Cin NL	5–5	.500	4.23	30	4	0	76⅔	80	34	55	0
1950	Cin NL	17–15	.531	2.97	40	32	18	261	203	112	188	1
1951	Cin NL	16–15	.516	3.45	38	32	11	232⅔	204	97	120	2
1952	Cin NL	4–12	.250	4.73	28	19	3	118	119	72	55	0
	(23G,3–12), (NY, AL, 5G, 1–0)											
1953	NY Al	2–0	1.000	3.66	8	4	0	19⅔	17	13	11	0
1955	KC AL	0–1	.000	6.75	2	0	0	4	3	5	2	0
1955	San Fran,	5–5	.500	4.09	23	16	3	112	120	47	31	1
	Seattle PCL											
Major League												
Totals		82–78	.513	3.30	236	169	69	1320⅔	1150	562	839	16
10 yrs.												

Asterisk indicates led league

World Series Record

Year	Team	W–L	Pct.	ERA	G	GS	CG	IP	H	BB	SO	ShO
1952	NY, AL	0–0	--	7.20	1	1	0	5	4	3	4	0

9   BOSTON'S BOO

DAVE FERRISS

> "He'll win in any league against
> any kind of pitching."
> MANAGER JOE CRONIN

In 1945 and 1946, Dave Ferriss, nicknamed Boo, was one of the best pitchers in baseball. He was 21–10 in 1945, a war year, and he improved to 25–6 in 1946, a post-war year when the "real major leaguers" were back from military service. Ferriss won 46 games his first two years in the big leagues, an outstanding feat. Numerous hurlers have captured 20 wins in their first season, but in the twentieth century all but three failed to repeat in the second. Besides Ferriss, the only pitchers to win at least 20 in each of their first two years were Jake Weimer of the 1903 and 1904 Chicago Cubs, and Vean Gregg of Cleveland, who holds the modern-day record of 20 or more wins his first three years he appeared in the majors. Wes Ferrell won 20 games in his first four full-time seasons, but he had pitched briefly in two previous years. Since Ferriss accomplished the feat, no one has won 20 in each of his first two seasons in the majors.

David Meadow Ferriss was born December 5, 1921, in Shaw, Mississippi. When Ferriss was only 12 years old and in the seventh grade, he occasionally played second base for the Shaw High School team in the closing innings of lopsided losses. On his first play for Shaw, a runner charged into him at second and broke Ferriss's right wrist. With his right hand in a cast, Ferriss decided to practice throwing left-handed. He became sufficiently adept with his left arm that he always played first base or the outfield left-handed, and he started hitting left-handed as well. He was a shortstop in high school, right-handed of course. In his second year of high school, Ferriss began pitching, as a right-hander. Ferriss was also a running back on his high school football team and a center on the basketball team.

He entered Mississippi State University in 1939 and pitched for the school's baseball team. When not on the mound pitching right-handed, he played as a left-handed first baseman. In the summer of 1940, he was the star pitcher and outfielder of a semipro team that won the Mississippi-Louisiana championship.

The next summer he played for Brattleboro, Vermont, in the highly competitive semipro Northern League. He gained valuable experience competing against several major league prospects — Hank Borowy and George Stirnweiss, for example — and he proved to be one of the better players in the league.

That summer, Ferriss made his first visit to Fenway Park in Boston, and he had the good fortune to meet Ted Williams. Aware of the competitive nature of the Northern League, the renowned Boston slugger, who was working toward a .406 batting average that summer, boosted Ferriss's confidence by telling him that if he could win in the Northern League, he could win anywhere.

The Red Sox signed Ferriss to a contract in 1942 and farmed their new protégé to pitch at Greensboro in the Piedmont League. He split 14 decisions for Manager Heinie Manush with a fine 2.02 earned run average. He won all three games he pitched in the postseason playoffs, and immediately he became a hot prospect for the Red Sox.

Instead of reporting to Tom Yawkey in Boston the next year, Ferriss reported to the U.S. Army Air Corps. He pitched for his Air Corps unit at San Antonio, compiling an 8–2 record the first year and 20–8 the second. He served Uncle Sam for 26 months before the Army released him because of severe asthma. Asthmatic attacks often disabled him for days. Doctors advised him to move to a dry climate, preferably Arizona, and to change his profession. Baseball fever, however, consumed young Ferriss more than hay fever, and he reported to Joe Cronin of the Red Sox for the 1945 season.

Ferriss didn't have a blazing fastball, but he threw a good, heavy sinker. Most of the time, the thick shouldered, six-foot-three-inch, long-armed phenom threw with a three-quarter arm motion; in spots, though, he would come overhanded, and he threw a deadly sidearm curve against right-handed hitters. Against left-handed batters, he threw the screwball. He seldom showed a hitter his best pitch until it really mattered. When he learned to throw his fastball and curve at varying speeds, something Bibb Falk taught him at San Antonio while Ferriss was pitching for the Air Force, Dave Ferriss became an outstanding pitcher.

Boston got off to a slow start, and Manager Cronin, in search of an antidote, started Ferriss against Connie Mack's Philadelphia Athletics on

April 29. The youngster was so nervous that he missed the strike zone with his first 12 pitches, filling the bases. When Roberto Estalella, the fourth hitter, stepped up to the plate, Earle Mack, coaching at first base, called Estalella down the line, and, instead of telling him to wait out the jittery rookie, instructed him to hit the first good pitch. Estalela swung at Ferriss's first offering and popped up. The putout seemed to calm the kid pitcher, and he settled down to retire the next two batters, allowing no runs in the inning. He won the game, 2–0, on a neat five-hitter.

Ferriss went on to win eight consecutive contests, four of them shutouts. After the fourth shutout, Joe King, a New York writer, labeled Ferriss "The Whitewash Kid." Below is a list of the Ferriss victory skein, all complete games except for one inning of relief:

- April 29, he beat Philadelphia, 2–0.
- May 6, he pitched a second consecutive shutout, whitewashing New York, 5–0.
- May 13, he beat Detroit, 8–2.
- May 18, he shut out the White Sox, 2–0.
- May 23, he beat the St. Louis Browns, 4–1.
- May 27, he again shut out the White Sox, this time on a one-hitter, 7–0.
- May 31, he defeated Cleveland, 6–2.
- June 3, he pitched a perfect ninth inning in relief to post a save in a 4–3 win over Detroit.
- June 6, he beat Philadelphia again, 5–2, for his eighth straight win.

The young Boston star was in pursuit of the all-time rookie record of 12 consecutive wins set by Atley Donald of New York in 1939. His ninth start was on Sunday, June 10, against New York in Yankee Stadium. Ferriss had blanked the Bronx Bombers easily in Fenway Park, but the House that Ruth Built was less congenial. Poor weather held the expected crowd of 70,000 to 41,216. They got their money's worth.

Boston's young phenom was pitted against Hank Borowy, a former foe in the Northern League. The Yankees scored on Ferriss in the first inning, and again in the third. Then Herschel Martin drove in the third and decisive run in the sixth. A double play got Ferriss out of that inning before the Yankees could inflict greater damage.

Going into the top of the ninth, only one run down, George Metkovich and Bob Johnson opened the inning with back-to-back singles. Manager Joe McCarthy countered by bringing in his bullpen ace, Milkman Jim Turner, to replace a tiring Borowy. The Yankee fireman smothered the Red Sox with three quick outs. When Johnny Lazor flied to Bud Metheny to end the game,

Ferriss's winning streak ended with a well-pitched 3–2 loss. He now was 8–1, the same as Borowy of New York.

The Yankees afterward were effusive in praising Ferriss's pitching. Manager McCarthy remarked, "He throws that fastball over the handle of your bat." George Stirnweiss, who won the batting title in 1945 and an old Northern League foe who touched Ferriss for a single and a double in the game, commented, "His sidearm curve ball is not one of the easiest pitches for a right-hander, believe me." Other hitters praised Ferriss' amazing control and pitching savvy for a rookie.

The mild-mannered, agreeable rookie was popular with fans, club officials and teammates alike. The fans in Boston chanted for Ferriss, just to see him, as a hitter or a pitcher. Every day, the Beantown phenom got a new pile of mail. He heard from almost all his old friends in the Army Air Corps, and from lots of other soldiers he didn't personally know, but who nonetheless sent him their best wishes and support. Letters came from Brazil, Germany, the South Pacific, and from all over the United States. At the ball park, he was a hot item for autographs. Ever modest and agreeable, Ferriss enjoyed contact with kids and seemed to get more kick out of signing autographs for them than they got from asking him. He always signed each autograph, "To my pal, Terence [or whatever the boy's name was]."

When the young pitcher had first reported to Boston, he discovered trainer Win Green's rule that lockers were only for regulars. Ferriss had to hang his clothes on a nail in the clubhouse. Even though the sensational rookie was compiling win after win during his streak, Green refused to give him a locker because he was afraid it would change Ferriss's luck. Ferriss, although not superstitious, went along without complaint. "What a modest guy," Green said at one point during the streak, "Why, I have to put a headlock on him to give him a rubdown." When the streak ended, the rusty nail never again felt the weight of Ferriss's clothes.

A left-handed hitter, Ferriss tended to help his own cause with timely hits, and he was often used as a pinch hitter. Hugh Duffy, an old Red Sox fixture who once hit .438, observed, "Ferriss is just as tough hitting against them as he is pitching against them." Ferriss hit .267 as a rookie. His career major-league batting average was .250.

On August 26, Ferriss beat Philadelphia, 4–3, in the first game of a doubleheader for his twentieth win. He also collected two hits, including a double. Writers speculated that the rookie would win 25 games his first year in the majors, an astounding feat. However, as the season moved into the month of August, asthma attacks became a problem. Ferriss had won his first eight games at the beginning of the season, but he took only three of his last 10.

His record for the season was 21–10, a great year for a rookie. His win total was second to Detroit Tiger Hal Newhouser's 25. His 26 complete games were second to Newhouser's 29. His 265 innings pitched were second to Newhouser's 313, and his five shutouts tied him with Al Benton of the Tigers for second behind Newhouser's eight. Newhouser was the dominant pitcher in baseball in 1944 and 1945, winning 54 games.

Rumors were circulating that doctors were advising Ferriss to give up baseball because of the asthma that had shortened his military career. Ferris pondered the question over the winter.

The other thing he pondered was the hex the Yankees seemed to have on him. After he shut them out in that first game at Fenway, he was winless against New York three straight times. The hex was so noticeable that it led Connie Mack to recall the experience of Lefty Grove. After Grove was sold to Boston, he started against the A's 19 times before he beat his old team. Once Grove broke the hex, he beat the A's regularly. Such hexes have been relatively common in major league baseball, affecting some of the game's greatest pitchers. Dazzy Vance and Dizzy Dean, for example, always had trouble with the Cubs; Carl Hubbell had a big career deficit against the cross-town Dodgers; and Kirby Higbe could not beat Pittsburgh.

Nineteen forty-five was the last war year. Some of the "real" major leaguers had already returned to play part of the baseball season. Bobby Feller, for example, returned to win five games for Cleveland. Hank Greenberg, who enlisted prior to Pearl Harbor and missed most of the 1941 season, returned to play 78 games for Detroit in 1945 and helped lead the Tigers to a World Series victory over the Cubs.

The actual changing of the guard took place in 1946 when the major-league ballplayers returned from military service. During the war, baseball had relied on a few old timers who returned to the major-league scene, any players physically unfit for the military, a few legitimate big leaguers who were deferred because of family hardship, such as Stan Musial from 1942–1944, and some players with minor-league talent who were forced into major-league roles.

Skeptics were certain that when the big hitters came back from the war, Boo Ferriss would find getting hitters out much harder. If the Yankees, with an outfield of Bud Metheny, Tuck Stainback, and Herschel Martin, had beaten Ferriss three out of four times in 1945, what would DiMaggio, Henrich, and Keller do to him? On the other hand, Ferriss now had Ted Williams, Dom DiMaggio, Johnny Pesky and a few other war veterans as part of his supporting cast.

Boston's Boo started the 1946 season slowly. He was knocked out of the

Dave Ferriss won 20 or more games each of his first two major league seasons (COR-BIS-BETTMAN ARCHIVES).

box by Washington on April 17 in the second game of the season and by Philadelphia on April 21 when Ferriss yielded six hits in two-and-two-thirds innings, a slugfest Boston eventually won, 12–11. After the second loss, whisperings were heard that Boo perhaps was a "wartime" pitcher. But on April 26, he shut out the A's, 7–0, in what proved to be the first of 10 straight victories for Ferriss, four of them shutouts.

"What a pitcher," Manager Joe Cronin exclaimed. "He'll win in any league against any kind of hitting." Cronin may not have understood that by winning ten straight, he was already doing that.

But after the 10-game streak, Ferriss lost four of the next six games. Then he got back on track, winning his twentieth game on August 14 against the A's. He stretched his record to 23–4, before Detroit, a team he had beaten six straight times, routed him on August 30 in six innings. He ended the season with a 25–6 record, as the Red Sox broke a 28-year drought and won their first pennant since 1918.

He faced New York three times in 1946 and won all three games. His winning percentage of .806 led the league. Only Feller and Newhouser topped his win total with 26; Ferris also ranked third in complete games with 26. One key to Boo's success was his continuing stinginess with bases on balls; he allowed only 2.33 walks per nine-inning game, third best in the American League. Especially noteworthy were Ferriss's 46 wins in his first two years in the major leagues, a figure topped only by Alexander's 47, compiled in 1911 and 1912.

Ferriss's performance in 1946 buried the charge that he was a wartime pitcher. Joe Cronin summed it up: "Everyone in baseball should doff his hat to him. He lived down the name of 'wartime' pitcher and showed that he had real stuff." Pitching against the real major leaguers, Boo Ferriss compared favorably with Bob Feller and Hal Newhouser, both enshrined in the Hall of Fame.

The 1946 World Series had considerable promise. Each side had a superstar: Boston had Ted Williams, St. Louis had Stan Musial. Each side had outstanding pitching: Boston had Tex Hughson, Mickey Harris, Joe Dobson, and, of course, Boo Ferriss; St. Louis had George Munger, Howie Pollett, Harry Brecheen, and Murry Dickson. The oddsmakers favored Boston to win. The series was equal to its promise and was one of the great series in history.

The Red Sox won the first game on October 6 in 10 innings, as Tex Hughson and Earl Johnson outdueled Howie Pollett. The next day Harry Brecheen beat the Sox, 3–0. Then, in game three on October 9, Ferriss shut out St. Louis, 4–0, on six hits. The victory made Ferriss 14–0 in Fenway Park for the year.

His pitching received high praise in the press. New York writer Dan Daniel said of Ferriss, "He has a free and easy motion. It looked as if he were skimming pebbles off a lake. He features that wicked snap of the wrist which is the mark of the truly great workman." Daniel further noted that Ferriss "is especially tough against the right-handed hitter. He sidearms that type and the ball rolls off the bat handle. He can three-quarter, and he can come overhand." Much was made of how Boo had closed out the game after Stan Musial's triple by striking out Enos Slaughter with a sinking fastball on a two-and-two count.

After the game, Ferriss went from locker to locker thanking his teammates for their roles in the victory. Ferriss was easily the best-liked member of the team.

With Boston leading the Series two games to one, Ferriss lamented, "Doesn't look as if I will get to pitch against them a second time." However, he was pleased that he could add a 47th baseball to his collection of balls from games he won as a major league pitcher in a display case in Mississippi. Dave Ferriss always remembered his roots.

The series, however, took a turn in game four. The Cardinals battered six Boston pitchers for 20 hits and a 12–3 victory. Boston won game five on October 11 in Fenway Park, and all they had to do was win one game at Sportsman's Park to win their first World Series since they sold Babe Ruth.

When the Series returned to St. Louis, Brecheen on October 13 beat Harris, 4–1, in game six, and it came down to the seventh game played October 15. The pitching matchup was Boo Ferriss against Murry Dickson, the same as in game three. Neither pitcher was around at the finish. Ferriss was removed in favor of Joe Dobson with one out in the fourth inning. Dickson pitched through the seventh, when he was replaced by Brecheen. In the bottom of the eighth, with Country Slaughter on first, Harry Walker hit a ball into the gap in left center field. Leon Culberson fielded it and threw to Pesky, the cutoff man, who hesitated a split second in relaying the ball to the plate, and Slaughter raced home with the winning run. It was one of the great moments in World Series history. Harry "The Cat" Brecheen was the pitching star of the Series with three victories.

The World Series loss was disappointing, but Ferriss went home knowing that he was one of the premier pitchers in baseball. His future seemed bright. After all, he was only 25 years old and he had already pitched a World Series shutout.

The Red Sox pitching staff in the spring of 1947 was strong. Tex Hughson, Joe Dobson, Mickey Harris and Boo Ferriss all were coming off good seasons. Earl Johnson seemed ready to help, and Dennis Galehouse came over from the St. Louis Browns early in the season. The batting order looked as power-laden as the year before. Baseball's seers believed that the Red Sox would repeat as American League champions.

The season, however, proved to be disappointing, both for the team and for Ferriss. The early weeks were an indication of the kind of year it was to be. Boo's control was off a bit, and he allowed more walks than he had the previous year. He was hit fairly hard on occasion, but he also pitched in a lot of games when the hard-hitting Red Sox failed to produce runs.

Ferriss won his first start of the year on April 18, beating Philadelphia, 9–3. In his second start on April 23, Boston's hitters failed him as Allie Reynolds of the Yankees shut out the Sox, 3–0. In his third start on April 27, Ferriss was shelled for 11 hits in five-and-two-thirds innings against Philadelphia, but the game ended in a 6–6 tie, called because of rain. Ferriss' next start on May 2 was another hard-luck performance. Cleveland beat him, 2–0, as Feller pitched a one-hitter.

On May 8, Ferriss won another game with relief help from Harry Dorish in the ninth inning because Ferriss injured his pitching hand fielding a line drive hit by Luke Appling. Ferriss and Dorish combined to shut out

Chicago, 3–0. On May 13, Ferriss started against the White Sox and lasted only five innings, allowing 10 hits. Boston won the game, 19–6, as Bill Zuber picked up the win in relief. On May 19, he was involved in another tough ballgame. He lost to Detroit, 3–2, in 12 innings. On May 24, Spud Chandler and the Yankees shut out Boston, 5–0, and in early June, Ferriss and the Red Sox were blanked by Detroit's Hal Newhouser. Thus, in Ferriss's first 10 starts, the Red Sox were shut out four times and lost a 3–2 game in 12 innings.

Ferriss's pitching for the month of June was inconsistent. In a night game on July 14, he was on. He outdueled Cleveland's Don Black, 1–0. Although it was not generally known at the time, the game was the watershed of Boo Ferriss's career. With the bases loaded, Ferriss cracked down hard with an overhand curve to George Metkovich. He felt a twinge as he threw the ball, and he experienced considerable pain as he continued to pitch, but he didn't think much of it. He finished the game, but the next day he could not lift his arm.

Ferriss's 12–11 win-loss record for the year was satisfactory, but certainly far from the 25–6 pinnacle of 1946. He was down in all statistical categories, but so were his pitching colleagues — Tex Hughson, Denny Galehouse and Earl Johnson. Hughson and Johnson both matched Ferriss' 12–11 record, and Galehouse was 11–7 as the Red Sox slipped to third place, two games behind the second-place Tigers, but 14 games behind the Yankees, who won the pennant for the first time since 1943. Ferriss' shoulder problem was probably a factor early in the season, explaining his inconsistency. The tendon in his shoulder simply popped that night in Cleveland. Although he occasionally showed flashes of his 1946 form, much of the time Ferriss' pitching was different from the previous two years. Always a respectable hitter, Ferriss was used as a pinch hitter during the year, and he batted .273 in 99 at-bats.

In the spring of 1948, Ferriss had difficulty getting in shape. Asthma sapped his strength, and his arm lacked the snap that had made him a respected pitcher. That overhand curve in Cleveland on July 14, 1947, had left him impaired. He had torn tendons in his right shoulder.

Writer Jack Hand, in a column predicting the finishes of both leagues, selected the Red Sox to win the American League, but noted that the club had pitching problems: Tex Hughson was coming off arm surgery, and "Ferris has been slow to hit his stride."

For a club with a reputation for being weak in pitching, the Boston staff that year was deep. The Red Sox had acquired Jack Kramer and Ellis Kinder from the St. Louis Browns, and young Mel Parnell was ready to become a starter, and with veterans Galehouse, Dobson, Johnson and Ferriss, their pitching was strong.

Ferriss started the fourth game of the year on April 22 and did well until the seventh inning. He was leading 2–1, when the A's chased him with a two-run rally. While he did not get a decision, he had pitched well. He allowed only six hits in six-and-one-third innings. On May 4, he made his second start and beat his favorite club, Detroit, going six innings and allowing eight hits. On May 10, Cleveland scored three times in the first inning against him, when Larry Doby, the first African-American to play in the modern-day American League, poled a tremendous home run into the right field seats.

From then on, Ferriss was not in the regular rotation. By the end of May, his record was 1–1. He relieved more than he started, often with success. He beat Detroit in relief of Kinder, allowing only three hits in seven-and-one-third innings. On June 27, he pitched a complete game against St. Louis and won, 6–3. His record at the All-Star Game was 4–1. With Boston involved in a pennant chase with Lou Boudreau's Cleveland Indians, Ferriss was used only nine times in a starting role in 1948, and he relieved in 22 games. While his final win-loss record was 7–3, his earned run average was 5.23.

"Something cracked in my shoulder in '47," Ferriss recalled some years later. "We never knew exactly what it was, but it became worse in '49. Today's medical care could probably have repaired it."

In 1949, Ferriss's arm went completely dead and he pitched a mere six-and-two-thirds innings in four games with no decisions. He made a final, futile comeback try in 1950, but he pitched only one inning. His major-league pitching career was over, cut short by arm problems and an asthmatic condition.

While Ferriss remained for four seasons in Triple A baseball, he never regained his former ability to pitch at a major-league level.

After his playing career, Ferris remained with the Red Sox organization as a pitching coach, serving in that role from 1955 until 1959, when former teammate Pinky Higgins stepped down as manager. When Ferriss relinquished his pitching coach position with the Red Sox, he did not disappear but launched a new, successful career. He became the varsity baseball coach, and ultimately athletic director, at Delta State College in Cleveland, Mississippi, not far from where he grew up.

Just as he had done as a pitcher for Boston in 1945 and '46, he lifted Delta State to baseball success in their NCAA Division II competition. In 26 seasons, his Delta State teams won 639 games and lost only 387. His last year, 1988, Delta State posted its best record in school history, winning 44 and losing only 13. His teams won four Gulf South Conference championships, three NCAA regional titles, and placed second once and third twice in the College World Series.

Ferriss was a player's coach. He sought to mold better citizens every bit as much as developing baseball talent. "Boys at the college age are at a very crucial point in their lives," Ferriss contended, "and it's gratifying to watch them mature. It's our job to help make better citizens." He became heavily involved in the Fellowship of Christian Athletes and exemplified the organization's goals in his own life. Many of his former players distinguished themselves in both professional baseball and in the larger game of life. Forty-three earned all-Gulf South Conference honors. Eighteen were All-American. Seventeen went on to professional baseball. Twenty garnered academic All-American honors. Ferris gained the respect of fellow coaches in college baseball. Small wonder that Delta State officials named the university's baseball field for him.

Boo was a mentor to his players and a model citizen in his community. His name often was associated with local events, and he helped to build civic pride in those around him. His principal concern, though, was for the youth. As such, he labored tirelessly to organize a Fellowship of Christian Athletes chapter at Delta State.

Boo Ferriss's name will never be enshrined in Cooperstown, but he has been inducted to the Mississippi Sports Hall of Fame, the Mississippi State University Sports Hall of Fame, the Mississippi Semi-Pro Baseball Hall of Fame, and the American Baseball Coaches Hall of Fame. Finally, upon his retirement from Delta State, Dave Ferriss in October of 1988 was enshrined in the *Congressional Record,* an honor not many athletes achieve.

When he was inducted in the Mississippi Sports Hall of Fame, congratulations came from many sources: Pinky Higgins, Neil Mahoney, Milt Bolling, and George Digby, all of the Red Sox family, and many others. However, the most appropriate wire came from Tom Yawkey, owner of the Red Sox — it simply read: "I wish you were going to be our opening day pitcher." Why not? Few ever pitched better in Fenway Park than Dave Ferriss in 1945 and 1946.

Boo Ferriss was an outstanding pitcher, one of the best in the business before he snapped that fateful, overhand curve that night in Cleveland — the pitch that short-circuited his career. For two wonderful years, he tasted glory — even while hanging his clothes on a nail in the locker room.

DAVID MEADOW FERRISS

Born Dec. 5, 1921, Shaw, Miss.   Batted left, threw right.

Year	Team	W–L	Pct.	ERA	G	GS	CG	IP	H	BB	SO	ShO
1942	Greens-boro, Pied	7–7	.500	2.22	21	n/a	n/a	130	94	53	98	n/a
1943–1944	In the U.S. Military.											
1945	Bos A	21–10	.677	2.96	35	31	26	264⅔	*263	85	94	5
1946	Bos A	25–6	*.806	3.25	40	35	26	274	274	71	106	6
1947	Bos A	12–11	.522	4.04	33	28	14	218	241	92	64	1
1948	Bos A	7–3	.700	5.23	31	9	1	115⅓	127	61	30	0
1949	Bos A	0–0	.000	4.05	4	0	0	6⅔	7	4	1	0
1950	Bos A	0–0	.000	18.00	1	0	0	1	2	1	1	0
Major League Totals 6 yrs.		65–30	.684	3.64	144	103	67	880	914	314	296	12

Asterisk indicates led league

World Series Record

Year	Team	W–L	Pct.	ERA	G	GS	CG	IP	H	BB	SO	ShO
1946	Bos A	1–0	1.000	2.03	2	2	1	13⅓	13	2	4	0

10 THE WESTERN WONDER

VEAN GREGG

"I never saw a young pitcher grasp
the finer points of the game or
the weakness of batters more quickly
than the Western Wonder."
BILLY EVANS, UMPIRE

Two highly touted pitchers arrived in the majors in 1911, one right-handed and the other left-handed. One came to the Philadelphia Phillies in the National League, the other to the Cleveland team which had been known as the "Naps" when Nap Lajoie was acquired in 1902. The righthander from Elba, Nebraska, was named Grover Cleveland (Pete) Alexander. The lefthander from Chehalis, Washington, was Sylveanus Augustus (Vean) Gregg.

Both pitchers had outstanding rookie seasons, with Alexander winning 28 games and losing 13, while Gregg won 23 and lost 7. After three outstanding seasons, Alexander amassed 69 victories pitching for a team managed by Red Dooin that finished fourth, fifth and second. While Alexander's win totals were impressive, he also lost 38, and his teams finished far behind McGraw's great Giant teams. Gregg, in the same three years, won 63 while losing 33. Gregg's combined ERA for the three years was lower than Alexander's. That is where the comparison stopped, in 1914. Alexander went on to win 373 games in a 20-year major-league career; Gregg was able to win only another 27 games in an eight-year career. Alexander stayed healthy; Gregg did not.

Gregg, like most American youngsters of that period, began playing ball early in life. He, like others his age, yearned to grow up to be a professional ballplayer. His chance of making it to the big leagues was no better than anyone else's back then in the early part of the century.

119

When he was old enough to get a job, Gregg learned the trade of a plasterer. He became quite accomplished and spent weekdays working without much thought of the sport that was sweeping America. On Sundays and holidays, however, he pitched for a local team. His pitching skill developed rapidly, and he soon became a well-known pitcher in the community. As his reputation spread, he attracted attention from other teams. Thus, in 1907, Vean Gregg gave up plastering and traveled to Idaho to pitch semiprofessional ball for Lewiston. By the end of that first season, Joe Cohen, manager of Spokane in the Northwestern League, signed him to his first professional contract.

While Gregg did not have an impressive season at Spokane in 1909, with only six victories against 13 losses, he was spotted by Walter McCredle of the Portland team of the Pacific Coast League. McCredle, acting on a tip, began watching Gregg. He liked what he saw and sent one of his scouts to watch the young lefthander. The scout observed Gregg often, and by the end of the season the Portland team purchased his contract before other teams had a chance to scout him.

At Portland, Gregg blossomed. In 1910, at the advanced age of 25 (for someone who had not yet pitched in the majors), Gregg had a final minor-league season that few could top. He won 32 while losing 18. He fanned 364 batters, an average of nine per game, and he pitched 362 innings. The season brought immediate results to his career. Cleveland purchased his contract from Portland along with teammates Ivy Olson, Gus Fisher and Gene (Rubber) Krapp. Olson, a shortstop, played in the majors 14 years. Fisher and Krapp had brief careers, but the key acquisition for the Naplanders on Lake Erie was Vean Gregg. As one columnist observed, "Gregg, like Abou Ben Adhem, leads all the rest."

Gregg was presumed to be younger than he actually was because his birthday was listed erroneously as October 27, 1887, rather than the actual date: April 13, 1885. It was common for ball players to be older than their listed ages.

Gregg, a tall, rangy lefthander, had an excellent fastball, but his best pitch was a curve. A writer in 1911 said of his curve, "It sweeps to the plate, and just as the batter sets to take a swing at the pill, the ball shoots toward him like lightning." Gregg had confidence in his curve ball and threw it often when he was behind in the count. The umpire Billy Evans said, "His nerve is unlimited. In one game with the Athletics, in which I umpired at the plate, I saw Gregg on five occasions, with the count three and two, use his curve ball in preference to grooving the fast one. On three of those occasions, a base on balls would have been costly, but each time the surprised batter watched the curve glide over, and he retired to the shade of the bench."

Gregg was a fast worker. The games he pitched were generally shorter than most. His wind-up consisted of a full, graceful sweep of the arms above the head, a motion that bothered many hitters. Moreover, according to Billy Evans, he had "two of baseball's greatest requisites, brains and nerve."

Gregg became a student of the game on the West Coast when the papers began calling him a big league prospect. He never before was interested in major league box scores, but once he felt he was headed for the majors, he studied them to learn what he could about individual hitters. In 1912, Gregg told Billy Evans, "I read every line of news I could see about the big stars. Any time a reference was made to the weakness of a certain player, I made a mental note of that information, intending to put it to the test at the very first opportunity. I'd gamble no ball player in the country studies the dope more closely than I do now."

When the 1911 season started, Gregg was not in the starting rotation. He made his first appearance in Cleveland's sixth game on April 18 when Detroit knocked George Kahler out of the box in the first inning by scoring five quick runs, and the young southpaw from Portland was brought into relief. Gregg was impressive in his debut, holding the Tigers scoreless the rest of the way. While Cleveland lost the game, 5–1, a star was born.

Gregg's relief effort resulted in a starting assignment on April 23 against the White Sox which he won, 5–2. He faced the Tigers five days later, losing 6–3 but pitching a complete game. In his third start on May 3, Gregg went the distance again, but was hit hard in an 8–7 Cleveland victory. With a record of 2–1, Gregg suddenly got hot and was virtually unhittable. He beat the Red Sox on a five hitter, 6–0. He beat the Yankees, 2–1, and on May 21, beat Washington, 8–1. One reporter wrote that Gregg was a mystery throughout.

The three consecutive pitching gems established Gregg as a legitimate major-league pitcher, so dominant that he was used in critical spots as a reliever. On May 28, he relieved Specs Harkness with Cleveland and Chicago tied in the ninth inning and the bases loaded. In the tenth inning, the game was called with two outs because of rain. On May 29, he got another win in relief against Detroit.

Gregg returned to the starting rotation in early June, beating Washington, 8–2, on June 6. The game was memorable because Gregg's teammate, "Shoeless" Joe Jackson, hit one of the "longest home runs recorded here," as reported by a Cleveland writer. From that point forward, Gregg was sensational.

Vean Gregg won 20 or more games in each of his first three full-time major league seasons (NATIONAL BASEBALL HALL OF FAME LIBRARY, COOPERSTOWN, NY).

His record was a spectacular 17–3 before he slumped slightly in late August, but he still finished the season with a 23–7 record. It was a great rookie season for the Washington native. Although his win total was exceeded by Philadelphia's Jack Combs, who won 28, Gregg tied for fourth with Eddie Plank, also of the A's, with 23. He led the league in ERA with 1.81, beating Washington's Walter Johnson. Gregg also led the league in fewest hits per game, 6.34. Gregg finished second in winning percentage with .767. He was nosed out by another A's hurler, Chief Bender.

While his team finished third to Philadelphia, Vean Gregg recorded one of the best rookie seasons for a pitcher in the twentieth century. Gregg's second season failed to equal his first year, but he was still among the pitching elite, and he won 20 again, going 20–13. His ERA was 2.59, good enough for sixth in the league, and he was second in strikeouts. Vean Gregg did not suffer a sophomore jinx.

During his second season, it became apparent that Cleveland liked to play when Gregg was pitching. Gregg had a habit of acknowledging good plays; he never criticized, regardless of the situation; and he always encouraged anyone who might have committed an error. Umpire Billy Evans said, "Fans express the opinion that the Naps seem to play better ball behind Gregg than any of the other pitchers. I know they perform better under such conditions because they have confidence in the big southpaw and are with him." This may explain why Gregg's winning percentage for the season was .606 and the overall team percentage was a mere .490 as Cleveland finished fifth in the league.

Pete Alexander in his rookie year led the National League with 28 wins, five more than Gregg. In 1912, however, Alexander failed to win 20, missing by one game while Gregg did win 20 again.

In 1913, Gregg set a mark that has never been equaled in modern day baseball. He won 20 games for the third straight season at the start of his career. No one before or since has been able to reach the 20-win level in each of his first three seasons. His record was identical to his 1912 ledger: 20 victories and 13 losses. A comparison of the records of Gregg and Alexander show how effective Vean Gregg was and how well he compared with the success of the Hall of Famer.

After failing to win 20 in 1912, Alexander bounced back to post a 22–8 record in the senior league in 1913, thereby exceeding Gregg's three-year totals by six games. At the same time, Gregg easily bested Alexander in earned run average each of the three seasons.

Year	Alexander	Gregg
1911	2.57	1.81
1912	2.81	2.59
1913	2.79	2.24

In 1913, Gregg's 166 strikeouts placed him second in the American League to Johnson's 243. Johnson clearly was the strikeout king of the era, but Gregg was among the league's best. His hits allowed per nine innings pitched was again excellent, 8.15. However, for the first time in his career, Gregg was wild, leading the league in bases on balls with 124. He tied for fourth in the league with 23 complete games.

Gregg started the 1914 season as if he were headed for a fourth straight 20-win season. But he developed soreness in his arm, a problem that first emerged during spring training. Because of the sore arm, Cleveland traded their three-time 20-game winner to the Red Sox on August 20 for three players — catcher Ben Egan, pitcher Fritz Coumbe and minor-league pitcher Rankin Johnson. Johnson never played in the majors; Egan played briefly for the Indians; only Coumbe lasted a few years, winning a high of 13 games for Cleveland in 1918. The trade marked the beginning of a shakeup for the Naps. Boston made the deal with the hope that it would help them in the pennant race with Philadelphia, which it did not. The Sox finished eight games behind Connie Mack's A's.

Gregg won only three games while losing four for Boston to close out the season. He was 4–2 in 1915 and 2–5 in 1916. Something was wrong with the lefthander's arm. Red Sox President Lanin sent Gregg to several specialists, and their diagnosis was that he was suffering from a peculiar form of rheumatism which they thought could be cured. Lanin paid the bills and said that it was "worth the gamble. If Gregg could be made fit again, the money would be well spent."

The specialists told Gregg to throw some each day until his arm felt stronger. He did as directed. When he could wind up without pain in his left shoulder, he would inform manager Bill Carrigan, and he would pitch. The results were splendid. Carrigan was ecstatic. With a healthy Vean Gregg, he would have four solid lefthanders, the other three being Babe Ruth, Dutch Leonard, and Ray Collins, who had won 20 in 1914. Pairing those lefthanders with four classy righthanders — Smoky Joe Wood, Ernie Shore, Rube Foster and Carl Mays — would give the Sox dominant pitching; in fact, seldom has anyone had better.

Boston won the 1915 pennant with a 101–50 record, and won the World Series from the Phillies in five games. But on July 15, 1915, the club sent Gregg to Buffalo of the International League to rehabilitate his arm. Hence, Vean Gregg missed an opportunity to be on a World Series championship team. Gregg returned to Boston in 1916, but his arm miseries persisted. His record fell to 2–5. Carrigan used Gregg mostly in relief. He appeared in 21 games and started only seven, finishing three. The Red Sox went on to win the pennant once more, but received little help from Gregg.

Over the winter, Gregg set out to strengthen his arm, giving it a careful course of treatment. The effort paid off.

He spent the 1917 season pitching for Providence in the International League, and he had an excellent 21–9 record. He compiled one of the best strikeout records in International League history, fanning 249 men in 267 innings. His peak performance came on September 2, when, in a 1–0 losing effort, he fanned 20 Newark batters in 18 innings. Additionally, his 1.72 ERA stood at the top of the league, and he finished second in wins. He allowed only 193 hits in 267 innings, walking only 76. He threw four shutouts and he beat every team in the league at least twice. Of his nine defeats four were by one run, and the real heartbreaker was the 18-inning affair against Newark. He reported to the Red Sox at the close of the International League season but did not get into any games.

The pitching-rich Red Sox traded Gregg on December 14, 1917, to the Athletics for the 1918 season. He was shipped with outfielder Merlin Kopp, catcher Pinch Thomas and $60,000 to Connie Mack for veteran outfielder Amos Strunk, star pitcher Bullet Joe Bush, and an established catcher, Wally Schang. The trade additionally paved the way for Philadelphia to trade Stuffy McInnis to Boston on January 10, 1918. The trade was controversial. To many A's fans, sending established performers like Bush, Schang and Strunk to Boston was foolish. Connie Mack responded, telling his critics to study the record Gregg had compiled in the International League the year before. The trade was the first time that Mack disassembled a star team. The second time occurred in the 1930s when he broke up a team led by Jimmie Foxx, Mickey Cochrane, Al Simmons, and Lefty Grove.

It was the second time that Gregg came to the majors on the basis of a great minor league performance. Bob Hurt, International League umpire, predicted that Gregg would make a highly successful comeback with the Athletics in 1918. He said that, in his opinion, Gregg in 1917 had more speed than any other pitcher in the International League and that he would be surprised if Gregg did not win big for Connie Mack.

Gregg's comeback, however, was unimpressive. He pitched in 30 games for the Athletics, starting 25 and completing 17. He won only 8 and lost 14, with his earned run average a respectable 3.12, slightly above the league average of 2.77. He allowed 180 hits in 199 innings, but his team finished last.

After the 1918 season, Gregg voluntarily retired and purchased a 480-acre ranch in Alberta, Canada, hoping for personal independence. He was too busy running tractors to play ball. Rising costs and falling prices, however, caused him to come out of retirement in 1922 to pitch for Seattle in the Pacific Coast League. The Alberta Ace, as he was known by then, toiled for three seasons and compiled respectable records, 19–20 in 1922, 17–15 in 1923, and 25–11 in 1924.

The Washington Senators decided to bolster their pitching staff and purchased Gregg from Seattle for $35,000. Incensed that he did not receive a larger bonus from his sale to Washington, the Alberta Ace went home to Alberta and threatened to retire from baseball. Wade Killifer, manager of Seattle, said that Gregg had been paid a $1,500 bonus "besides paying his expenses back home contrary to the general rule. Gregg is unreasonable if he asks for more."

Gregg eventually thought the better of retiring and celebrated his 40th birthday back in a major league uniform on the day the 1925 season opened, April 13. The veteran southpaw pitched in 26 games for the Nats, mostly in relief, winning two and losing two. He was released to New Orleans in the Southern League before the end of the season and finished with a 3–3 record.

After the season, Gregg returned to Alberta. During the 1926 season, he farmed and pitched a little in Aberdeen, Washington. Prior to the 1927 season, William A. McCarthy, president of the Mission club of the Pacific Coast League, contacted Gregg and arranged for a tryout. McCarthy envisioned using Gregg as a reliever "to pull endangered games out of the fire." Besides, he thought the veteran Gregg's experience might be an influence on his younger pitchers.

The silver-haired Gregg, now past 40, worked hard to get in shape. He threw until his arm was sore. He was sure he could work his way through it, however. "I've done it before, and I can do it again," Gregg predicted. "It was a question of how the old souper would act up in training. I'm satisfied with it."

That was Gregg's final year in professional ball. He returned to Alberta. Eventually, he moved to Aberdeen, Washington, where he retired. He died on July 29, 1964.

Gregg was two years older than Alexander when he came to the majors in 1911. Hall of Fame careers usually begin earlier than age 26. Warren Spahn, for example, was 26 when in 1947 he launched his first 20-win season. Spahn won 21 in 1947, 15 in 1948, and a league-leading 21 in 1949, six fewer victories than Gregg accumulated in the same time span. Of course, Spahn, like Alexander, went on to a great career. Spahn was 42 the last year he won 20 for the Milwaukee Braves in 1963, the same age that Gregg closed out his career on the Pacific Coast.

In terms of performance and testimony, Vean Gregg was a great pitcher. He had a tremendous curve and a great fastball. He had good control and was a student of the game. But for an arm injury, complicated by rheumatism, the Western Wonder, alias the Alberta Ace, might well be in Cooperstown.

SYLVEANUS AUGUSTUS GREGG
Born Apr. 13, 1885. Died July 29, 1964. Batted right, threw left.

Year	Team	W–L	Pct.	ERA	G	GS	CG	IP	H	BB	SO	ShO
1909	Spokane-Northwestern	6–13	.316	n/a	n/a	n/a	n/a	n/a	n/a	n/a	n/a	n/a
1910	Seattle PCL	32–18	.640	n/a	n/a	n/a	n/a	n/a	n/a	n/a	n/a	n/a
1911	Cle AL	23–7	.767	*1.81	34	26	22	244	172	86	125	5
1912	Cle AL	20–13	.606	2.59	37	34	26	271⅓	242	86	184	1
1913	Cle AL	20–13	.606	2.24	44	34	23	285⅔	258	124	166	3
1914	Cle AL	12–7	.632	3.44	29	21	10	165	159	85	80	1
1915	Bos AL	4–2	.667	3.36	18	9	3	75	71	32	43	1
1916	Bos AL	2–5	.286	3.01	21	7	3	77.2	71	30	41	0
1917	Prov IL	21–9	.700	1.71	n/a	n/a	n/a	267	193	76	249	4
1918	Phil AL	8–14	.364	3.12	30	25	17	199⅓	180	38	18	3
1922	Sea PCL	19–20	.499	n/a	n/a	n/a	n/a	n/a	n/a	n/a	n/a	n/a
1923	Sea PCL	17–15	.532	n/a	n/a	n/a	n/a	n/a	n/a	n/a	n/a	n/a
1924	Sea PCL	25–11	.694	2.90	49	25	n/a	326	341	75	175	n/a
1925	Wash AL	2–2	.500	4.12	26	5	1	74⅓	87	38	18	0
1925	New Orl. Southern	3–3	.500	2.62	9	n/a	n/a	48	47	10	19	0
Major League Totals 8 yrs.		91–63	.591	2.70	239	161	105	1391⅓	1240	552	720	14

*Asterisk indicates led league

11   THE NO-HIT KID

STEVE BUSBY

> "I've never seen such an accomplished
> pitcher who has been in pro ball
> such a short time, unless it was Seaver."
> COOKIE ROJAS

An article written by William Barry Furlong in 1974 was appropriately titled "Steve Busby: The No-Hit Kid." Busby was, and is, the only pitcher in history to hurl no-hitters in each of his first two full-time major-league seasons. But for a rotator cuff injury, complicated by a knee injury, Steven Lee Busby, not George Brett, might have been the first Kansas City Royal to be enshrined at Cooperstown.

Busby, of English-German descent, was born in Burbank, California, on September 29, 1949. He grew up in the middle of what is now California State–Fullerton. At that time, it was mostly orange groves, and he and his brothers had numerous orange fights. Even then, Steven could throw hard.

His brother Mike, who was 10 years older, and his father were a big influence on his development. His father was a good athlete who played football with the old Los Angeles Dons of the All-American League. When Steve was old enough, his father coached him in Pony League ball. Steve began dreaming of playing big league baseball. Living in the Los Angeles area, he came to admire Sandy Koufax and Don Drysdale, the two great Dodger pitchers of the 1960s. His brother Mike was a pitcher, and every chance Steve got, he watched Mike pitch.

When Steve reached high school, he was already an accomplished pitcher for his age. In fact, he began the no-hit habit early, twirling two hitless gems for the Fullerton High School team. In retrospect, Busby credits much of his pitching success to his high school coach, Jim Bass. Bass was a stickler for mechanics. He taught his pitching protégé the wind-up, body control and fluidity of motion. He had the young hurler practice the proper motion with a count of one, two, three, four, with each number representing a certain spot in the delivery, and he made him repeat it over and over. When asked about it, Busby in an interview said that he still sometimes dreams about it and finds himself mentally counting from one to four.

Busby starred in football as well, although a broken shoulder blade kept him out of action much of the time. By the time he was a senior, he was team captain, and he had a 120-yard rushing night and ran back an interception for a touchdown. He was on the way to stardom, but he injured his knee the next game and twice needed surgery to repair it. His football career moved to the background.

No matter, baseball was his first love. He spent summers playing American Legion ball. His performances soon attracted major league scouts, and he almost signed with the San Francisco Giants in 1967. Carl Hubbell, the Giant scout, was talking about a big bonus, but Busby's knee gave out — the knee he had injured in football — and the Giants greatly decreased their offer. Busby decided to go to college instead of signing, a decision he never regretted.

He attended the University of Southern California and majored in business. While baseball was his passion, he did not neglect his studies. He had a strong intellectual bent, and at one time tried his hand at writing science fiction. He attended college the full four years and received his degree in business.

"To me the college degree is a big thing," Busby told reporters, "something no one can take away. College gave me a chance to mature physically and mentally. I learned a lot about life and people." He made good use of his business education as a financial consultant and for making good investments.

Busby pitched and played the outfield at USC. Rod Dedeaux, the team coach, was highly professional. He wanted his teams to be better prepared than the opponents. He thought that they should be a full level better than other teams.

On the basis of an 8–3 pitching record and a .422 batting average, Busby was named USC's Most Valuable Player as a freshman in 1968. He missed the entire 1969 season because of an arm injury that required surgery. Surgeons relocated a nerve in his pitching arm, producing a 10-inch scar running from his right elbow down his forearm.

The operation may have been a turning point in Busby's career. Before the operation, all he had was a good, live fastball; afterward, he became a pitcher. Busby has said, "After the operation the strength in my forearm was gone and so was my fastball. I knew I had to come up with something else if I wanted to stay around. I learned to pitch that year." He added a good curve, a wicked slider, and a deceptive changeup to his repertoire. In time, the strength in his arm came back — and so did his fastball.

The year following his surgery, 1970, he posted a 3–0 record with a 2.06 ERA. Then he came on strong his senior year. He won 11 and lost only two, and he led USC to the Pac-Eight championship, the NCAA District Eight title, and the College World Series championship. In the College World Series, he lost his first start to Southern Illinois, but he came back to defeat the Salukis, 7–2, in the championship game. He was named to All-Conference, All-District, and NCAA College All-American first teams.

In the summer of 1970, he pitched the Boulder Collegians to the Colorado state semipro title and to a fourth place finish in the National Baseball Congress tournament in Wichita.

Busby was drafted by Kansas City in the second round of the 1971 amateur-player draft and he signed his first contract with the Royals for a modest bonus.

Buzz's first minor league stop was San Jose. In his second California League start, he shut out Reno on two hits. He won three and lost one in his abbreviated minor league rookie season, good enough to earn him a promotion for 1972 to Omaha, the Royals' Triple-A franchise.

In the off-season, disaster almost struck. On January 2, Busby tore an ankle ligament playing basketball. The doctor recommended surgery, but Busby called Dr. Paul Meyer, Kansas City's team physician. Dr. Meyer had them put Busby's leg in a cast. The cast came off only two weeks before he was to report to Florida for spring training. The ankle responded well, and he went to Omaha as scheduled.

Busby compiled an undistinguished 12–14 record in the American Association, but his supporting stats were spectacular. His 221 strikeouts led the league, as did his 217 innings pitched and his 17 complete games. He tied for the league lead with 30 games started, and his 3.20 ERA was the sixth best. On May 4, he tied an American Association record by striking out eight consecutive Tulsa batters; and on August 14, he tied another league record by striking out 16 Tulsa batters in a nine-inning game. On July 31, in a seven-inning game, after the Oklahoma City leadoff batter singled, Buzz retired the next 21 batters in order. He was voted Minor League Player of the Year by the Southern California Hot Stove League.

Kansas City brought Busby up from Omaha at the close of the American Association season. He distinguished himself by winning three of four games.

In his third major-league start on September 20, 1972, Busby added a second dimension to his game — hitting. He came up to bat with the bases loaded and hit what appeared to be a grand slam home run, but the play was nullified because the first base umpire had called time out just before the pitch was being thrown.

The disappointed rookie went back to the plate and hit a two-run single.

Always a good hitter, Busby disliked the American League designated-hitter rule. He felt that players should be expected to go both ways in all sports. He didn't even like defensive and offensive platooning in football. He thought that basketball was the perfect sport because the nature of the game forced a player to play both defense and offense.

Busby went to spring training in 1973 with a starting position in the Kansas City pitching rotation virtually assured. The Royals, who debuted on the major league stage in 1969, had already enjoyed unprecedented success for an expansion franchise. Kansas City finished fourth in a seven-team division the first two years, and then in 1971 moved up to second place.

Their success was greatly the result of the trading ingenuity of Cedric Tallis, their first general manager. Before the Royals ever played a game, Tallis traded Steve Whitaker, whom they had gotten in the expansion draft from New York, to the Seattle Pilots, the other expansion team, for Lou Piniella, whom the Pilots had taken in the draft from Cleveland. Then Tallis virtually turned Joe Foy, taken from Boston in the expansion draft, into a franchise. He traded Foy to the New York Mets for Amos Otis and Bob Johnson. He then used Johnson as a key player in a trade with Pittsburgh for shortstop Freddie Patek and Ed Kirkpatrick. Tallis next sent the Royals' first expansion choice, Roger Nelson, along with Richie Scheinblum, whom he had purchased from Washington, to Cincinnati for Hal McRae. He got Cookie Rojas from St. Louis for outfielder Fred Rico, and John Mayberry from Houston for pitcher Jim York. Additionally, the Royals had chosen Paul Splittorff in the twenty-second round of their first amateur player draft in 1968. After splitting two seasons between Omaha and Kansas City, the big lefthander came to the Royals to stay, and in 1972 posted a 12–12 record.

By 1973, the team was starting to jell, and the Royals' starting pitching rotation seemed set with Dick Drago, Roger Nelson, Paul Splittorff, and Wayne Simpson, acquired from Cincinnati. When a veteran pitcher asked new manager Jack McKeon, who had managed Busby the year before in Omaha, why Busby was listed as a starter, McKeon simply replied, "Because Buzz can throw the ball. What's more, he's got the mental toughness to be a 20-game winner, even in his first full year in the majors."

Busby himself felt confident. He had developed the capacity for positive thinking under Rod Dedeaux at Southern California. "Dedeaux," Busby said, "is one of the all-time great positive thinkers. He is one of those coaches who can take a mediocre team and win the national championship. He just doesn't accept the idea of losing." Dedeaux had boosted Busby's confidence by recommending that he sign with the Royals when they drafted him with one year of collegiate eligibility remaining. He felt that Busby had gotten all he could out of college ball and that he was ready for the challenge of professional baseball.

The spring after his first year in the minors, there was speculation that Busby might make the Kansas City roster. He had the poise of a veteran, and he understood the fine art of pitching. He had prospered under McKeon's tutelage at Omaha. "Jack really helped me," Buzz said. "For example, I had four pitches last fall — fast ball, curve, slider and change-up. But I was having trouble with my curve. It was hanging. Jack told me to quit worrying about it. He said I should throw something else. That's when I decided to concentrate on my slider. Now when I feel the pressure, I go to my slider."

Buzz started slowly in spring training, but on March 24, he pitched six innings of no-hit ball against Detroit. Doug Bird, another rookie, came on to finish the springtime no-hitter by holding the Tigers hitless over the final three innings. McKeon afterward remarked, "There isn't a hitter who can intimidate Busby." Busby himself said, "Why should I go out there afraid and worried?"

Some predicted that Busby might win 20 games his rookie year. Busby responded, "Twenty games? Sure I think I can do it, but I'm not going to be counting them." However, McKeon emphatically vouched, "Twenty, I'll tell you. Take my word for it."

For an encore, Busby pitched seven innings of no-hit, no-run baseball against St. Louis on March 31. As an added feature, he retired 17 men in a row. Afterward, Galen Cisco, the Royals' pitching coach, categorically stated that he "wouldn't trade Busby for any pitcher in the American League." Busby had a phenomenal spring training; he allowed only one earned run in his last 28 innings pitched.

Although a rookie, Busby was honored by being given the opening-day assignment against California at Anaheim, 10 minutes from where he grew up. He was matched against Nolan Ryan, then in his second year in the American League. The Angels had acquired Ryan the year before in one of the all-time one-sided trades, sending Jim Fregosi to the Mets for Nolan Ryan. Buzz lasted only four-and-one-third innings, yielding seven hits and three runs. Ryan went the distance to defeat the Royals, 3–2. He struck out 12 Kansas City batters and went from there to set an all-time season strike-out record with 383 whiffs.

In Busby's second start, he was rocked for seven hits and four runs in three-and-one-third innings. The Royals went on to win the game, 9–6, on the basis of Jan Garber's nifty relief pitching. In his third start, Busby beat the Chisox, 12–5. He worked seven innings and allowed eight hits and three earned runs. By April 27, the phenom had not looked phenomenal at all. He had an ordinary 2–2 record, having given up many hits and runs.

When he went to work in his first game at Detroit's Tiger Stadium, on a numbing, blustery Detroit spring evening, his mound opponent was the veteran Jim Perry. This time, the raw Kansas City rookie announced his arrival to the league: no hits, no runs. Busby was already in the record books: a no-hitter in his first full major league season.

Throughout the game, Buzz had nasty, sailing stuff that was hard to hit but also hard to control. He walked six batters in the game. According to Buzz, "Every inning was a new adventure. My fastball was running more than usual and I had trouble getting it over. About the fourth or fifth inning, I changed my grip so I could get the ball to straighten out a bit."

In most no-hitters, the pitcher tends to get help from at least one fielder who makes an outstanding play, denying the batter a safety. Busby got that help in the second inning when, with two out and a man on, Dick McAuliffe nailed a line drive to right that was hauled down by Ed Kirkpatrick. Buzz later remarked, "That was a great catch. Without that we wouldn't have been worrying in the ninth."

There was plenty to worry about in the final inning. Perry had shut the Royals down until the fifth inning when Kirkpatrick hit one into the right-field seats. Three innings later, Amos Otis blasted one out to left field. As the Tigers came to bat in the ninth, Buzz not only needed to protect his no-hit game but the Royals' three-run lead for the win. Duke Sims, pinch-hitting for Aurelio Rodriquez, opened the final stanza by drawing a walk. Rich Reese, the Detroit left fielder, stepped to the plate. He had been in a similar situation once before. In 1968, playing for Minnesota, he made the final out to complete Catfish Hunter's perfect game. This time, however, he almost broke up the no-hitter. He hooked a line drive foul, then rocketed one down the line toward John Mayberry, who reached across his body to catch the ball and stepped on first base to double Sims. Busby had no idea what had happened on the play; his cap had fallen over his eyes as he delivered the pitch.

"I heard how hard he hit it," he said. "I was worried he might have hit back to me."

Steve Busby is congratulated after pitching a no-hitter on April 27, 1973 (Corbis-Bettman Archives, New York, NY).

If Sims had not been on base, Reese's smash would have gone into the right-field corner for a double.

Mayberry's play took some of the pressure off Buzz. What he needed to do was to retire Bill Freehan, Detroit's hard-hitting catcher. Freehan swung at a fastball and hit a sky-high pop behind shortstop into a strong wind blowing in from left. Freddie Patek backpedaled, wandered somewhat perilously tracking the ball, and then fielded it in short center, while Busby hopped joyously toward second base.

"It was blowing all over," Patek later revealed, "but there was no way I was going to let that ball get away. I wanted that ball too bad to miss it. I think I could have caught anything, I was so psyched up."

On the other side of the field, Freehan told reporters, "I outguessed myself. I was looking for a breaking ball, and he threw me a fastball — right down the middle, and I didn't do anything with it."

McKeon observed that Galen Cisco deserved much of the credit for Busby's no-hitter. Buzz had been letting his pitching arm dip to the side before delivery. "Tonight was the first time Galen was able to get him to come on top with his pitches," bringing his arm straight down overhand. According to Busby, he threw 75 percent fastballs, and virtually all the rest were sliders. "I threw two change-ups and only one curve," he reported.

Kansas City					Detroit				
	AB	R	H	RBI		AB	R	H	RBI
Patek, ss	4	0	0	0	Northrup, rf	4	0	0	0
Hovley, dh	4	0	1	0	A. Rodriguez, 3b	3	0	0	0
McRae, dh	1	0	0	0	Sims, ph	0	0	0	0
Otis, cf	4	1	1	1	Reese, lf	3	0	0	0
Mayberry, 1b	3	0	0	0	Freehan, c	2	0	0	0
Piniella, lf	4	0	2	0	G. Brown, dh	3	0	0	0
Kirkpatrick, rf	4	2	3	1	Cash, 1b	1	0	0	0
Rojas, 2b	3	0	1	0	McAuliffe, 2b	3	0	0	0
Schaal, 3b	4	0	0	0	M. Stanley, cf	3	0	0	0
Healy, c	4	0	0	0	Brinkman, ss	3	0	0	0
Busby, p	0	0	0	0	J. Perry, p	0	0	0	0
TOTALS	35	3	8	2	Scherman, p	0	0	0	0
					TOTALS	25	0	0	0

											R	H	E
Kansas City	0	0	0		0	1	0		0	1	1	—	3	8	0
Detroit	0	0	0		0	0	0		0	0	0	—	0	0	2

E — Cash, A. Rodriguez. DP — Kansas City, 2, Detroit 1. LOB — Kansas City 8, Detroit 1. HR — Kirkpatrick (3), Otis (4). S — Rojas.

	IP	H	R	ER	BB	SO
Busby (W, 2–2)	9	0	0	0	6	4
J. Perry (L, 2–2)	8⅔	8	3	2	2	2
Scherman	⅓	0	0	0	0	0

WP — Busby. PB — Healy, Freehan. T — 2:18. A — 16, 345.

The pitching masterpiece was historic. Busby became the tenth rookie of the twentieth century to hurl a no-hit game, and it was the first major league no-hitter by a Kansas City pitcher in the century. Henry Porter threw a 4–0 no-hitter for Kansas City against Baltimore on June 6, 1888, when Kansas City was in the American Association, then a major league. In the modern era, Kansas City had five no-hitters as a Triple-A American Association franchise. The last nine-inning no-hitter was a perfect game in 1947 by little-known Carl DeRose, who never pitched in the major leagues.

One week after his no-hitter, Busby took the mound against the Milwaukee Brewers. Buzz, like every other pitcher since 1938 who has pitched a no-hitter, desired to match Johnny Vander Meer's record of two in a row. For five innings, he set the Brewers down without a hit, allowing only a pair of walks. More than a few hearts were pounding when Pedro Garcia opened the sixth with a bounce to shortstop which Patek easily turned into an out. Busby only needed 11 more outs to match Vander Meer's record. But then Buzz made a mistake to the next hitter, Dave May. He got one in May's power zone and watched him hit a line drive over the outfield fence. Disconcerted, the rookie hurler walked four of the next five batters and was removed from the game after five-and-two-thirds innings. While Busby got the victory, 5–3, Vander Meer remained alone in pitching back-to-back gems.

Whether this failed effort affected Buzz, or if he just went into a slump, is conjecture, but after the Milwaukee game, he did not win again until June 24. He floundered repeatedly as he struggled with his control. In his next five appearances, he worked 24-and-one-third innings and gave up 36 hits, 20 earned runs, and 15 walks. He was the loser in all five games. Not only did he walk batters, but his pitch location was bad. His record fell to 4-9.

Busby refused to let the pressure get to him. "Thing that bothers me," he said, "is that the team is losing when I pitch." McKeon remained steadfast, though, and kept the rookie hurler in the starting rotation.

The All-Star Game gave Busby needed time off and it seemed to settle him down. He surged back after the break. Pitching against Milwaukee in mid–July, he broke the Kansas City strike-out record by fanning 13 Brewers. The old record of 12 was shared by Catfish Hunter, Jim Nash, and Bob Johnson. Busby won 10 out of 13 games during one stretch and finished the season with 16 wins and 15 losses, striking out 174 batters.

Busby was a leading candidate for Rookie of the Year. He received strong support from his manager, the coaches and his teammates. Jack McKeon said, "He is a rookie pitching like he has been in the major leagues eight or 10 years." Galen Cisco, pitching coach, commented, "I've never seen a rookie pitcher as good or with his potential on any club I've been associated with in my 16 years in pro ball." Charley Lau, the hitting coach and himself a former catcher, chimed in, "Buzz is the most mature young pitcher I've ever been associated with." The veteran Cookie Rojas noted, "I've never seen such an accomplished pitcher who has been in pro ball such a short time, unless it was Seaver."

Not only did Busby's raw talent impress people, his poise and overall pitching maturity drew equal notice. Nothing seemed to bother him. He fielded his position well and had an excellent ability to hold the runners. With runners on first and third, he perfected what has been referred to since as the "Steve Busby Pickoff Move." He faked a throw to third and then whirled and threw behind the runner at first, a move he had learned from Jim Bass, his high school coach. Seven times he caught a runner napping with that move in 1973. Numerous pitchers have tried this move since, but seldom have they been successful; baserunners have become more wary of the possibility.

Busby was also adept at picking runners off third base. He would signal the third baseman, who would take a step toward third, and Busby threw the ball half the distance between the baseman and the base and the baseman fielded it on the run to get the runner returning to the base.

In the postseason, Busby was appropriately honored by being named American League Rookie Pitcher of the Year.

There was no sophomore jinx with Busby; he was even better than the year before. His 22 victories in 36 decisions tied him for third in the American League for most wins. He lowered his earned run average to 3.39 and struck out 198. He pitched 20 complete games and toiled 292 innings.

The high point of Busby's 1974 season came on June 19, the day of his wedding anniversary, when he threw his second annual no-hit, no-run game, this time against the Brewers in Milwaukee's County Stadium. Only a second-inning walk to George Scott deprived him of a perfect game, but he was helped considerably by several fielding gems. Rookie George Brett backhanded Don Money's smash over third, Al Cowens chased down a long drive to the right-field warning track, and Freddie Patek speared Bob Coluccio's smash in the hole at short. The real game-saver, however, was made by the veteran Cookie Rojas at second base. Bob Hansen, Milwaukee's designated hitter, hit a sharp two-hopper through the right side of the infield, but Rojas dived headlong at the ball, fielded it, and threw from his knees to John Mayberry at first for the out. Buzz retired the next 24 batters in order.

Kansas City					Milwaukee				
	AB	R	H	RBI		AB	R	H	RBI
Patek, ss	4	0	2	0	Money, 3b	4	0	0	0
Rojas, 2b	4	0	1	0	Yount, ss	3	0	0	0
Otis, cf	4	0	1	0	May, rf	3	0	0	0
Mayberry, 1b	3	1	0	0	Scott, 1b	2	0	0	0
McRae, dh	4	0	1	0	Briggs, lf	3	0	0	0
Wohlford, lf	4	1	1	0	Porter, c	3	0	0	0
Cowens, rf	3	0	0	0	Hansen, dh	3	0	0	0
Brett, 3b	3	0	1	1	Coluccio, rf	3	0	0	0
Healy, c	3	0	0	0	Johnson, 2b	3	0	0	0
Busby, p	0	0	0	0	Wright, p	0	0	0	0
TOTALS	32	2	7	1	TOTALS	27	0	0	0

									R	H	E
Kansas City	0	0	0	0	0	0	0	0	0	—	2	7	0
Milwaukee	0	0	0	0	0	0	0	0	0	—	0	0	2

E — Yount, Porter. DP — Milwaukee 2. LOB — Kansas City 5. Milwaukee 1.

	IP	H	R	ER	BB	SO
Busby (W, 8–6)	9	0	0	0	1	3
Wright (L, 5–8	9	7	2	1	2	2

T — 2:03. A — 9,019. U — Brinkman, Bremigan, Chylak, McCoy.

After the game, Busby modestly considered himself lucky. "There were at least a dozen balls hit hard enough to be hits," he pointed out. "My best pitch was my slider. Then later I went mostly with my fast ball."

Fran Healy, who caught both of Busby's no-hitters, added, "He also had a pretty good curve, and when he has that, well — the rest is history for the hitters."

While others have pitched at least two no-hitters in their careers, Busby was the first to do so in each of his first two full seasons. Vander Meer pitched his consecutive no-hitters in his second season.

Busby did not slump after this no-hitter. Rather, he went on to retire an American League record 33 consecutive batters, surpassing Lindy McDaniel's and Vic Raschi's 32, but three shy of Harvey Haddix's major league record of 36. He faced 54 batters without allowing a hit. In his next start, at home against Chicago, he again pitched hitless ball into the sixth inning, when with one out Pat Kelly ruined Busby's bid to join Vander Meer. A home run by Ron Santo in the seventh kayoed Buzz and he lost the game. But Busby came right back in his next effort with a 2–0 victory over Oakland's Vida Blue. Until the eighth, Oakland had only one hit. Busby called it his best effort in the majors, because, he said, "I probably had the best stuff of the year."

Busby's pickoff move, if anything, was even better in 1974. In an interview in September 1996, Busby recalled two moments. The first occurred in Chicago. With the White Sox trailing in the bottom of the ninth, Dick Allen came in to pinch-hit with runners on first and third, one out. Buzz toed the rubber, faked a throw to third, wheeled and threw to first to pick Carlos May off base for the second out. With Allen eagerly swinging the bat back and forth at the plate, Buzz stepped on the rubber and picked Pat Kelly off third for the final out. Allen had been sent up to bat with only one out, yet he never saw a pitch. The moody Allen, who loved hitting, muttered epithets to himself and yelled at Busby, "Pitchers are supposed to throw the ball to the plate."

In another game, Buzz picked Charley Spikes of Cleveland off third base twice, for which, to no one's surprise, Spikes received a stern tongue-lashing from Manager Ken Aspromonte. Busby's favorite pick-off target was Pat Kelly, who was never able to fathom Buzz's move. One time Busby picked

Kelly off first; when hearing the ball strike Mayberry's glove, Kelly made no attempt to return to base but proceeded directly to the dugout. Mayberry never tagged him.

After 1974, Busby, who had pitched 38 victories in his first two complete seasons, was ready for stardom.

By 1975, the Kansas City Royals were ready to challenge the powerful three-time world champion Oakland Athletics for the American League West championship. The Royals seemed tailored for spacious Royals Stadium. They had great speed, tremendous defense, line-drive hitters and strong pitching headed by Steve Busby.

The year, however, was marred by controversy, much of it involving Busby and Manager McKeon. In mid–July, *The Topeka State Journal* reported that Busby might quit the team and return home. Buzz resigned as player representative for the team, an action that was interpreted as freeing him to quit if he wanted to. The article pointed out that Busby had been critical of the Royals organization since the fall of 1974 when Charley Lau, very popular with the players, was fired as batting coach. Buzz was quoted at the time as saying that the Royals organization seemed unsure if it really wanted to win, "and if that's the case, then I don't want to be part of it."

The first half of the season, the team played poorly and McKeon became the focus of dissension. Much of the team had lost confidence in him. The press reported that Busby was convinced that the Royals could not win the pennant with McKeon as manager. It was also reported that Busby wanted Buck Martinez to be the regular catcher, not Fran Healy, as McKeon apparently had decided. The Royals' front office replaced McKeon with Whitey Herzog. The team caught fire and, except for a late season slump, might have defeated the A's for the championship. They finished seven games behind.

In June 1975, Busby pitched in a game that was tied 2–2 after nine innings. Buzz felt something different in his shoulder, but he bowed his neck and kept on going. The game went 12 innings, and Busby threw an amazing 195 pitches. As Buzz put it, they were hard pitches, because his mechanics were off and he was struggling with his stuff. Later, he felt a dull sensation in his shoulder. Little did he know at the time that it was an injury to his rotator cuff.

Pitching with only three days' rest, Busby started against Texas. He had no pop in his arm, and as he tired, his arm seemed to lag. It felt different from normal tiredness, or even an ordinary inflammation.

After the game, Herzog asked Buzz, "How're you doing?" Busby responded, "Give me an extra day here and there." With the competitive spirit of a gladiator, Busby continued to pitch despite the pain. Things did not improve in the second half, however. He would have one good day and then a bad one, followed by a "really sloppy one." He finished the season with 18 wins and 12 losses and a highly respectable 3.08 ERA.

After the season, Busby spoke with Dr. Bob Kerlan. Kerlan thought that Busby had encapsulated tendonitis and that he should ice it down every day, which Buzz did faithfully.

The spring of 1976 began with a 16-day lockout of the players, and spring camp was delayed. Busby went to see Dr. Kerlan during this time, and Kerlan gave him a cortisone shot. Busby was in pain when spring camp finally opened. Herzog sent him to Kerlan again, and Kerlan told him to pitch.

In 1976, the Kansas City Royals finally replaced the A's and won their first of three consecutive AL West championships. But, sadly, they had to do it without Steve Busby, their pitching ace, who won only three games in six decisions. He struggled from the beginning of the season. He was scheduled to start the second game of a doubleheader on July 6. He could throw only about 75 miles an hour warming up. He threw for only seven minutes and told pitching coach Galen Cisco that his arm was gone, but Busby did start the game. For seven innings he threw "nothing pitches" successfully. He found himself behind 2–1, and was relieved in the eighth. In Detroit the next day, he could not lift his arm above his shoulder.

Busby told Herzog of his problem. "We have to find out what is going on," Herzog responded. Herzog contacted Dr. Frank Jobe. As soon as Herzog identified himself, Dr. Jobe said: "I know why you are calling." Busby flew out to Los Angeles to see Dr. Jobe, who did an analysis. He found a hole the size of a half dollar in Busby's rotator cuff. Additionally, he found bone spurs.

Dr. Jobe told Busby that they had done operations on tennis players with rotator cuff problems and "We will try it on you if you wish."

Dr. Jobe did surgery on July 19. Afterward, he told Busby that it went fine, but the prognosis was for him to look for another line of work. He told Busby that he would have to wait 18 months to find out the real verdict.

Kansas City lost the American League pennant in 1976 in the fifth and final game of the playoffs when Yankee first baseman Chris Chambliss swatted a three-run homer late in the contest. Royals fans were convinced that if their big hammer, Steve Busby, had been healthy, they would have won easily, a feeling that repeated itself in 1977 and in 1978 as the Royals lost to New York twice more.

Busby missed the entire 1977 season, a real blow for the Royals. With a healthy Busby, they might have been the best team in baseball. Whitey

Herzog, years later, said that the 1977 Royals were the best team he ever managed, including the 1982 world champion Cardinals. The Royals put together a tremendous 16-game winning streak in September and went on to win the American League West by eight games over Minnesota.

In 1978, Busby sought to rehabilitate himself at Omaha, but instead he faced a new problem: a bad back. After the All-Star break, Sid Borden wrote an article in the Kansas City paper suggesting that Busby retire. The article made Buzz more determined to return. On August 30, he threw batting practice in Kansas City and seemed to be throwing very well. He pitched a total of 21 innings in seven games, winning one while losing none, but he posted a 7.59 earned run average.

In the spring of 1979, Busby was upbeat. The season, however, was less than kind to him. He won six and lost six. At times, he was effective, and at other times, he was hit hard. To complicate things, his back flared up again, as did an old football injury. Baseball people who saw him pitch knew that Buzz was pitching more with his heart than with his once-golden arm.

Buzz was reasonably impressive in early camp in the spring of 1980, but he had still another setback when he had to have arthroscopic surgery on his left knee. He started the season in Omaha and pitched effectively. He threw a one-hitter on July 14 against the Iowa Oaks, winning 5–0. A radar gun clocked Busby's fastest pitch in the low eighties; he used to throw in the nineties. Kansas City was sufficiently impressed that they called him back, but Buzz had little success.

On August 30, 1980, Steve Busby, with a 1–3 record and a 6.21 ERA, was released by the Royals two days before he would have been eligible for postseason play. It was a bitter moment for Steve, but the Royals were making room for Ken Brett, a lefthanded pitcher. Thus, Busby missed the one chance he had to play in a World Series. Busby acknowledged that it was difficult "not to be able to pitch in all those play-off games."

In the spring of 1981, Whitey Herzog, who had signed as manager of the St. Louis Cardinals after Ewing Kauffman fired him from the Royals at the close of the 1979 season, invited Busby to the Cardinals' spring camp, but his playing days were over at age 31. Actually, they had ended at age 26.

Busby was an intense competitor, and quitting baseball was difficult. He spent hours talking to Paul Splittorff and Charley Lau, his one-time roommate, trying to face the situation. He even turned to a professional counselor. The competitive fires died slowly in him. Busby hoped that he might return to baseball in some capacity.

While recuperating from injuries, Busby spent much time in the Royals' broadcast booth as an analyst, gaining valuable broadcast experience. He received strong encouragement from Bud Blattner, the Royals' veteran broadcaster, and close friend Fred White of the Royals' crew to seek a career in broadcasting. Busby hoped to be a broadcaster for the Royals, a team to which he felt strong ties, but Kansas City was committed to another Royal stalwart as their television analyst, the articulate and respected Paul Splittorf.

Not to be denied, Busby was hired to work for Channel 4 in Kansas City in 1981. In 1982, Boston and Texas both had broadcast jobs open. Busby flew to Boston, interviewed and was offered a job the same day. The next day, he interviewed in Texas. Again he was offered the job. He decided to take the position in Texas.

Merle Harmon, the Rangers' play-by-play broadcaster, worked with Buzz on the finer aspects of the trade. The effort paid off, as Busby was hired by the CBS radio Game of the Week.

Busby worked as a Rangers broadcaster from 1982 until 1995, when an opening occurred on the Royals' television broadcast team. Busby was hired to work with Paul Splittorf, giving the Royals' broadcast crew the best pitching duel of any franchise in baseball.

"I don't feel cheated," Busby said. "Because I did everything I was able to. But I get mad at myself, because if I hadn't been so stubborn about a lot of things — insisting on pitching when my arm was sore, for instance — I think I could have prevented the serious damage. That's why I still go through a lot of ifs, ifs, ifs."

When the Kansas City Royals inaugurated a team Hall of Fame, the first two players chosen were Amos Otis and Steve Busby. At the time, Ewing Kauffman, the Royals' owner, paid appropriate tribute to the "No-Hit Kid": "Buzz was outstanding. I think he's the best pitcher in club history. Steve overmatched hitters to the point where it was embarrassing." Paul Splittorf expressed it well: "There's no telling what Buzz could have done if he hadn't been injured."

STEVEN LEE BUSBY

Born Sept. 29, 1949, Burbank, Calif.   Batted right, threw right.

Year	Team	W–L	Pct.	ERA	G	GS	CG	IP	H	BB	SO	ShO
1971	San Jose Calif.	4–1	.800	0.68	8	7	2	40	31	14	50	2
1972	Omaha AA	12–14	.462	3.20	30	30	17	217	197	61	221	2
1972	KC, AL	3–1	.750	1.58	5	5	3	40	28	8	31	0

Year	Team	W–L	Pct.	ERA	G	GS	CG	IP	H	BB	SO	ShO
1973	KC, AL	16–15	.516	4.24	37	37	7	238	246	105	174	1
1974	KC, AL	22–14	.611	3.39	38	38	20	292⅓	284	92	198	3
1975	KC, AL	18–12	.600	3.08	34	34	18	260	233	81	160	3
1976	KC, AL	3–3	.500	4.38	13	13	1	72	58	49	29	0
1977	Daytona B. Fla. St.	0–1	.000	15.00	1	1	0	3	11	1	2	0
1978	Sarasota Gulf Coast	1–0	1.000	0.00	2	2	0	13	7	0	9	0
1978	KC, AL	1–0	1.000	7.59	7	5	0	21⅓	24	15	10	0
1979	KC, AL	6–6	.500	3.64	22	12	4	94	71	64	45	0
1980	KC, AL	1–3	.250	6.21	11	6	0	42	59	19	12	0
Major League Totals 8 yrs.		70–54	.565	3.72	167	150	53	1060	1003	433	659	7

12 A STROKE OF MISFORTUNE

J. R. RICHARD

"Boy, that is some kind of smoke!"
BOB THURMAN, K.C. SCOUT

His mother called him Rodney, but playmates in Louisiana called him J.R. Others referred to him as "The Big Fellow"—for that was how he looked to hitters in the batter's box.

Baseball was not J.R.'s first love. Given his size as a teenager, he was attracted to basketball. He played the hoops game so well that as a senior at Lincoln High School in New Orleans, he gained the coveted All-American designation by averaging 35 points and 22 rebounds a game. Over 140 colleges sought his services as a cager.

Football also got J.R.'s interest. He played all the line positions and sometimes quarterbacked. But it was as a punter that he excelled. He boomed the football a phenomenal 67.5 yards a kick. Seven college coaches offered football scholarships, thinking that if Richard could not make it as a lineman, he could certainly do the punting.

J.R. played a little softball in the summertime, but did not try baseball until he was 15, and then only because friends talked him into it. At six feet, eight inches, and possessing a powerful arm, it was natural that he should be the team's pitcher.

Success came quickly. His overall high school record was 28–0 and included four perfect games. His senior year, he posted an 11–0 mark with a perfect 0.00 ERA. In a game which his team won 48–0, J.R. hit four consecutive home runs and drove in 10 runs. For the season, he batted .378 and hit six round-trippers. To no one's surprise, major league scouts clamored to meet this pitching Goliath. "Boy, that is some kind of smoke!" exclaimed Bob Thurman, scout for the Kansas City Royals, when he saw the strapping, young J.R. Richard throw the baseball. Mel Didier, scouting director

144

for Montreal, remarked, "It was unbelievable the arm that guy had. He was raw, real raw. But you knew if it all came together for him, this boy was going to be something special." "The raw ability was just awesome," Tal Smith, Houston Astros director of player personnel, reported after seeing this gangly, 19-year-old, 222-pound righthander from Lincoln High School intimidate would-be hitters. Smith felt Richard had the kind of arm "that a scout might see once about every 500,000 miles." Scouts agreed that J.R. was a cinch to become a superstar.

In the spring of 1969, the Astros, who had the second choice in the June player draft, narrowed their choices to Charlie Spikes, an outfielder from Bogalusa, Louisiana; Alvin McGrew of Fairfield, Alabama, another outfielder; and the flame-throwing Richard from Vienna, Louisiana. While Spikes and McGrew seemed more certain commodities, the Astros felt J.R. Richard's potential was too great to pass up, and they chose him second in the 1969 June draft. Houston signed Richard to a contract for $100,000.

J.R. debuted in pro ball at Covington, West Virginia, in the Appalachian League. In 12 games, he pitched 56 innings, struck out 71 batters, and posted a 5–4 record. In 1970, he pitched for Cocoa in the Florida State League. The hard-throwing righthander struck out 138 batters in 109 innings, but posted only a 4–11 record for a dismal minor league team.

Richard's next stop was at the Triple-A level in Oklahoma City. As is typical of young hurlers, Richard struggled to gain control of his breaking pitches. When he was on, he was tough. For example, he struck out 15 against Tulsa and 12 against Denver in back-to-back four-hit shutouts. For the season, he struck out 202 batters in only 173 innings, but he also led the league in walks with 105. He was unanimously selected for the American Association All-Star team.

The Astros brought the young flame-thrower to Houston at the end of the season and started him in four games. His first appearance was on September 5, 1971. Richard wasted little time in establishing himself as a legitimate major leaguer. In his major league debut in San Francisco, he tied Karl Spooner's first game record by striking out 15 Giant batters. He won two and lost one for Houston and allowed 3.43 earned runs per nine-inning game while striking out 29 in 21 innings.

In 1972, the Astros sent Richard back to Oklahoma City so he could pitch regularly. He went 10–8 and fanned 169 in 128 innings. He pitched four times for Houston late in the season and won one while losing none.

Everybody knew Richard was going to be an outstanding pitcher if he could get better control of his pitches. So J.R. split 1973 between Denver of the American Association and Houston of the N.L. He was 6–2 at Houston and 2–4 at Denver. The next year was also disappointing. He won two and lost four for Houston and went 5–8 in Triple-A ball at Columbus. Wildness and nagging injuries plagued the big righthander throughout the season.

As the 1975 season approached, writers and baseball personnel agreed that this was the year that Richard needed to step up and establish himself as a major league pitcher. He had bounced up and down between Houston and the minor leagues enough. Richard himself was beginning to experience mental anguish about the uncertainty of the situation. He lamented, "They tell you there's not enough room for you on the big club, and they say, 'Go down. Keep your chin up. We'll call you.' They make it sound easy. But it's not easy. It sets you back a great deal."

The 1975 season looked promising for Richard, now 25 years old. The untimely death in January of hard-throwing Don Wilson had left a big hole in the Astros pitching staff. Richard had a chance to step in and take Wilson's place. Only Tom Griffin, Dave Roberts and Larry Dierker loomed as certainties in Manager Preston Gomez's starting rotation. Richard himself acknowledged, "It looks to me like I have a better chance than ever before. I would say I am 100 percent ahead of last year."

J.R. proved to be prophetic. Not only did he stick with Houston in 1975, he was relatively free of the small, nagging injuries that had plagued him, and he pitched consistently enough to achieve a winning 12–10 record. He fanned 176 but walked a league-leading 138 batsmen. Richard, despite wildness, finally ascended to the pitching rotation.

In 1976, Richard established himself as the dominating pitcher that scouts had predicted. Richard's fastball hummed by National League hitters for a third strike 214 times, and despite issuing a league-leading 151 walks, he reached the 20-win plateau while losing 15. By allowing only 221 hits in 291 innings, he lowered his ERA to an excellent 2.75.

The next three years, 1977–79, J.R. Richard was steady and consistent, winning 18 games each season. His loss totals were 12, 11 and 13, and in 1978, he led the league in strikeouts, fanning 303 hitters. When you think of the outstanding fastball pitchers in National League history, pitchers like Sandy Koufax, Don Drysdale, Bob Gibson, Tom Seaver, and Dizzy Dean, only Koufax fanned more in a season. Richard came back in 1979 to strike out 313, and he reduced his walk total from a league-leading 141 in 1978 to 98 in 1979. Despite wildness, J.R.'s ERA was among the league leaders in these years: 2.97 in 1977; 3.11 in 1978; and a league-low 2.71 in 1979. His hits allowed per inning ratio was outstanding each year. For example, in 1978 he allowed only 192 base hits in 275 innings.

J. R. Richard twice struck out more than 300 batters in one season (CORBIS-BETTMAN ARCHIVES, NEW YORK, NY).

Richard finished the 1979 season with a rush. On July 24, his record was 7–11, with a 3.84 ERA. From that point on, J.R. was scored on in only 11 innings, including four unearned runs. He finished with a 2.71 earned run average, and won 11 while losing only two, for an 18–13 record. Richard concluded the 1979 season with 25 consecutive shutout innings.

His best friend on the team, Enos Cabell, proclaimed, "Maybe people will realize now that J.R. is probably the best pitcher in baseball." Richard himself assented, "I do think this is as good as I've ever pitched because my rhythm is good. Rhythm is the big key for me. In the past, I would sometimes try to overthrow; then I would overcompensate for that problem, and all of sudden I would be in trouble."

At the end of the year, according to the major league player agreement, J.R. Richard of Houston and Nolan Ryan of California were the top-billed pitching free agents. Consensus was that the Astros would not let Richard get away, and Ryan was talking about a desire to return to his home state of Texas, creating the prospect that Houston might have the two hardest-throwing righthanders in baseball on the same pitching staff in 1980. Tal Smith, now the general manager, made it top priority to keep Richard in Houston. After all, J.R. had won 74 games the past four seasons, and if he were to participate in the November re-entry draft, he would be the subject of an intense bidding war. Smith signed Richard to a four-year contract valued somewhere between $2.5 and $3 million. Smith said the amount would vary because of contingencies and guarantees.

Richard, who celebrated his 30th birthday prior to the 1980 season, was elated. "My wife, Carolyn, and I like Houston and want to stay there," Richard said. He further explained that his teammates had something to do with his decision. Also, things looked promising for the Astros. They had won 89 games in 1979, and a division championship seemed within reach. "I didn't need more money," Richard added. "I was content with what the Astros offered."

As was predicted, Nolan Ryan, a big winner for California the previous eight years, signed with Houston for $1 million a year, giving the Astros two of the most dominating pitchers in baseball in their rotation. Hopes ran high in East Texas as the year began. The club had lost the National League's West Division championship to Cincinnati by only a game-and-a-half in 1979, and the signing of Ryan and Richard made them favorites for 1980. Even Richard predicted, "We're going to win it. We've got the best pitching staff in baseball, we've got speed, and we've got defense."

Richard disappointed no one at the beginning of the new season. He was brilliant. He seemed on course for his best season and toward becoming the top pitcher in the game. He posted a 10–4 record with a 1.89 ERA during the first half. His fastballs repeatedly were clocked at 100 mph and his sliders at 90 mph. The trajectory of Richard's slider made it tough to see or hit. It looked just like his fastball coming up to home plate but then took an explosive dive into the dirt around the plate. Catcher Joe Ferguson indicated that the batter loses the ball about 10 feet in front of home plate. "He's already tracked the ball and made his decision. If the pitch changes, he's got no time to react." Many a hitter swung at pitches from Richard that bounced in the dirt.

Richard started the All-Star Game and pitched two scoreless innings. His fastball was clocked at 100 mph during that stint at Dodger Stadium. J.R. had become the superstar that his admirers had predicted.

There was one disturbing element, however. Richard had completed only four of his 17 first-half starts and repeatedly complained of arm fatigue. The press began to criticize Richard's change in pitching stamina. A steady barrage of articles inferred that J.R., in the words of his agent Tom Reich, "was a faker, a malingerer, a head case." Both Houston newspapers, on the same day, compared J.R.'s pitching troubles to the highly hyped "Who shot J.R.?" episode of the popular soap opera of that era, *Dallas*. "Who Shot J.R.'s Arm?" one headline asked.

Richard responded by keeping to himself, which made him seem aloof to his teammates and an obvious malingerer to much of the press. Nolan Ryan later said of the problem, "The fact that J.R. didn't seem to have a specific injury like a broken bone or an ulna nerve or a torn rotator cuff made his complaints seem suspect." There was no physical ailment people could pinpoint.

In Chicago, Richard pitched five excellent innings, but came in saying that he did not feel well, that he had a weakness in his arm, that his arm was "just not right." When asked where he hurt, he reported that he had no pain, just fatigue. Athletes characteristically are expected to play through minor pain, and if they do not, they are subject to criticism. Reggie Smith observed that he had found over the years "if you don't play hurt, you're a sissy. If you're knocked down, it's 'Get up, you're not hurt that bad, you're still breathing.'"

All Richard could report was arm fatigue, which was unconvincing. How could he be hurt if he could throw 100-mph fastballs? His stuff was good, but he would come into the dugout and say he did not feel right, and when asked what was wrong, he would say, "My arm is weak." But then he would go for another inning, and his stuff would still be good.

He started the All-Star Game July 8 in Los Angeles and pitched two perfect innings. Afterward he told reporters, "I feel fine now. I just needed rest. I don't anticipate any more problems."

However, on July 11, J.R. went to see Dr. Frank Jobe for an examination. After the examination, Richard falsely told the press and his teammates that Dr. Jobe had prescribed 30 days' rest. Three days later, on July 14, he admitted that he had made up that story and asked to start that night against Atlanta. He was outstanding for three innings, but in the fourth he called Manager Bill Virdon to the mound and asked to be relieved. Later, he told people that he left the game because he felt a bit nauseous. He said that he had a stomach problem that had resulted from eating too much spicy food.

The Houston press criticized Richard for leaving the game. One columnist sarcastically proposed a new soap opera, "As the Stomach Turns." The next day, news leaked out that Richard had not complained of a stomach problem at all but that he had told Virdon his arm was tired. "I didn't know anything about a stomach ache," Virdon confirmed. "He was woozy but not woozy enough to come out of a game. He just told me he had a tired arm, and when he does, I'm taking him out." Richard's leaving the game early did not sit well with his Astro teammates. One of them said, "We're in a pennant race, and he pulls this?"

Some people thought that Richard was unhappy because Nolan Ryan was making $1 million a year whereas he was making $700,000. Yet, Richard had never expressed dissatisfaction with his contract to anyone.

Team physician Dr. Harold Brelsford held a press conference in which he publicly advised Richard "to eat better, sleep more and cut down his social life"— all matters involving Richard's mental outlook, not physical maladies.

The next day, Richard threw 22 minutes on the sidelines and reported that his arm felt weary. "We don't want to take any chances," Virdon said. The Astros put their star hurler on the 21-day disabled list. To be safe, they scheduled three days of diagnostic testing at Methodist Hospital.

Medical tests found no neurological, arthritic, or muscle disorders, but an arteriogram revealed a blockage of the "distal subclavian and auxiliary arteries on the right arm." In layman's terms, J.R. had a blood clot on his right or pitching side. Dr. Charles McCollum, a surgeon at Methodist Hospital, and team physician Dr. Brelsford decided that "no surgical intervention" was needed. Rather Richard "should be allowed to resume activities and work out under close control and observed conditions."

Four days later, while engaged in a light workout at the Astrodome, J.R. Richard collapsed to the turf. He was rushed by ambulance to the hospital where it was discovered that he had suffered a stroke and "that he had no pulse in his right carotid artery."

In a 90-minute operation, vascular surgeons Dr. George Noon and Dr. Charles McCullom, in consultation with Dr. Michael DeBakey, the famed Houston surgeon, surgically removed a large clot from the arteries (innominate, carotid, and subclavian) of his neck. This procedure restored the circulation to the carotid artery and once more improved circulation in his right arm. But team physician Dr. Brelsford reported, "The right side of his brain did not get sufficient blood for several hours (between the time of the stroke and the time of the operation) and this resulted in the weakness to his left arm and leg." When Richard regained consciousness, he discovered that he was totally paralyzed on his left side and that he could not speak.

Doctors said they were unable to predict if the effects of the stroke would be temporary or permanent, nor could they predict if Richard would ever be able to pitch again. They defended their original decision to let Richard work out after their original diagnosis of a blood clot.

Dr. Brelsford explained, "The original thrombosis was there at least two months and probably a long time before that. It likely was the result of the effects of his pitching; I cannot explain why he developed an extension of that thrombosis."

When queried about why Richard had been allowed to return to workouts under those conditions, Dr. Brelsford added, "It was a medical judgment that the clot was a chronic situation. I don't think it is that uncommon in baseball to find pitchers with circulatory problems in their arms."

Controversy over the incident spread. Enos Cabell, when he heard the medical report, said with a hint of bitterness, "If Jay were white, maybe they would have checked him more thoroughly, and maybe he wouldn't have been out there throwing. Most black athletes play hurt, and he pitched when he was hurt."

Dr. Brelsford responded, "I've gone over this thing 100 times in my own mind, and I've talked with 50 other doctors, and I can truthfully say that none of us could figure anything to do differently. Something happened between July 25 and July 29. But what that was, I just don't know." He added, "His first clot was due to his pitching, but the second one we may never know why."

Doctors involved with the case believed that stress might have been a factor that brought about the stroke. Pitchers generally experience worry and concern about their pitching arms — their livelihood — and Richard had experienced constant arm fatigue before the incident.

Richard's agent, Tom Reich, blamed the media for causing the stress. He said that the press had placed awesome pressure on his client with their charges of malingering, and especially with the comparison of J.R. Richard with J.R. Ewing of the television program *Dallas*.

"In the name of God, how could you people do this?" Reich exclaimed. "I'm sure nobody meant any personal harm to J.R., but I think the coincidence of metaphors of a fictional soap opera program involving J.R. Ewing to a real-life J.R. Richard was just too damn enticing to pass up. How could you do this? It's despicable, and it stinks." The comparison, he said, had caused great strain on Richard and all "I can say is shame on you people. I like to think I have sympathy, but I'm not sorry. I don't have sympathy for these sick people who wrote things like that."

Besides, Reich charged, how could anyone familiar with Richard's previous record and the number of innings he had pitched even think he was faking when he kept reporting arm fatigue in the first half of the 1980 season? "This was a great injustice," he said. "How could anyone conclude that J.R. was a dog? This was more like a crucifixion than anything I have ever seen."

While Richard was in the operating room, the Astros were losing to

Philadelphia behind Nolan Ryan's pitching. The players did not find out about the operation until after the game had started, and a pall fell over the dugout when the word got to them. Manager Bill Virdon, upon hearing the news aptly observed, "At least, it will put an end to all the speculation."

Two days after the operation, Richard regained some movement in his left side. The third day, he sat up and took fluids. By August 3, he was described as being in "very good spirits." A month later, he was back on his feet and walking without a limp. He got out of the hospital in September, but his spirits were down because of the probability that he would never play baseball again. He found it hard to cope with his enormous misfortune. He moped and pouted, and his mood was generally morose. He knew that patience was the key, but it was so difficult to be patient.

Houston went on to win the National League West without J.R. and played the Phillies for the championship. Appropriately, Richard was asked to throw out the first ball in Houston. To those in attendance at the Astrodome, the tall 30-year-old, once a powerful pitcher, was a pitiful sight. The left side of his face drooped from the paralysis, he walked with the cautious gait of an old man, and he declined to say anything in public.

The playoffs between Houston and Philadelphia produced much excitement. Steve Carlton outdueled Ken Forsch in the first game, 3–1, but Nolan Ryan and the Astros evened the series the next day with a 7–4 win. The third game was in Houston, and it was a classic pitchers' battle that the Astros won in the eleventh inning, 1–0. Philadelphia won the next two games, 5–3 and 8–7, the last game being decided in the tenth inning when Gary Maddox drove home Del Unser with the deciding run. It is easy to speculate that had a healthy J.R. Richard been able to pitch in the series, Houston, not Philadelphia, would have played Kansas City for the world's championship.

On the day of the first World Series game, Richard was back in the hospital undergoing 18-hour surgery by Dr. Jack Wiley to graft an eight-inch segment of artery into his pitching shoulder. Doctors felt that the procedure would improve circulation in the right shoulder and might allow J.R. to return to baseball. The operation brought new hope to Richard. As he was leaving the hospital, Dr. Wiley asked him, "What are you going to do first?" Richard said, "Going fishing, Doc." So Dr. Wiley asked, "And after that?" The tall, one-time flame-thrower replied, "Going to pitch."

Within 30 days, Richard showed improvement as a result of the latest surgery. His face no longer drooped, his speech was nearly normal, and he was jogging three miles a day. Hope surged through his mind as his body began rebuilding. His neurologist gave him the go-ahead to start throwing a baseball after New Year's. Richard's spirits soared, and he announced, "There's no doubt in my mind now that I'll be back. I feel terrific. I've already been out throwing a football with the kids." Unfortunately, it was too early to write a happy ending to the story.

Official verdicts labeled Richard's baseball future problematic. But J.R. wanted to prove something to the public. So he pointed toward opening day, 1981. He set a schedule for himself and began working out in January. "I know I'll come back," he said. "Everybody's on my side, I know that. But everyone doesn't believe like I do. When I do come back, when people see me pitch again, they'll be shocked off their feet." Working at a Houston fitness club, he began throwing Frisbees, then basketballs from the free-throw line, and finally a baseball at progressively faster speeds. Every day, he threw 10 or 15 minutes to Luis Pujols, the backup catcher for the Astros.

But things didn't go so well for Richard in Florida. Although his arm and his speech had returned sufficiently, he still had neurological deficits. J.R. had a problem with ground balls, especially to his left side, the area that was partially paralyzed by the stroke. Then one day Gene Coleman, the exercise specialist, was trying to hit a ground ball to Richard when he accidentally hit a line drive right back at the pitcher's mound. The ball sailed by Richard's head, and he never so much as blinked. His reflexes had not even reacted in self-defense. Richard, however, persisted. When Dr. William S. Fields asked him what he would do if a ball were hit back at him during a game, Richard confidently replied, "Doc, the best way to handle that is just not let 'em hit the ball."

The season opened with Richard on the inactive list. The 1981 season was interrupted by a long and bitter players' strike. Richard kept working avidly during the strike. When play resumed, he frequently pitched batting practice. His velocity usually was good, although not at the previous level, but his control was spotty. Although he pitched batting practice from behind a protective screen, his reaction to balls hit past him seemed to improve.

In early August, Richard asked Bill Virdon if he might pitch in an August 7 exhibition against the Rangers. Virdon responded tentatively. However, two days later, General Manager Al Rosen announced, "Short of a major breakdown tonight, J.R. will pitch against the Rangers."

"He will pitch one inning," Dr. William S. Fields, Richard's physician, said. "There is no danger. I wouldn't approve his pitching if I felt he were in danger." But Richard responded, "I won't decide whether I'll pitch Friday night until I see how I feel Friday. I feel pretty good today. But I may feel lousy Friday. I think they owe me the respect of consulting me."

Richard did not have the final say. On the day of the game, Virdon announced, "I just don't think he is quite ready. Those would be competitive hitters he'd be facing." Virdon's firm decision may well have come as a relief to the recovering hurler.

Both the pitcher and the club retained hope that Richard might be activated in September, but as the season progressed, it became clear that Richard would not pitch during the 1981 season. His comeback would have to wait until 1982.

In the spring, Richard reported to camp 25 pounds overweight. Bill Virdon was disappointed, because, he said, J.R. "needs everything going for him he can." In early workouts, J.R. had problems with his fastball, and the strike zone seemed to be elusive. Even his motion seemed out of sync. Astros President Al Rosen indicated that Richard would probably be asked to start the season in the minors. "It seems like the most logical thing for both J.R. and the club," he said.

Although during the 1981 season a comeback by the big righthander seemed plausible, in the spring of 1982, it seemed remote. Richard did not pitch to major league hitters again. For two years he toiled, facing Class A hitters who once would have trembled to stand in the box against him, but who now stepped up and teed off at his servings. Richard made it to the Astros' Triple-A club in Tucson, but that is where his comeback ended. J.R. had gotten to the point where he could again throw a 90 mph fastball, but he could not field. Enough neurological impairment remained that he had difficulty moving quickly.

The Astros decided that Richard's comeback attempt was futile. They gave J.R. his unconditional release. The career of one of the most overpowering pitchers of all time, a possible Hall of Famer, had run its course. It ended when he was 34 years old. Richard was stricken by a stroke of misfortune.

Instead of sulking about his fate, J.R. sought a new career as a car salesman, and he found inner peace through God and family. He described what had happened to him as "The Big Trade." "I traded baseball for a life of God. God wanted it to be this way," he said. Richard felt he had exchanged pitching glory for the glory of God.

JAMES RODNEY RICHARD

Born Mar. 27, 1950, Vienna, La.   Batted right, threw right.

Year	Team	W–L	Pct.	ERA	G	GS	CG	IP	H	BB	SO	ShO
1969	Covington Appal.	5–4	.556	6.59	12	n/a	n/a	56	51	*52	71	n/a

Year	Team	W–L	Pct.	ERA	G	GS	CG	IP	H	BB	SO	ShO
1970	Cocoa Fla. St.	4–11	.267	2.39	19	n/a	n/a	109	67	68	71	n/a
1971	Okla. City, AA	12–7	.632	*2.45	24	n/a	n/a	173	116	*105	*202	n/a
1971	Hou NL	2–1	.667	3.43	4	4	1	21	17	16	29	0
1972	Okla. City, AA	10–8	.556	3.02	19	n/a	n/a	128	94	79	163	n/a
1972	Hou NL	1–0	1.000	13.50	4	1	0	6	10	8	8	0
1973	Denver AA	2–4	.333	5.71	8	n/a	n/a	52	54	26	66	n/a
1973	Hou NL	6–2	.750	4.00	16	10	2	72	54	38	75	1
1974	Columbus Southern	5–8	.385	5.38	13	n/a	n/a	87	103	61	77	n/a
1974	Denver AA	4–0	1.000	0.00	4	n/a	n/a	33	15	12	26	n/a
1974	Hou NL	2–3	.400	4.15	15	9	0	65	58	36	42	0
1975	Hou NL	12–10	.545	4.39	33	31	7	203	178	*138	176	1
1976	Hou NL	20–15	.571	2.75	39	39	14	291	221	*151	214	3
1977	Hou NL	18–12	.600	2.97	36	36	13	267	212	104	214	3
1978	Hou NL	18–11	.621	3.11	36	36	16	275	192	*141	303	3
1979	Hou NL	18–13	.581	*2.71	38	38	19	292	220	98	*313	4
1980	Hou NL	10–4	.714	1.89	17	17	4	114	65	40	119	4
1981	Out of baseball.											
1982	Daytona Beach, Fla.	3–1	.750	2.79	6	6	2	42	36	15	28	0
1982	Tucson, PC	0–2	.000	13.68	6	6	0	24	27	13	24	0
Major League Totals 10 yrs.		107–71	.601	3.15	238	221	76	1606	1227	770	1493	19

Asterisk indicates led league

13   THE HOME RUN KID

TONY CONIGLIARO

> "I kept saying to myself, 'Oh, God,
> let me breathe.' I didn't think about my future
> in baseball. I just wanted to stay alive."
> TONY CONIGLIARO

The proud Boston Red Sox franchise fell on hard times in the early 1960s. In the period following World War II, the Red Sox were always competitive, winning the pennant in 1946 and finishing second twice and third once. Throughout the 1950s, they resided in the first division, finishing third or fourth four times each. With the great Ted Williams, and quality players like Jackie Jensen, Frank Malzone, Billy Goodman, and Walt Dropo, the Boston team always was respectable.

The 1960s began with a seventh-place finish and the retirement of one of the greatest hitters of all-time, Ted Williams. Despite boasting the batting champion for three of the first four years of the decade, 1960–1963, the Red Sox finished seventh, sixth, eighth, and seventh. The team had aged badly, and their pitching was terrible. The staff finished near the bottom of the league in ERA the first four years. Managerial changes were frequent.

Entering the 1964 season, Johnny Pesky, one of their stalwart players of the 1940s, took over as manager. It was Pesky's first managerial assignment and he was 43 years old. Carl Yastrzemski in his fourth year was the only legitimate star of the squad. The rest of the team was made up of retreads like Eddie Bressoud, Dick "Strange Glove" Stuart, Lee Thomas, and a host of no-names. Making the team for the first time was a sensational rookie who had a phenomenal minor-league year as an 18-year-old in 1963.

The hype for Anthony Richard Conigliaro was continuous and extravagant. He was a true phenom. One reporter observed that a bumper crop of rookies emerged in 1964 and all of them achieved something of merit in the early games of the season. The writer listed Tony Oliva, Dick Allen, Jay Alou, and Sam Bowens, and went on, "but above them all stood Tony Conigliaro, 18-year-old center fielder of the Red Sox [a slight error; Conigliaro was 19 in 1964]. Mr. Conigliaro must be accounted a baseball natural, if not to say phenom."

Conigliaro's one minor league season at Wellsville of the New York–Pennsylvania League was a smash. In only 333 at-bats, the young slugger amassed 70 extra base hits among his 121 safeties, and he finished with a robust .363 batting average and an unbelievable slugging percentage of .730. He was named MVP and the league's Number One Rookie. An early season injury caused him to miss 30 games and denied him the league's batting title because of insufficient at-bats.

Winning a minor-league batting title was not Conigliaro's goal. He wanted to start and star for the Red Sox. When he first signed with the Sox, 13 other major league teams were at his doorstep. Conigliaro and his family narrowed the choices to three: the Red Sox, the Orioles, and the Yankees. He chose Boston when they matched all other offers. He received a reported bonus of $25,000.

The Red Sox had another highly touted 19-year-old in their farm system, a big first baseman named Tony Horton. Horton got more money. One report put Horton's bonus at $125,000. Most reports agreed that Boston fans should drool at the prospect of seeing two young right-handed sluggers shooting at the "Green Monster."

With Conigliaro coming up, Red Sox management in 1964 was heartened and optimistic about the future. While finishing seventh in 1963, they had young Carl Yastrzemski, Ted Williams' replacement, winning his first batting title. When young Conigliaro had a sensational spring, Pesky installed him in center field for opening day. Could a 19-year-old rookie make it?

If reputation was a factor, he could. Conigliaro was already being compared to great players past and present. Red Sox Vice President Pinky Higgins said of young Tony, "He stands up to the plate like Al Kaline." (Kaline, the Detroit Tiger star, had won a batting title as a 20-year-old nine years earlier.) Manager Johnny Pesky said, "Tony can be another Joe DiMaggio, but he must take care of himself." Another veteran American Leaguer, Birdie Tebbetts, said early in 1964, "The Red Sox could come up with the best one-two batting punch in the American League"—Conigliaro and Yastrzemski. Talk about pressure.

The new Red Sox phenom was simply known as Tony by his family and as Tony C. to the sports writers. He was born in Revere, Massachusetts, right in the heart of Boston Red Sox country, and was raised in Swampscott, a few miles northeast on the water. He graduated from St. Mary's High School in Lynn in 1962. Lynn is a city that has produced many outstanding ball players, including Bump Hadley, Jim Hegan, and Harry Agganis. In his senior year, Conigliaro, batting .580, led St. Mary's to its first Catholic title. He was a three sport athlete and was voted MVP in all three: baseball, football, and basketball.

Tony C. grew up with the Red Sox teams that boasted Williams, Doerr, Pesky, and Dom DiMaggio. He had drawn throngs of major league scouts to his ball fields, and his story was developing considerably before his twentieth birthday.

Conigliaro debuted impressively. While the higher priced Tony Horton played most of 1964 with Reading, Conigliaro established records in Boston. He played 111 games and batted 404 times, clubbing 24 home runs — the most ever by a 19-year-old rookie, breaking Mel Ott's long-standing record. At 19, Ott had hit 18 home runs in 1928. Conigliaro broke the record on July 26, despite missing many games because of a broken bone in his left hand that he suffered May 24. In the second game of a doubleheader on July 26, he was hit by a pitch on his right arm. He fell to the ground in pain. X-rays showed a fracture of the ulna. The doctors thought he was through for the season, but he returned September 1.

While he made quite an impact throughout the season, his opening game in Boston was particularly noteworthy. It was a game dedicated to the memory of the late President John F. Kennedy, who had been assassinated the previous November. In the stands, along with Conigliaro's mother and father, Mr. and Mrs. Sal Conigliaro, were the governor of Massachusetts, a United States senator, the mayor of Boston, and a host of Hollywood and baseball celebrities.

Young Conigliaro did not disappoint them. In the second inning, White Sox pitcher Joel Horlen threw a fastball that Conigliaro hit out of the park onto Lansdowne Street beyond the famous left field screen.

In the spring, General Manager Gabe Paul of the Cleveland Indians said of Conigliaro, "He's the finest young prospect I have ever seen in the Cactus League." After the season got under way, first baseman Dick Stuart said about his young teammate, "This boy has everything; he can hit, run, field, and throw."

Conigliaro confirmed all the lavish comments in his rookie season. Tony Oliva of the Twins won Rookie of the Year honors, but one must consider the fact that Conigliaro missed over 50 games, whereas Oliva missed none, and Conigliaro was only 19. The next season, 1965, was historic. In a league that boasted sluggers like Killebrew, Colavito, Howard, Cash, Mantle, and

Tony Conigliaro talking with another pretty good hitter, Ted Williams, Boston batting advisor, in 1965 (CORBIS-BETTMAN ARCHIVES, NEW YORK, NY).

Maris, 20-year-old Tony C. won the home run title, becoming the youngest player in history to achieve that honor. He homered 32 times in 138 games. The Red Sox finished seventh, 40 games behind the champion Twins, but Conigliaro made the record books. In two seasons, he had amassed 56 home runs before his 21st birthday.

In 1965, Conigliaro again suffered injuries that kept him from an even greater home run total. Tony C. broke his wrist late in July, missing 24 games. He had made a wager with a sports writer that he would play in at least 140 games in the 1965 season, but his wrist injury, caused by a pitch thrown by Kansas City A's Wes Stock, cost him the bet.

Conigliaro got the attention and the admiration of numerous people. He caught the eye, for example, of Ron Santo of the Cubs. "He's the most aggressive young hitter I've ever seen. I hope he never changes," Santo said.

Frank Lane, serving as a scout for Baltimore, predicted great things for Tony C. "He's going to have a terrific season in 1966," Lane prophesied. "He's a fine hitter and he will have his feet solidly on the ground by then. He might be a super-star." Lane went on to suggest that Red Sox pitchers needed to brush back opposing hitters more in order to protect Conigliaro from being crippled by an excessive number of inside pitches.

Conigliaro was concerned that the Red Sox had finished eighth and ninth his first two seasons with them. He thus approached 1966 with the goal of playing a full season uninterrupted by injury. Tony C. achieved his goal: he played 150 games in 1966. He drove in a team-leading 93 runs. While his home run total dipped to 28, it was tops for the team. Another slugger, George Scott, joined the Sox that year, and he contributed 27 home runs, but the final result for the Red Sox was the same. They finished in eighth place, 25 games behind the young, pitching-rich Baltimore Orioles.

Red Sox pitching was the worst in the league, although Jim Lonborg debuted and gave promise for the future. Lonborg was a hard thrower with an excellent curveball. The Red Sox fired Billy Herman, their manager of two years, and finished the season with Pete Runnels. Dick Williams was signed to manage in 1967.

Boston's record to that point in the decade was terrible. Their best finish was sixth in 1961. Although hope is eternal in baseball, there was no reason to assume that 1967 would be different for the Red Sox. Perhaps climbing two, three, or four notches was possible. Finishing in the first division would be an enormous accomplishment. But the pennant? There were no such predictions as the team went to spring training for the 1967 season.

Conigliaro was pleased when the tough Boston writers voted him the most valuable Red Sox player of 1966. The award had been won the previous year by Yastrzemski. Tony was particularly pleased because he had had such a dismal start. Rookie George Scott got most of the headlines and was voted starting first baseman in the All-Star Game while Conigliaro wasn't even in the running. By the end of the season, he had gotten back to form and boosted his career home run total to 84 at the age of 22. He was gaining respect as an outfielder, having mastered the tough Fenway Park right field.

After Conigliaro signed his contract in January, General Manager Dick O'Connell revealed that Charlie Finley, owner of the Kansas City Athletics, had bid $500,000 for Conigliaro. "He offered a half a million, but I turned him down," said O'Connell. Some were surprised by the offer since Conigliaro's batting averages for his first three years were .290, .269 and .265. The offer, however, indicated that Tony C. was considered one of the top players in the majors as the 1967 season dawned.

Conigliaro was sidelined in late March with a hairline fracture of the scapular bone when he was hit by a pitch from teammate Johnny Wyatt. It was the fifth time he had suffered a broken bone, but the Red Sox trainer was sure that Tony C. would be ready for opening day. And he was.

Conigliaro enjoyed a good season through the All-Star Game. He played in the game and demonstrated his prowess as an all-star outfielder by making several excellent plays, including a sensational catch of a blast off the bat of Orlando Cepeda. It was Conigliaro's first All-Star appearance and owner Tom Yawkey sent him a letter of congratulations.

Conigliaro had set three goals for himself for 1967: he wanted to bat .300, hit 30 home runs, and drive in 100 runs. As August approached, he was batting close to .290 with 20 home runs and nearly 70 RBIs. Further, the Red Sox were finally making a run for the pennant. Lonborg was pitching brilliantly, and rookie center fielder Reggie Smith was having an excellent season. Conigliaro's season was interrupted when he was called into military service for two weeks. The absence affected his timing. Still, he was ecstatic at the prospect of a World Series appearance. Tragically, it was not to be.

Baseball history is dotted with significant dates: October 1, 1961, when Roger Maris hit his 61st home run off Tracy Stallard; July 17, 1941, the day Joe DiMaggio's 56-game hitting streak was stopped in Cleveland; August 16, 1920, the day Ray Chapman was beaned by Carl Mays; May 7, 1957, the day Gil McDougald hit a line drive that struck Herb Score; and October 8, 1956, the day Don Larsen pitched a perfect game in the World Series.

For Anthony Richard Conigliaro, the critical date of his baseball life was August 18, 1967. The Red Sox were in the midst of their miracle year. They were involved in a fierce pennant race, one of the closest of all time. Four teams were involved: the Detroit Tigers, the Minnesota Twins and the Chicago White Sox, along with Conigliaro's Red Sox. The team's pitching staff finally boasted a legitimate ace in Jim Lonborg.

On that date, August 18, the pennant race ended for Boston's star slugger. Tony C. was at bat, facing California Angels pitcher Jack Hamilton. With the count 0 and 2, Hamilton threw a fastball that came straight for Conigliaro's head. The ball hit him, and he fell.

The 22-year-old slugger later described the incident with these words: "His pitch came in tight. I jumped back and my helmet flew off. There was this tremendous ringing noise. I couldn't stand it. Just a loud shriek all over me. I was trying to find some place in my mouth where I could get air through, but I couldn't breathe. I kept saying to myself, 'Oh, God, let me breathe.' I didn't think about my future in baseball. I just wanted to stay alive."

Buck Rodgers, the Angels catcher, remembers that Conigliaro "was bleeding from the ear, the mouth and the nose, and I didn't want to look any more. I told Jack, 'Get out of here, get away.' Jack came up to the plate; he was concerned. But I pushed him back. I said, 'Jack, you don't want to see this.'"

The on-deck hitter was Rico Petrocelli. He knelt beside Tony and told him over and over, "You're going to be OK, it's going to be fine." Conigliaro lost consciousness, and he was taken by stretcher into the clubhouse, where he regained consciousness.

Initially, it was uncertain how badly Conigliaro was hurt and how badly his eye was damaged. The doctor's report indicated that the ball had fractured Tony's cheekbone in three places and had dislocated his jaw. It left him blind for 48 hours after the accident.

Conigliaro remained in the hospital for eight days. When he was released, the imprint of the baseball's stitches were visible, and the effect of the collision of the ball with his face was apparent. His vision was blurred, and experts were quietly predicting that his career was over. The force of the blow had punched a tiny hole in his retina, thus causing a loss of depth perception, a critical skill for a batter.

The Red Sox, after the beaning, swept the four-game series from the Angels and vaulted into first place. They successfully held on for the rest of the season and won their first pennant since 1946.

Lonborg pitched brilliantly in the World Series against St. Louis, but the Sox succumbed to the Cardinals in seven games. Bob Gibson won three of the four games for St. Louis and emerged as the pitching hero of the Series. Conigliaro's bat was sorely missed by the Red Sox. His replacements, Jose Tartabull and Ken Harrelson, hit .154 and .077, respectively, garnering three singles in 26 at-bats between them.

In the post-season, Dick Williams was praised for his managerial talents in achieving what so many other Red Sox managers had failed to do: a pennant flying above Fenway Park. During the winter, however, Conigliaro stirred up controversy when he was quoted as saying, "All of the credit is going to Dick Williams. The main credit should go to the ball players. They deserve all the credit." When asked for his reaction, Williams agreed that the players deserved the credit, and he continued, "Tony Conigliaro is one who deserved a lot of the credit." The manager's comments defused the controversy.

Conigliaro attempted to return to baseball the following spring despite frequent headaches and spells of dizziness. His depth perception was faulty. He had a terrible spring, and after several highly embarrassing at-bats, flew to Boston for an examination. Doctors told him that his career was finished. His vision in his left eye, the one that had been injured, was 20/300.

Tony sat out the entire 1968 season. Not only had the Red Sox lost their big slugger, but pitcher Jim Lonborg had broken a leg in a skiing accident and was lost to the club for months. In May, team owner Tom Yawkey said he would offer Conigliaro a job with the Red Sox organization if "he wants and needs it." Yawkey, expressing sympathy for Conigliaro's plight, went on to say, "I think what happened to Tony was a sickening and saddening thing." The Red Sox finished fourth without their young slugger, 17 games behind the champion Detroit Tigers.

In 1969, Conigliaro startled the baseball world by making an impressive comeback. It was opening day, April 8, in Baltimore. After a good spring, Conigliaro started in the outfield. When he came to the plate in the first inning, Orioles fans responded to the pathos of the moment by giving him a big ovation. Conigliaro struck out. He walked in the third, but got a solid base hit in the fifth. He flied out in the eighth, and the game went into extra innings. Tony came up in the tenth after Ken Harrelson had reached base on an error. After attempting a sacrifice, Conigliaro got the hit sign and swung at a 2 — 2 pitch from Pete Richert, blasting a home run deep into the left field seats. As he rounded the bases, his teammates could not wait. They stormed the field to greet him. Manager Dick Williams kissed him on the cheek. It was a dramatic and beautiful moment.

Conigliaro played in 141 games in 1969, connecting for 20 home runs and driving in 82. While his .255 batting average was the lowest since coming into the majors, no one complained. Tony C. was back, and while the Red Sox finished third, his return was celebrated and he was only 24 years old. They looked to 1970, when Conigliaro's vision would be improved and his hitting would return to form. Perhaps, Conigliaro was ready for his .300 average, one hundred RBI, and 30 home run season.

In the offseason, Boston picked up lefthander Gary Peters from the White Sox to solidify their pitching staff. They brought Carl Yastrzemski in from the outfield to play first base. They installed Tony Conigliaro's brother Billy in the outfield and hired Eddie Kasko to manage. It was the 38-year-old Kasko's first assignment as a big league manager. With these changes, the Red Sox felt confident they could challenge for the pennant.

Boston did not improve its record, finishing the year with the same win-loss total as in 1969, but Conigliaro had a great year, finishing with 36 home runs and 116 runs batted in, totals that exceeded any of his previous numbers. In the home run category, only Frank Howard had more in 1970. The Red Sox led the league with an impressive total of 203 round trippers, the most for an American League team since Minnesota in 1964, and his little brother Billy hit 18 homers.

Tony C. started spring training in 1971 by breaking a rib trying to catch a Texas Leaguer but recovered in time to start the season. On May 25, General Manager Dick O'Connell asked him to undergo an eye examination to determine if he was suffering any ill effects from the beaning. The Red Sox were concerned with Conigliaro's vision problems in the outfield, especially in night games, rather than at the plate, where he seemed to be doing all right.

While the examination did not reveal anything, Conigliaro was understandably touchy when pitchers attempted to move him away from the plate with inside pitches. A major melee occurred the Sunday before the All-Star Game, July 12. The Red Sox were playing the Indians in Cleveland. Pitching for the Tribe was reliever Fred Lasher. Conigliaro had hit a home run off Lasher on July 4, and a reporter in the Boston *Herald-Traveler* quoted Lasher as saying, "Tell Tony Conigliaro he'd better be a little careful the next time he faces me. The next time he may just get a little jammed."

The next time was Sunday, July 12. Lasher started for Cleveland, and his first pitch to Conigliaro hit him on the left forearm. Irate, Tony C., the holder of a brown belt in karate, charged out to the mound and instead of throwing a punch as Lasher anticipated, threw him a leaping kick. The kick spiked Lasher's left thigh. A bench-clearing brawl ensued.

The result was the same as countless other brawls in baseball — a lot of scratching, hair pulling, and wrestling, but no injuries. Other pitchers had previously tested Conigliaro's resolve since the beaning. In fact, Lasher's errant pitch was the seventh Tony C. received to his body since he returned from the beaning in 1969. Plainly, Conigliaro had his fill of intimidation. That, and the fact that Lasher advertised his intentions, aroused his ire.

Later in the season, Conigliaro, in a *Sports Illustrated* story, spoke of the beaning and made unfavorable remarks about his former manager, Dick Williams. He said that he and Williams had never gotten along well and that Williams' behavior after the beaning irked him. "I felt that I had contributed something to the ball club and had given the man everything I had. I was hit in the face by a baseball and nearly lost my life, and I felt the least he could do was show me he knew I existed. Sure, my relationship with Williams hadn't been a great one, but I did my job, I played ball and didn't give him any trouble."

He also had words for Jack Hamilton, the pitcher who had thrown that fateful pitch. "I didn't feel one way or the other about Hamilton before he beaned me, and I don't hate him for what he did. I have no grudge against him, but I wouldn't invite him over to the house for dinner, either. Only one person in the whole world knows if Jack Hamilton was trying to hit me that night."

Jack Hamilton was traded by California after the 1968 season to Cleveland, and the Indians dealt him to the White Sox the following June. He was released following the season and did not pitch again in the majors after 1969.

Conigliaro's autobiography was published in 1970. It was written by reporter Jack Zanger and was appropriately titled *Seeing It Through*.

But Conigliaro experienced considerable difficulty "seeing it through." He became increasingly impatient with the constant questioning about his eyesight. "I'm tired of people suggesting I have my eyesight checked. My eyes are 20/20 and there isn't the slightest reason for concern," Tony assured the baseball world.

It wasn't his hitting but his continued lapses in the field that caused the newspaper talk. Several times Conigliaro misplayed fly balls in right field. In a game in Baltimore, a fly ball landed behind him, and that error resulted in a Red Sox defeat. It again raised questions about his eyesight. GM Dick O'Connell talked to him, trying to reassure him that the club had faith in him. Afterward, O'Connell expressed high praise for Conigliaro's courage and abilities. But Tony C. said, "If this team isn't going well, someone always suggests I have my eyes checked. I've had enough of it."

Despite his difficulties, Conigliaro anticipated a new season at the ripe age of 26, an age when most successful players are only beginning to hit their stride. But the 1971 season was not to be spent with Boston. The Sox traded Tony C. to the California Angels on October 11, 1970, along with pitcher Ray Jarvis and catcher Gerry Moses, for infielder Doug Griffin, outfielder Jarvis Tatum, and reliever Ken Tatum, the only time in baseball history that someone with the first name of Jarvis was traded for someone surnamed Jarvis.

Conigliaro learned about the trade from his father Sal, who had been told about the deal by Boston's GM, Dick O'Connell. Upon receiving the news, Tony C. exclaimed, "You're kidding, it's impossible." O'Connell defended the trade by telling Sal that in Ken Tatum, who had 17 saves in 1970, the Sox had obtained the best relief pitcher in the American League.

As it turned out, only Doug Griffin of the six players involved became a regular and had a decent record.

As for Conigliaro, Angels General Manager Dick Walsh made huge predictions for Tony C. "If Tony Conigliaro does for us what he has done while hitting behind Carl Yastrzemski, then I can't help but think in terms of a pennant," Walsh predicted.

Angels Manager Lefty Phillips was also enthusiastic. "We've just added the home-run punch that we've been lacking. Tony will bat fourth and Alex Johnson now will bat third. I'll move [Jim] Fregosi up to second and keep Sandy Alomar in the leadoff position," Phillips said.

It was not to be. In early July, Tony Conigliaro quit baseball when he received an extraordinarily negative report from his doctor, Charles Regan. The medical report showed a drastic loss of vision in his left eye. The findings told him, "There is no doubt that all tests show that the functional ability of your left eye has decreased in the past 13 months."

Conigliaro tried to be philosophical about the news. He said that he loved baseball deeply but was unable to play because of his vision problem. He talked to Angels owner Gene Autry and told him that he was willing to consider the disabled list. Tony C.'s baseball career was over several months before his 27th birthday.

"I can't believe I'm through. I'm not sure what I'll do. Maybe a baseball school. I'm not certain. I discussed it with my family and want to do something that'll make me happy. We'll just have to wait and see," Conigliaro told the public.

The news caused brother Billy to become involved in a controversy with two of his teammates, Reggie Smith and Carl Yastrzemski. Billy alleged that Yaz had pushed management to trade Tony. When Reggie Smith heard Billy's charge, he was irate. "The club should take disciplinary action," he heatedly exclaimed. "If he doesn't want to play anymore, let him go."

On October 11, 1971, Boston traded brother Billy to Milwaukee. After the 1972 season, the Brewers sent Billy to Oakland where he played part-time in 1973. He appeared in 48 games, batting only .200. However, he did get into the World Series, something that had eluded big brother Tony. Billy was released after the 1973 Series and was out of baseball at the age of 26, about the same age as big brother Tony when he departed the majors.

Tony C. attempted a comeback with the Red Sox in 1975 as a designated hitter. After talking to reporters about how his vision had improved, he said, "I know this much. The ball looks good to me up there, and I'm swinging well. What I need now is competitive sharpening. The other night, against the Mets, was the first time I'd been in left field since 1971. I'm only 30, and the way I feel now, I have a lot of baseball left in me."

But, alas, there was little baseball left for Tony C. After 21 spring games, 15 as the DH, Tony Conigliaro quit baseball for good.

Tony's frustrated mother said of Tony's retirement, "I couldn't take having another boy in baseball. Not after what has happened." She was referring to Tony's misfortune, Billy's early departure from the majors, and to her youngest son Richie who was also an outfielder, thought to be a good prospect, but who never made it to the majors.

On January 9, 1982, Tony Conigliaro suffered a massive heart attack at the age of 37. He was on his way to the Boston airport with his brother Billy when he was stricken. He went into a coma that lasted four months. His heart had stopped and the lack of oxygen to the brain caused brain damage. It was almost four months before he was able to utter a word and his doctors were "cautiously optimistic." According to Dr. Wesley Woll, director of rehabilitation medicine at Shaughnessy Rehabilitation Hospital in Salem, Massachusetts, Conigliaro had suffered a sudden cardio-pulmonary arrest that caused a lack of oxygen to all the brain's cells.

Both of his feet were spastic, but one day he looked at his mother and said, "Hi, Mom."

Publicity of his saying, "Hi, Mom," brought mail for Conigliaro from all over the country. In sympathy, several hundred letters and cards a day poured in for the stricken slugger.

On January 7, 1985, almost three years later, Tony Conigliaro celebrated his fortieth birthday. He was now living with his parents in Nahant, Massachusetts. His youngest brother Richie told the press that "Tony improves every day, but it's a very slow process. He's aware of what's going on around him. He can walk about 10 steps with the aid of a walker. He can talk, but he's very moody." Then he added, "He's starting to eat Italian food again, so he must be getting better."

Five years later, on February 24, 1990, Tony Conigliaro died in Salem of kidney failure. He was 45. "For eight years I cried for Tony," his mother grieved. "He suffered so much. God finally took him, and now he's at peace."

A story in the *New York Times* noted that baseball links certain batters and pitchers. Ralph Branca and Bobby Thomson; Ray Chapman and Carl Mays; Tracy Stallard and Roger Maris; Gil McDougald and Herb Score. The writer suggested that there will be such a lasting connection between Tony Conigliaro and Jack Hamilton.

At the time of Conigliaro's death, Hamilton was interviewed, and he said, "I've had to live with it. I think about it a lot."

So ended the tragic story of Anthony Richard Conigliaro. As one eulogizer commented, "Who knows how many home runs Tony C. might have hit? Who knows how much of Tony C. died that night in 1967?" One fateful pitch, one dull thud of ball striking bone, probably kept Tony Conigliaro from being listed among the all-time home run greats.

ANTHONY RICHARD CONIGLIARO

Born Jan. 7, 1945, Revere, Mass.   Died Feb. 24, 1990, Salem, Mass.   Batted right,
threw right.

Year	Team	Pos.	G	AB	R	H	2B	3B	HR	RBI	BB	SB	Ave.	Slug.
1963	Wells-ville, NY-PA	OF	83	333	65	121	*42	4	24	74	26	2	.363	*.733
1964	Bos A	OF	111	404	69	117	21	2	24	52	35	2	.290	.530
1965	Bos A	OF	138	521	82	140	21	5	*32	82	51	4	.269	.512
1966	Bos A	OF	150	558	77	148	26	7	28	93	52	0	.265	.487
1967	Bos A	OF	95	349	59	100	11	5	20	67	27	4	.287	.519
1963	Out of baseball.													
1969	Bos A	OF	141	506	57	129	21	3	20	82	48	2	.255	.427
1970	Bos A	OF	146	560	89	149	20	1	36	116	43	4	.266	.498
1971	Cal A	OF	74	266	23	59	18	0	4	15	23	3	.222	.335
1972–1974	Out of baseball.													
1975	Bos A	DH	21	57	8	7	1	0	2	9	8	1	.123	.246
Major League Totals 8 yrs.			876	3221	464	849	139	23	166	516	287	20	.264	.476

14　L'IL BROTHER DAFFY

PAUL DEAN

"He's even better than me —
if that's possible."
DIZZY DEAN

Dizzy and Daffy, The Great Deans, as they were labeled, were victims of arm trouble. While Dizzy pitched long enough to be voted into the Hall of Fame before his career was cut short by a shoulder injury, Paul was less fortunate. Dizzy endured to win 150 games, winning over 20 four times in a season and once winning 30.

Paul, on the other hand, had only two great seasons before arm trouble ended his career. His lifetime win-loss record was 50–34. How great Paul Dean would have been had he not injured his arm we will never know, but for two short seasons he was so outstanding that the immodest Dizzy declared, "He's even better than me — if that's possible."

Paul was born at Lucas, Arkansas, two years after his famous brother. Neither Paul nor Dizzy attended school regularly, spending most of their youth picking cotton. Their average daily income was about 38 cents a day. Nobody in their neck of the woods was very well off, but the Deans were really poor. Whenever the boys got a chance, they threw rocks or played with a homemade ball made by winding string or yarn around a rock. Their bat was a stick they cut and whittled themselves.

The Deans moved to Oklahoma and took up sharecropping. Dizzy and Paul enrolled in the local school and were placed in advanced grades because of their baseball abilities. Dizzy pitched, and Paul played shortstop. Paul didn't start pitching until 1929 when he was 17, probably because Dizzy was older and could throw harder. Perhaps it was also because Dizzy did most of the talking for the two — including all the bragging.

Not wanting to pick cotton all his life, Dizzy joined the Army and was stationed in Texas. Thus it was that Ab Dean, the father, took his other two sons, Elmer, who was handicapped, and Paul, and moved to Texas to begin sharecropping west of Houston. After a year and a half in the Army, Dizzy had had his fill of military life and was itching to play semipro baseball, so he bought his way out of the Army, which was possible then, with $120 Paul loaned him from his cotton-picking earnings.

Dizzy signed with the St. Louis Cardinals in 1930. Paul remained behind, picked cotton, and played with an amateur baseball team in San Antonio. Paul played shortstop until one day his club needed a pitcher and, since he was Dizzy's little brother, he was drafted. From that day forward, he remained a pitcher. He won 11 out of 13 games. His fame spread, and he was scouted by Don Curtis of the Cardinals.

The Cardinals decided that having two Deans would be even better than one, especially since Paul possessed hardly any of the brashness and braggadocio of the elder Dizzy. He preferred to let his fastball do the talking. The Cards signed 17-year-old Paul to a contract with Houston in 1931. He appeared in two games for the Texas League Bisons, pitching three innings in relief. Since the Columbus Red Birds badly needed right-handed pitching, Paul was moved up to the American Association. He pitched 36 innings in 12 games at Columbus with an 0–2 record.

Paul developed wild spells at Columbus. The Cardinals decided that they were advancing him too rapidly, so they shipped him to the Springfield Midgets in the Western Association where he could work regularly under the tutelage of Eddie Dyer, an old pitcher. While at Springfield, things started to turn around for Paul. He compiled an attention-getting 11–3 record in 19 games pitched, with 119 strikeouts in 136 innings and a 3.64 ERA.

Paul spent all of 1932 with the Columbus Red Birds. He pitched 212 innings in 40 games, but he posted a disappointing 7–16 win-loss record, reflecting both Paul's inexperience and in part the team's woeful offense. Still, on August 7, the 18-year-old hurler showed signs of future greatness by throwing a no-hit, no-run game against the Kansas City Blues, the first night-time no-hitter ever thrown in the American Association.

In 1933, the 19-year-old Paul came into his own at Columbus. He overpowered the opposition in the American Association. A high point of the season occurred July 31 when the parent St. Louis team came to Columbus for an exhibition. It was the only time Paul pitched against Dizzy in an organized game. Each brother started and went two innings. Paul fanned two Cardinals and did not allow a hit. Dizzy gave up two hits, one of them to his little brother, Paul, who hit a smash right past Dizzy's head into center field, ran to first and stood there laughing and shaking his fist at Dizzy.

Paul wanted to stay in the game another inning and pitch to Dizzy, but Ray Blades, the Columbus manager, took him out. That Dizzy pitched in the exhibition game at all was peculiar, because only the day before he had set the National League strikeout record of 17.

On the train to Pittsburgh that night, Dizzy revised his list of baseball's top three pitchers, "I'm number one. Paul's second. And I guess Carl Hubbell is third." Some observers were beginning to wonder if, in the long run, Little Brother might not become number one. At any rate, National League batters would soon have to face two Deans "foggin'" them past them when they played St. Louis.

Columbus was also scheduled to play an exhibition game with the New York Yankees. Paul begged manager Nemo Leibold for a chance to pitch. "I may never get another chance to fan Babe Ruth," he pleaded. "He'll probably be through next year when I go to the Cardinals, and I'll never know how it feels to fool him." Leibold gave Paul the chance, and the younger Dean fanned the Bambino twice. He struck out Lou Gehrig as well. Columbus beat the Bronx Bombers behind Paul Dean, 3–2. This performance really got the attention of the St. Louis brass.

For the 1933 season, Paul won 22 and lost seven, struck out 222, and posted a 3.15 earned run average in 254 innings for Columbus. Paul's performance caught the eye both of the parent Cardinals and other major league clubs as well, chiefly the Yankees and Red Sox. Boston reportedly offered St. Louis $50,000 for Paul — cash that was not easy to turn down in those depression years. But, general manager Branch Rickey and owner Sam Breadon of the Cardinals decided that Paul, in the long run, had more value as a member of the St. Louis pitching staff than that amount of money, so they exercised an option to purchase him from Columbus themselves.

After a brief ruckus about how much the Cardinals would pay Paul — generated, of course, by Dizzy — Paul reported to the St. Louis training camp in 1934. Young Paul had all the natural talent of the illustrious Dizzy: great speed, a good curve, an occasional knuckler, an easy, graceful motion, and good pitching sense.

He also threw a slider when it was not only a rare pitch but, as a matter of fact, was in disrepute. The slider's reputation was, "The pitcher throws the ball and the batter slides into third." It was frequently referred to as a nickel curve or a fade-away.

Paul threw a pitch that darted away from right-handed hitters as they swung, and none of them catalogued it as a curve. With Paul's terrific speed, the slider was a highly effective pitch for him — it frustrated a lot of hitters who could not understand how he got them out.

Paul threw his sinking fastball sidearm or three-quarter arm, depending to some extent on whether the batter was right- or left-handed. Player-manager Frank Frisch said Paul threw the "heaviest sinker you ever saw. When a batter hit one of those pitches, his hands stung as painfully in July as if he'd swung at an icicle in December." Paul had problems with wildness in his minor league days, but his control got better each year.

"Me and Paul," as Dizzy referred to himself and his brother, were an immediate sensation. Dizzy told everybody who would listen, "I've got a great fastball, but Paul's is just as good. Me and Paul will win the pennant for the Cardinals." The senior Dean predicted that he and Paul would win 45 between them in 1934. It proved to be one of the few times in his life that "ol' Diz" was too modest, for the brothers finished the season with 49 wins.

Paul pitched his first spring game March 14, shutting out the Philadelphia Phillies for three innings. Mimicking Dizzy, he crowed about his performance and claimed that he would win 25 games "just to prove I got more stuff than Dizzy."

Paul's initial regular season game came April 19 against a Pittsburgh Pirates' team featuring the Waner brothers. It was the Cardinals' second game of the year. Dizzy had won the first, 7–1. Although Paul claimed that he and Dizzy never were nervous in their lives, he seemed tense on the mound until Dizzy yelled at him, "Fog one in there, boy." That's just what he did. He struck out Lloyd Waner, the first batter, on three pitches. Freddie Lindstrom, the second batter, also went down swinging. But before getting the last out, the Pirates scored twice on a Paul Waner single and a Pie Traynor homer. In the second, he allowed two more runs when Gus Suhr hit one out of the park with a runner on. Paul was taken out of the game, but he averted a loss when the Cardinals rallied for the win, 7–6.

Paul's next outing was on April 22 in relief of Dizzy, who was shelled by the Chicago Cubs in the first inning. It was an all-around bad day for the Deans, because Paul also was driven from the mound in the fourth after allowing six hits in two innings. On May 3, Paul was sent in to relieve in the fourth inning against the Phillies with the score tied, 2–2. Again, he was hit freely in the five innings he worked, yielding seven hits, two walks, and three runs. Fortunately, Joe Medwick hit a grand slam home run late in the game, and Paul got his first big league win as the Cardinals outscored Philadelphia, 8–7.

Some of the Cardinal pitchers complained in postgame discussions that Paul wasn't showing a thing and that he belonged back in the minors. Tex Carleton was especially critical. Carleton had developed an intense dislike

of Dizzy when they were at Houston together. The college-educated Carleton thought that Dizzy was a "loud mouth," and he transferred some of
his dislike for Dizzy to Paul. Carleton felt that experienced pitchers such as
himself should be preferred to a rookie.

Bill Hallahan, who referred to the Deans as "the clods from the sticks,"
felt that Paul belonged back in the minors. The consensus was that "If Paul
wasn't Dizzy's brother, he'd be long gone." Dick Farrington reported in *The
Sporting News*, "There is grave doubting about the junior Dean."

Frisch, on the other hand, knowing that he was a pitcher short, stayed
with the younger Dean. It also did not hurt knowing that if Paul could make
it, the box office would be helped considerably by the brother act.

Being convinced that Paul's problems stemmed from trying to imitate
Dizzy too much, Frisch started Paul against the New York Giants on May 11
and told him to pitch his own game. Paul realized that his immediate future
with the club probably depended on this showing. Teams carried only a 21-
man roster in that era and could not afford a nonperformer, especially con-
tending clubs. Pitted against Paul was the Giant ace, King Carl Hubbell.
Dizzy advised L'il Brother, "Beatin' him is gonna take another great pitcher,
and that's you, boy, so go on out there and do it."

That is exactly what Paul did. He went the distance and beat the Giants'
Meal Ticket, 3–2. The win seemed to give Paul the impetus to pitch up to
his ability. He won his next start, 5–3, on May 17 against the Boston Braves
with the help of home runs by Frisch and Spud Davis. By the end of May,
Paul's record was a sparkling 5–0.

Dizzy began agitating for more money for his younger brother. He said
that Paul was worth at least $5,000 instead of the paltry $2,000 he was being
paid. On June 1, the two brothers went on strike for a day. Rumor had it
that Paul was given a $2,000 raise, but the likelihood is that he got a promise
from Breadon that if he continued to pitch well he would be amply rewarded
the next year. Cardinal management, thrifty at best, miserly at worst, was
not in the habit of giving midseason raises.

Dizzy had a strong argument for Paul's raise. Between them, they won
11 games in June, while the rest of the pitching staff won two. Paul's record
was 5–2 for the month. After winning eight consecutive games, extending
back into May, Paul lost to the Philadelphia Phillies on June 19 and to the
Cincinnati Reds on June 30 in relief. At the All-Star Game break, Paul's
record was 10–3.

On August 13, the Cards were scheduled to play an exhibition in Detroit
the day after a Sunday doubleheader in which both Deans had pitched. In
that era, teams played a 154-game schedule, but some clubs scheduled enough

exhibition games to approximate a contemporary 162-game season. The Cardinals, for example, tended to play exhibitions with their top farm clubs. The exhibition in Detroit was for charity, and it had been presented to the public as a chance to see the Great Deans. Not enamored by an overnight train ride, the Deans decided to skip the trip. After all, they had won a combined total of 34 games by now, and stars should have rights. Cardinal management responded to their absence by fining Dizzy, always the ringleader, $100, and Paul, $50.

When he heard of the fine, Dizzy threw a tantrum. He ripped up his uniform and announced that he would never play for the Cardinals again. Frisch promptly suspended both of them. In an unbylined August 15 story about the suspension in the *Brooklyn Eagle*, Paul was called Daffy for the first time. From that point on, the Deans were called Dizzy and Daffy. After a brief walkout, the Deans returned to the team. The club accepted Paul back at once, but felt that Dizzy, as the instigator, needed extra punishment. So they kept him out an additional 10 days at a cost of $50 a day. A hearing was held before Commissioner Kenesaw Mountain Landis, and as one would expect, the Judge sided with the ballclub. In a week, peace was restored in the Cardinal family, and both Deans were back on the job.

And what a job they did. The Cardinals were five games behind the Giants going into Labor Day and then went six down as the Deans lost a doubleheader to Pittsburgh, Paul losing 12–1, and Dizzy 6–5. But after that, Dizzy and Daffy went to work. All year Frisch had used them to pitch doubleheaders. For example, on June 17, both beat Philadelphia. On July 8, Dizzy beat Cincinnati, but Paul lost. Both of them beat the Cubs on August 12, and both beat the Giants on September 16. Then on September 21, in a doubleheader against the Brooklyn Dodgers, Paul Dean pitched a gem.

Dizzy pitched no-hit ball in the first game until one had been retired in the eighth inning, when he yielded a hit. He finished with a three-hit shutout. Starting the second game, Paul was on a roll, having allowed only two runs in his last 32 innings.

Paul accomplished what Dizzy never achieved. He threw the only no-hit, no-run game in the National League during the 1934 season. Only a first-inning walk to Len Koenecke kept him from hurling a perfect game. The no-hitter in his first year in the majors placed Paul in history with such pitching stalwarts as Christy Mathewson (New York Giants, 1901), Jeff Tesreau (New York Giants, 1912) and Nick Maddox (Pittsburgh Pirates, 1907). A number of other rookie hurlers have joined the list since then.

After the game, Dizzy expressed disappointment that Paul did not tell him ahead of time what he was going to do, because if he had, he would

In the second game of a doubleheader on September 21, 1934, Paul Dean no-hit the Brooklyn Dodgers, a feat big brother Dizzy never accomplished (ROCHESTER *DEMO-CRAT AND CHRONICLE*).

have worked a little harder "and struck out a few more of the Dodgers" himself in the first game, so that both would have pitched no-hitters. Dizzy praised Paul as the "greatest pitcher in the world — next to me — and if he had my change of pace, nobody'd ever touch him again."

	St. Louis						**Brooklyn**				
	AB	**R**	**H**	**O**	**A**		**AB**	**R**	**H**	**O**	**A**
Martin, 3b	4	0	1	0	1	Boyle, rf	4	0	0	2	0
Rothrock, rf	4	0	0	1	0	Frey, ss	3	0	0	4	3
Frisch, 2b	4	0	0	1	3	Koenecke, cf	2	0	0	1	1
Medwick, lf	4	2	2	6	0	Leslie, 1b	3	0	0	10	1
Collins, 1b	4	0	1	9	1	Cuccinello, 3b	3	0	0	3	0
DeLancey, c	4	0	1	7	0	Frederick, lf	3	0	0	2	0
Orsatti, cf	3	0	0	1	0	Jordan, 2b	3	0	0	1	6
Durocher, ss	3	0	0	1	3	Lopez, c	2	0	0	3	1
P. Dean, p	3	1	2	1	2	Bucher, ph	1	0	0	0	0
TOTALS	33	3	7	27	10	Benge, p	2	0	0	1	1
						McCarthy, ph	1	0	0	0	0
						TOTALS	27	0	0	27	13

Bucher batted for Lopez in ninth. McCarthy batted for Benge in ninth.

										R	**H**	**E**
St. Louis	0	0	0		0	0	1		1 0 1	3	7	1
Brooklyn	0	0	0		0	0	0		0 0 0	0	0	1

Errors-Jordan. RBI — Martin, Collins 2. Two-base hits — P. Dean, Martin, Medwick. Three-base hit — Medwick. Umpires — Klem, Sears and Rigler.

	IP	**H**	**R**	**ER**	**BB**	**SO**
Benge (14–12)	9	7	3	3	0	1
P. Dean (18–9)	9	0	0	0	1	6

After his no-hit gem, Paul lost twice in quick succession. Dizzy, in the meantime, turned red hot. On September 28, Diz shut out Cincinnati, 4–0, with only two days rest, and St. Louis finally pulled into a tie with the idle Giants. The next day, Paul bounced back to beat Cincinnati, 6–1, and the Cards led New York by a game.

The Giants finished the season against the Brooklyn Dodgers. The Dodgers were mad about Bill Terry's ill-considered question, "Brooklyn? Are they still in the league?" Fueled by Terry's verbal gaffe, the Dodgers swept the Giants. On the same day, September 30, Dizzy won his 30th game when he shut out Cincinnati again, this time 9–0, to win the National League flag for the Cardinals — St. Louis's fifth pennant in nine years. Lefty Grove won 31 for the Philadelphia A's in the American League in 1931, but Diz was the first to win 30 in one season in the NL since Grover Cleveland Alexander turned the trick in 1917. No one has achieved that level of excellence in the senior circuit since. In the AL, Denny McLain won 31 for Detroit in 1968.

The Cardinals at one point of the season were 10 games behind the Giants. Then the last three weeks of the season, Dizzy pitched just about every second day, either starting or relieving, and Paul went to the mound most other days.

Dizzy and Paul had combined for 49 wins and the rest of the Cardinals' pitching staff combined for 46. Paul led the league in strikeouts per nine innings, 5.79, tied for fifth in wins, 19, was third in strikeouts, 150, and tied for second in shutouts, 5. He appeared in 39 games, starting 26 and completing 16, registering two saves. He pitched a total of 233.1 innings. His 3.43 earned run average was .63 below the 4.06 league average for the year.

Dizzy contributed mightily, winning 30 while losing only seven, and accumulating a 2.66 ERA, which was second to Hubbell's 2.30. He saved another seven games, only one fewer than Hubbell's league-leading eight. Fifty times Dizzy went to the mound, tying for second in games pitched. He started 33 times and completed a league-leading 24. He led the league in shutouts with seven and in winning percentage with .811. He struck out a league-leading total of 195 batters and finished second to Paul in strike-outs per nine innings, with a 5.63 average. Dizzy was also second in fewest hits per nine innings, 8.32, and third in innings pitched, 312. In any era, this was a truly remarkable brother act.

The Detroit Tigers won the American League pennant in 1934 by seven games over the Yankees and were strong favorites to top St. Louis in the World Series. Their powerful lineup of Mickey Cochrane, Hank Greenberg, Charlie Gehringer, Gee Walker, and Goose Goslin seemed too potent for St. Louis. Even Marv Owen at third base, one of their weaker hitters, had a .317 year. Their pitching was anchored by Schoolboy Rowe, 24–8, Tommy Bridges, 22–11, Eldon Auker, 15–7, Firpo Marberry, 15–5 and late-season acquisition General Crowder, 5–1, making for a strong staff. Some managers spend a career hoping for one pitcher who can a establish a winning percentage of .716. Here was the nucleus of a staff that accomplished it in one year.

The World Series opened on October 3 in Detroit. In the first game, the Cardinals were the beneficiaries of five errors by the Detroit infield, and got a four-hit attack, including a home run, from Joe (Ducky) Medwick. Dizzy Dean bested General Crowder, Firpo Marberry and Chief Hogsett, 8–3.

Wild Bill Hallahan started the second game on October 4 for St. Louis against Schoolboy Rowe. Detroit came from behind to tie it, 2–2, in the ninth inning when Gee Walker, given a second chance on a missed pop foul, singled home the tying run. A Goose Goslin single off Bill Walker in the twelfth won the game for Detroit, 3–2.

Daffy and Dizzy Dean pitched the 1934 St. Louis Cardinals to the world's championship (National Baseball Hall of Fame Library, Cooperstown, NY.

The third game on October 5 pitted Tommy Bridges, the renowned curveballer, against Paul Dean. L'il Brother responded by pitching a remarkable game. Paul was wild early, hitting Marv Owen and yielding five walks for the game. Additionally, Detroit drove out eight hits, because Paul's "curve wasn't working." "I guess the reason I wasn't workin' so good," Paul explained, "was because I was too rested. I hadn't pitched none in six days." Yet, he pitched out of dangerous situations with courage and finesse, stranding 13 baserunners.

Frisch later observed, "The boy was cool as ice out there." He didn't lose his shutout until the ninth inning. In the meantime, Pepper Martin led the attack for St. Louis with a double and a triple, and the Cards won 4–1, going one up in the series.

Eldon Auker and the Tigers handily beat Tex Carleton in the fourth game, 10–4 on October 6. When Tommy Bridges bested Dizzy 3–1 in game five on October 7, the Cardinals were reeling.

Game six on October 8 matched Schoolboy Rowe, with three days' rest, against Paul Dean, with only two days' rest. If Detroit won, they would be the world champs. The game belonged to Paul, however. He not only set the Tigers down on seven hits, but in the seventh inning he stroked a high, hanging curveball to right for a single that scored Leo Durocher with the game-winning run. The final score was 4–3.

The rookie pitching whiz now had two wins for the series.

Even though Dizzy had lost the fifth game, everybody knew that he would come back with only a day of rest to pitch game seven on October 9.

The game belonged to St. Louis. They scored seven runs in a third-inning barrage and went on to post an 11–0 victory.

The greatest excitement of the game occurred when left-field bleacher fans pelted Medwick with fruits and vegetables because of his hard slide into Marv Owen at third base. The situation got so out of hand that Judge Landis, who was in the stands, removed Medwick from the game so that order could be restored and the game finished.

The next day, Dan Daniel in the *New York World Telegram* called the 1934 Cardinals, because of their rough-and-tumble play in the Series, the "Gas House Gang." While there are varying accounts of how and when the Cardinals acquired the Gas House Gang designation, most point to late 1934 or early 1935. Although the term did not catch on for several months, it was a label that stuck with the team and made them legendary.

The Cardinals were world champions. As Dizzy had promised, they had grabbed the Tiger by the tail. The Dean brothers got all four wins. Dizzy was 2–1, Paul 2–0. Dizzy and Daffy literally pitched St. Louis to the championship. Children soon were seen wearing "Me and Paul" T-shirts. Had there been a Rookie of the Year award, Paul Dean would have been a strong candidate.

The colorful 1934 Cardinals drew only 325,000 fans, but they still made money. So, Sam Breadon, in a moment of generosity, gave the Deans $500 bonuses for their heroic and yeomanlike work of the final month of the season. The Tigers, losers in the World Series, gave Schoolboy Rowe a $2,500 bonus.

Despite having pitched almost every other day in the last month of the season, the Deans began an extensive barnstorming tour immediately after the World Series. "The Dizzy and Daffy Road Show" played every day for two weeks, and the star pitchers pitched almost every day until Paul fell and hurt his arm while chasing a fly ball. Paul was scared. Doctors, however, told him it was not serious, but that he should get plenty of rest. After that, he only played a few innings in the outfield, and he threw underhanded in order not to strain his arm. Dizzy himself was glad to end the tour, because, he admitted, "We have too much at stake, me'n Paul, to be fiddlin' around the country."

Diz signed an $18,500 contract for 1935, and Paul, after a brief protest, agreed to $8,500. The club entered the season shorthanded on the mound. They had four starters: Dizzy and Paul, Bill Walker and Wild Bill Hallahan. Tex Carleton, an unhappy trouper who had been extremely resentful of the swaggering Dizzy, was traded to the Chicago Cubs. Branch Rickey was certain one or more of his latest crop of pitchers from the Cardinal farm system would easily replace Tex, but none of them worked out.

St. Louis was slow getting started in 1935. Only Dizzy, Paul and Bill Walker could be counted on steadily. Paul started the year by shutting out the Chicago Cubs on April 9, besting Larry French, 1–0. By contrast, Hallahan floundered early, although he eventually finished the season with a 15–8 record and a strong 3.43 ERA. Three weeks into the season, St. Louis was in fourth place, and things got worse. Dissension on the team was rampant as Dizzy berated some of his teammates for shoddy fielding and for poor hitting. Dizzy feuded bitterly with Ripper Collins and Ducky Medwick.

Paul, after getting off to a good start, was battling his old foe — wildness. He began to blame the umpires for his problems. On June 21, the Philadelphia Phillies hit him hard, and he got so frustrated that he threw one duster after another at the hitters.

In July, the Giants were leading St. Louis by nine-and-a-half games. But then New York slumped, and the Cardinals got hot. The Red Birds won 14 in a row between July 2 and July 18. After that streak, they lost five of six. Then on August 1, they started another winning streak by winning 10 of their next 11.

St. Louis had a showdown series with the Giants coming up, and Paul usually did well against them. In the opener on August 14, Paul lost to Hubbell, 6–4, yielding five hits in two innings of work. In the second game, Paul pitched in relief of Hallahan, and the Cards won, 3–0. St. Louis went on to win the series, and things looked good for the Cardinals because all their September games were at home.

This was the time frame when the term "Gashouse Gang" really stuck, because the club did not get their uniforms cleaned from August 9 until Labor Day. They looked like a gashouse crew.

In September, the Chicago Cubs passed both the Cardinals and the Giants. Who were these upstart Cubs? On July 9, they were ten-and-one-half games out, and few saw them as headed for a championship. But then they got great hitting from Gabby Hartnett, Billy Herman, Frank Demaree, Augie Galan, Stan Hack, and the former Philadelphia home run king,

Chuck Klein. At shortstop they had the reliable Billy Jurges and at first they had a hard-hitting young Italian, Phil Cavarretta. Their pitching also rounded into shape. Big Bill Lee headed their staff, but Lon Warneke, Larry French, Charlie Root, Roy Henshaw and none other than former Cardinal Tex Carleton were also having good years.

The Deans pitched in 23 of the last 28 games, but they were not invincible this time. The St. Louis pitching situation got so dire that at the end of the season, Frisch simply alternated Dizzy and Paul. In a critical game on September 25 against Chicago, Lon Warneke beat Paul Dean, 1–0, on a Phil Cavarretta home run. Paul allowed seven hits in the game and struck out seven. However, the Arkansas Humming Bird hurled a neat two-hitter to win the game, and the Cubs clinched a tie for the pennant. The next day's game was canceled because of rain, but on September 27 Bill Lee bested Dizzy, 6–2, in the first game of a doubleheader, and the Chicago Cubs were the National League champions. The Cubs won their final 21 games, and they won the pennant by four games over the Cardinals.

The Deans had given it their best. Between them, they won 47 games, almost half of the team's 96 victories. Dizzy was 28–12, and Paul 19–12. Paul had a chance to win the critical twentieth game at the end of the season but was unable to do it. In two seasons, the Dean brothers had won a total of 96 games, one more than the rest of the Cardinal staff.

Small wonder that as the 1936 season approached Dizzy and Daffy expected to be rewarded with handsome salary increases. Paul bought an 80-acre farm at Garland, Texas, just outside of Dallas, with the thought that his father would live there and tend to things. Besides, Paul could live there all summer if the Cardinals didn't meet his demand for a $15,000 salary, almost double his pay of the year before. When he was told that he was only 22 years old and nobody so young had ever made that kind of money in baseball, Paul replied, "They ain't never had no Paul Dean before." Dizzy's expectation was even greater. He wanted a contract for $40,000.

When Paul's contract came, it was for the $8,500 he had made in 1935, considerably below what he was expecting. He suggested that he would rather slop hogs during the summer than pitch for that amount. Dizzy had also been sent a contract calling for no raise. Rickey piously told Dizzy that even though in 1934 he had won 30 games and that in 1935 he had fallen off to 28, the club was not going to cut his salary accordingly, but, magnanimously, they were going to pay him the same amount as they did the year after he had won 30. Dizzy found this difficult to take, considering he had led the league in total wins, games, games started, complete games, innings pitched and strikeouts.

In mid–March, J. Roy Stockton, a prominent St. Louis writer, arranged for a peace meeting between Rickey and Dizzy, who had been verbally lambasting the Cardinals' front office, and after some negotiation Dizzy signed for $22,300, the highest salary in the National League. Paul capitulated shortly thereafter and signed a contract calling for $12,500.

Their abbreviated spring training, resulting from holding out, caused the Deans to start slowly in the 1936 season. They were hit hard in the spring, and early in the regular season it got no better. Paul reported to the club overweight and did not have enough time in the spring to get the weight off.

Chicago routed Dizzy 12–7 in the season opener April 14, as Billy Herman went 5-for-5 for the Cubs. Two days later, Paul failed to hold an early two-run lead and lost the third game of the year to the Cubs, 5–3, yielding 10 hits. Paul also lost his next outing on April 23 to the Cincinnati Reds, 6–5.

Then on April 30, Paul won his first game against the New York Giants, 3–2. He walked no one in the game but allowed 11 hits. Paul always had great ability to pitch out of tough jams and demonstrated that trait in this game as inning after inning the Giants had runners in scoring position.

After a slow start, Dizzy got going and hit a hot streak. By June 20, he had won 13 games and promised everyone within earshot that he would win 40 for the season.

Paul also began to heat up in May. He beat the New York Giants, 3–2, on April 30. But then he lost a 1–0 heartbreaker to Danny MacFayden and the Boston Bees on May 5. But on May 10, he bounced back to beat Chicago, 5–1, on a neat three-hitter in a five inning rain-curtailed game. Then he got revenge and beat the Boston Bees, 7–5, on May 16. On May 22, he turned back the Giants, 4–2, and thereby pitched the Cardinals back into first place in the National League.

On Sunday, May 31, Paul was clobbered by Cincinnati, 10–1. On June 2, he came back to pitch scoreless baseball against Brooklyn for six innings. Then with one out in the seventh, the Dodgers jumped on him for three runs. With relief help from Bill Walker and Ed Heusser, the Cardinals managed to hold on to win the game, 5–4.

Two days later, in the same series with the Dodgers, Paul was brought in for late-inning relief. Pitching to Buddy Hassett with the bases loaded, Paul reached for a little extra on a high, hard one and felt a sting in his right shoulder. He dismissed it and stayed in the game, but the Dodgers scored twice to beat him, 4–3.

The next day in a pepper game, he discovered he could hardly raise his arm. The doctors said he had torn a piece of cartilage on the underside of his arm joint.

Rest would probably take care of the problem, so he was given 10 days off. He started against Philadelphia on June 14, but he did not last through the second inning, walking four and allowing three hits. Paul left the mound complaining about sharp pains in his shoulder. Although the term was not used at that time, in all probability, Paul had torn his rotator cuff on that fateful pitch to Hassett.

Paul got two more starts, on July 4 and August 24. He could not throw hard and had very little stuff. He was removed from the game in the third inning each time. Paul was through for the season, having compiled a 5–5 record in 1936. The Cardinals hoped that five months of rest would make him ready for 1937.

At first, Paul blamed his arm problem on an ulcerated tooth, but he later felt certain that it had resulted from insufficient spring training. He explained, "Me 'n' Diz came down there to Florida a month after the other boys, and I had some extra weight on me, and that kept me from gettin' the soupbone in the kinda shape it shoulda been — there wasn't enough time — but I didn't think it'd matter none because of the kinda strong arm I thought I had, but it did — and that's what fixed me."

Overuse may have been a contributing factor. For two successive years, the Cardinals relied on the Deans to carry the load. Dizzy and Paul frequently started with two days rest, and then came in two days later to pitch late-inning relief. During one stretch in 1935, Paul Dean pitched 37 innings in six days, an average of slightly more than six innings a day. Both brothers had adhered to Dizzy's notion that the "Deans ain't ordinary," and "Good pitchers don't get sore arms." Dizzy, despite Paul's fate, continued at the same pace for the rest of the season.

Dizzy's record for the year was 24–13, and he also had a league leading 11 saves, and three of his losses came in relief.

Paul went home to the farm, proclaiming that "I don't need baseball none for my milk and eggs." His farm could provide him all the grub he needed. Paul had always talked about going back to the hills from whence he had come. He liked being with Dizzy, and he liked Pepper Martin and Bill DeLancey. Otherwise, he often said that he preferred the hills, "living a natural life, with no frills, no fanfare and all that sort of thing."

Paul, however, loved baseball too much to give it up so easily. He pitched in one game for St. Louis in 1937, against the Cubs on April 24, but failed to get anyone out, giving up a hit and two walks.

It was a fateful year for Dizzy as well. Pitching perhaps the best baseball of his life, he was chosen for the All-Star team on the basis of his 12–7 record and 110 strikeouts. In his last start before the summer classic, he hurled a brilliant 1–0 shutout against the Cincinnati Reds. Diz started the All-Star Game and pitched well into the third inning. He quickly got two outs but then ran into trouble. Joe DiMaggio got a key hit, and Lou Gehrig hit one of Diz's fastballs out of the park, putting the American League in front of the National League, 2–0.

Next up was Earl Averill, Cleveland's hard-hitting centerfielder. Averill hit Diz's first pitch back through the box, and the ball caromed off Diz's left foot over to Billy Herman at second who threw Averill out at first. Dean got an assist on the play. Diz retired from the game after his three inning stint. Later it was discovered that he had a broken toe.

The Cardinals were desperate for pitching, having missed Paul badly, so they brought Dizzy back to pitch even though he was still limping from the toe injury. He changed his delivery to take the pressure off his toe, putting extra pressure on his arm, and a shoulder injury resulted. "I was unable to pivot my left foot because my toe hurt too much," Diz explained. "I was pitchin' entirely with my arm and puttin' all the pressure on it. I shouldn't a been out there."

Now both Deans were injured.

Rickey wanted to send Paul to Houston of the Texas League where he could work his arm back in shape. But Paul did not want to play in the minors and suggested he could work his arm in shape on his own. So he requested voluntary retirement, and went home. Soon he began pitching for various semipro teams in Texas. Reports came to St. Louis exaggerating his effectiveness. In truth, he was getting the free-swinging semipro hitters out with junk pitches. He could no longer "fog 'em in" Dean-style.

In the spring of 1938, Paul seemed to be throwing freely and easily in training camp. However, on March 14, he was so badly roughed up by the Boston Bees that Rickey declared Paul's arm to be dead and that he had "given up all hope that he ever is coming back." "It's pathetic about Daffy," wrote Wayne Otto of the *Chicago Herald and Examiner*. "It's sad, sad."

Prior to the regular season, the Cardinals traded Dizzy to the Cubs. He had a 7–1 record and a 1.81 earned run average in 75 innings for Chicago in 1938, and he pitched in one World Series game that October against the Yankees. With no fastball left, Dizzy gamely battled the Yankees in the second game on October 6, holding them to five hits in seven innings for a 3–2 lead. But Tony Lazzeri connected for a two-run homer in the eighth to bat in the tying and winning runs, and the Yankees had a 6–3 victory on their way to a series sweep.

Paul, in the meantime, stayed with the Cards. He pitched in five games and posted a 3–1 record, with a commendable 2.61 ERA. He did it with slow curves, which he kept low and on the corners of the plate, but the smoke was gone completely.

He was subsequently sent down to Houston in the Texas League, who loaned him to Dallas which was nearer to Paul's home. He pitched 201 innings in 29 games in the Texas League, and although his ERA was a respectable 3.69, his win-loss record was a disappointing 8–16.

In 1939, Paul pitched in 16 games for St. Louis, with no wins and one defeat. His ERA zoomed to 6.07. The next year, the New York Giants drafted him from the Columbus Red Birds, where the Cardinals had sent him for rehabilitation, but he made no appearances. He pitched in 27 games for the Giants, working in 99 innings, more than in any season since 1935, and won four and lost four, mostly in relief. In 1941, he made five no-decision appearances with the Giants before they traded him back to St. Louis on May 14, along with pitcher Harry Gumbert, for pitcher Bill McGee.

St. Louis shipped Paul to Columbus for the 1941 season, but he did not pitch, leaving baseball for the next two seasons. He came back briefly with the St. Louis Browns in 1943, pitching 13 innings in three games. That was the official end of Paul Dean's major league career. Unofficially, it had ended years earlier with the sting in his shoulder. He was 30 years old when he retired.

Paul did not leave baseball entirely and take up farming. In 1944, he was briefly on the roster of the Little Rock Travelers, but he never played. In 1945 he was out of baseball, but he came back in 1946 to pitch for Little Rock. He appeared in four games, winning two while losing one; his ERA was an inflated 7.37. In 1947, Paul turned to managing. He signed with the Ottawa franchise of the Class C Border State League. He led the club to the league championship with an 82–42 record.

Then in 1949, he managed Clovis, New Mexico, in the Class C West Texas-New Mexico League. This time, his club finished last, 31 games behind the league champion with a 52–87 record. He managed again in 1950 but was replaced by Harold Hoffman during the season, with the team accumulating a dismal 53–92 record.

In 1952, he served as coach for Lubbock, Texas, also in the Class C West Texas-New Mexico League.

At one time or another, Paul owned four Class C teams: Clovis, New Mexico; Lubbock, Texas; El Paso, Texas; and Hot Springs, Arkansas. In his own words, he was "president, groundskeeper, clubhouse boy and manager. I did it all."

In 1965, Paul quit baseball entirely and moved to Phoenix, Arizona, to manage Dizzy's carpet business. Dizzy explained that he had gone into the carpet business because it was a nice clean, respectable business. "The whole family can come in here, shop around, and talk baseball with me and Paul. If we had a tavern, we'd never get to meet and talk with the kids. They come in here all day, asking questions, and wanting autographs. It makes a fellow feel important."

But after a year in the carpet business, Paul moved back to the Dallas area. When Robert Morris, president of newly founded University of Plano, called him in 1966 and offered Paul a job as athletic director and coach of baseball and track, Paul was both surprised and puzzled. He had never heard of the school before, which was not surprising because it was brand new. The institution was founded especially for young people with reading problems. It began operating in obscure quarters on a side street in downtown Dallas, and then moved to a new campus about 20 miles north at Plano.

Morris told Paul to take the job and make what he could of it. At the time Paul said, "Everything is brand new at that school, so we'll just have to build from the ground up."

Paul had prior experience working with handicapped kids and home-less boys. He had taken some of them into his family, reared them, and sent them off to college. "Dawgonnit, I know I can teach 'em baseball," Paul said.

As a coach, he believed strongly in discipline. "I think more should be done with today's generation," he said. "Look at all the problems, the juve-nile delinquency and all that. These kids need more discipline.... They need to learn about fellowship ... just getting along." And then he added: "It takes a big man to be a winner and it takes a big man to give what a lot of kids don't like today, advice. But I've given it to my own children, and I'll give it to others."

Paul had definite ideas about coaching pitchers. In the first place, he thought it was important to handle each one as an individual. He felt that differences extended beyond temperament. "For instance, some work better at night, and some are better in the afternoon. Some are more effective on overcast or sultry days, while others are better when the air is cool and dry. Some liked to pitch against the wind, and some with the wind.... I always slept with a sweat shirt on the night before I was going to pitch, and I did it no matter how hot the weather. It made my arm and shoulder muscles more loose the next day."

The University of Plano was a short-lived venture. Its doors closed in 1978.

Paul moved to Arkansas and operated a couple of filling stations in Springdale. When he was offered a job as a goodwill ambassador by A. Ray Smith, a wealthy Tulsa owner of the Springfield, Illinois, Redbirds, Paul readily accepted, for he was asked to do what he had been doing for at least 15 years, hit the road for good will, make personal appearances and give speeches.

But his health soon failed. In January 1980, Paul was stricken by two heart attacks.

His heart condition was complicated by adult diabetes, and he died 14 months later, on March 17, 1981, at Springdale, Arkansas.

He was buried at Clarksville. He was survived by two sons and two daughters.

Big brother Dizzy had passed away nearly seven years earlier, on July 17, 1974.

Never has baseball seen a more colorful brother act than Dizzy and Daffy Dean. While Gaylord and Jim Perry, and Phil and Joe Niekro, compiled far greater victory totals than the Deans, both Dizzy and Paul, before their injuries, could pitch with the best of them. Even though he had only 150 career wins, Dizzy was such a dominant pitcher in his day that he was chosen for the Baseball Hall of Fame on the basis of eight seasons. Paul, who had 50 wins, will never make it. Yet, when he came onto the major league scene, some observers felt that, in the end, he would be better than Dizzy. Diz may have even agreed with that, but may have been just too stubborn to ever let it show on the field. How good Paul was in relation to Dizzy is moot. For two years, Paul was outstanding. His 38-win total for that time span ranks him twelfth on the all-time list of pitchers for the first two years in the majors.

The Cardinals exploited both Dizzy and Paul. The boys thought they were indestructible and that they could pitch every day forever. And the Cardinals let them do it. The Deans' motto was, "Give me the ball." In both 1934 and 1935, time after time, the Deans pitched in relief a day after they had gone nine innings.

Paul blamed only himself for his untimely demise. He believed his injury did not stem from overwork but from improper conditioning. "I'd let myself get up to 225 pounds." He felt that "there's never any excuse for a pitcher to have arm trouble. If he's handled right, he'll always be ready to pitch."

Paul Dean had great pitching sense, excellent breaking pitches, and, in Dizzy's words, "... a fastball that'd skin a rabbit from the kitchen to the barn."

PAUL DEE DEAN

Born Aug. 14, 1913, Lucas, Ark.   Died March 17, 1981, Springdale, Ark.   Batted right, threw right.

Year	Team	W–L	Pct.	ERA	G	GS	CG	IP	H	BB	SO	ShO
1931	Houston TL	0–1	.000	n/a	2	n/a	n/a	3	n/a	n/a	n/a	n/a
1931	Columbus AA	0–2	.000	n/a	12	n/a	n/a	36	n/a	24	11	n/a
1931	Spring-field, WA	11–3	.786	3.64	19	n/a	12	136	118	68	119	n/a
1932	Columbus AA	7–16	.304	n/a	40	n/a	n/a	212	191	113	169	n/a
1933	Columbus AA	22–7	.759	3.15	43	n/a	n/a	254	228	117	222	n/a
1934	St.L. NL	19–11	.633	3.43	39	26	16	233⅓	225	52	150	5
1935	St.L. NL	19–12	.613	3.37	46	33	19	269⅔	261	55	143	2
1936	St.L. NL	5–5	.500	4.60	17	14	5	92	113	20	28	0
1937	St.L. NL	0–0	---	00	1	0	0	--	1	2	0	0
1938	St.L. NL	3–1	.750	2.61	5	4	2	31	37	5	14	1
1938	Houston/Dallas, TL	8–16	.333	3.69	29	25	16	201	n/a	36	102	n/a
1939	St.L. NL	0–1	.000	6.07	16	2	0	43	54	10	16	0
1940	NY NL	4–4	.500	3.90	27	7	2	99⅓	110	29	32	0
1941	NY NL	0–0	---	3.18	5	0	0	5⅔	8	3	3	0
1942	Out of baseball.											
1943	St. L. AL	0–0	---	3.38	3	1	1	13⅓	16	3	1	0
1944	Out of baseball.											
1945	Out of baseball.											
1946	Little Rock, TL	2–1	.667	7.37	4	n/a	n/a	19	29	4	3	0
Major League Totals 9 yrs.		50–34	.595	3.75	159	87	44	787⅓	825	179	387	8

World Series Record

Year	Team	W–L	Pct.	ERA	G	GS	CG	IP	H	BB	SO	ShO
1934	St.L.	2–0	1.000	1.00	2	2	2	18	15	7	11	0

15 "TWO-WIN JOHNNY"

JOHNNY BEAZLEY

> "Here was the Yankee power in the big clutch
> ... and you would have thought young Beazley
> ... was pitching in a kid's game back of
> his house. He was that icy cold."
> JOE WILLIAMS, NEW YORK WRITER

October 1, 1942 — game two of the World Series. The St. Louis Cardinals were facing the New York Yankees — the prewar Yankees of Joe DiMaggio, Charlie Keller, Joe Gordon, Bill Dickey, Phil Rizzuto, Red Rolfe, and Red Ruffing. Tommy Henrich had entered the military late in the season. To replace him, the Yankees acquired Roy Cullenbine, one of the most underrated players of the era. Cullenbine always had one of the best on-base percentages in baseball.

Red Ruffing had beaten St. Louis, 7–4, in the first game, his seventh career World Series win. The Yankee ace had held the Redbirds hitless until there were two out in the eighth inning. In the ninth, St. Louis bats came to life, and the Cardinals scored four times, giving them encouragement for game two.

The Yankees sent Ernie Bonham, their new pitching ace, to the mound for game two. Tiny, as the strapping six-foot, two-inch, 215-pound righthander was often called, had recorded 21 wins against only five losses during the 1942 season for a league-leading .808 percentage. His opponent was 23-year-old rookie Johnny Beazley, the surprise of the year on a talent-laden Cardinal pitching staff.

From 1937 through 1940, like a true nomad, Beazley wandered through the Southern minor leagues, pitching for 10 different teams. Beazley started with Leesburg in the Florida State League in 1937 as an 18-year-old and won four games while losing three. But before long, he moved to Tallahassee in the Georgia-Florida League. At Tallahassee, he won only once while losing seven times. He ended the season in the Kitty League with Lexington, for whom he won two and lost five. His record for 1937 was an undistinguished 7–15.

He began 1938 with Greenville of the Cotton State League, winning two while losing four. He moved next to Abbeville of the Evangeline League, winning six while losing eight, a second losing season. His third season was not much better. In 1939, he toiled briefly for New Orleans of the Southern League before being optioned to Montgomery of the South-East League for the rest of the year. In 1940, he suited up a few times for New Orleans before being moved to Columbus, Georgia, of the South Atlantic League, where he won five and lost three. He ended the 1940 season with Mobile of the South-East League, where he also had a winning record, 4–2.

As a 21-year-old in 1941, Beazley seemed to break through a barrier at New Orleans. He pitched for the Pelicans the entire season, winning 16 while losing 12. His performance was impressive, and the Cardinals brought him to St. Louis at the end of the season. He started one game and pitched a complete game victory.

There was no reason to predict that Beazley would suddenly mature in 1942 and become the Cardinals' number-two starter behind ace Mort Cooper. Howie Pollett was a much better candidate. He was coming off two consecutive 20-win seasons for Houston in the Texas League, while losing only 10 games in the two-year span. Beazley, on paper, did not compare well to the rest of the St. Louis staff, consisting of highly promising Max Lanier; Howie Krist, who was 11–0 in 1941; Harry Gumbert, the old Giant hurler; Ernie White, who had a brilliant 16–5 rookie year in 1941; Murray Dickson; Clyde Shoun; the veteran Lon Warneke, who had tossed a no-hitter the year before; and Mort Cooper, the ace of the staff. It was a formidable group.

As the 1942 season began, Cooper, Gumbert, White, and Warneke started the first four games. On April 20, Manager Billy Southworth started 23-year-old Beazley against Pittsburgh. For eight innings, the rookie from Tennessee pitched shutout ball, but in the ninth he walked the first two batters and was relieved by Gumbert, who walked a third Pirate. With the help of two errors and a wild pitch, two runners scored. However, St. Louis held on to win, 3–2.

Despite this strong performance, Beazley was used only in relief. Southworth started seven different pitchers during the first month of the season in an effort to sort out the starters on his talented pitching staff.

The Cardinal infield was equally unsettled. At first was another rookie,

Ray Sanders, who had the task of making St. Louis fans forget Johnny Mize. Over the winter, the St. Louis front office, whom many saw as penny-pinching, had sold Mize to the Giants over a salary dispute. At second was Creepy Crespi, who seemed to come into his own in 1941 when the Cards lost the pennant to Brooklyn by three games. At short, the slick-fielding Marty Marion was a fixture, and veteran Jimmy Brown, who had hit a career-high .306 the year before, looked set at third. Terry Moore and Enos Slaughter were in center and right, respectively. In left, the rookie Stan Musial was slated to take over. Although Musial had hit .426 in 12 games at the end of the 1941 season, Southworth opened the season by platooning him with Coaker Triplett against left-handed pitching.

Despite their obvious talent, the Cards got off to a so-so start. Their record fell to 19–17 when they lost a doubleheader on May 24, dropping them to third place, one game behind Boston and six-and-a-half behind Brooklyn. The next day Southworth took action. He moved Brown to second base and installed Whitey Kurowski as the regular third baseman. This new lineup won four straight. On May 27, Southworth acted again. He replaced Sanders at first base with the speedy Johnny Hopp. This change might have been made sooner but for Hopp's injured thumb.

At about the same time, two members of the Cards pitching staff, Howie Pollett and Ernie White, developed arm problems. Pollett's was temporary, but a large lump swelled on White's left arm, and he could not raise his arm to throw. White pitched and won the day Kurowski made his debut on May 25, but he was unable to pitch again until July 1.

The situation led Southworth to make the most critical move of the season. He had started Johnny Beazley now and then, but mostly had used him in relief. Each time Beazley entered the game, he pitched with such poise and confidence that Southworth decided to move the lanky rookie into the starting rotation. To make room for him, St. Louis, on July 8th, the day after the All-Star Game, sold popular veteran Lon Warneke back to Chicago for the minimum $7,500 waiver money (and thereby got rid of Warneke's $12,500 salary as well).

The move was so controversial that critics were certain the Cards were conceding the race to Brooklyn. "The pattern is too familiar here," wrote New York writer Joe King. "Hafey and Dean and Medwick and Mize, to name a few, go down the river when they go up in the salary brackets and the public esteem."

The move proved to be some concession: From July 19 until the end of the season, the Cardinals won 63 games while losing only 19.

Beazley made Southworth look like a genius. On July 9, the day after

Warneke was sold, Southworth started him in the first game against the Giants. Beazley pitched brilliantly and helped his cause by clearing the bags with a triple in a six-run sixth inning. Then in the eighth, he came out to the mound wearing Warneke's old No. 18 instead of his usual No. 21. The gesture signified who was going to replace the Arkansas Humming Bird in the rotation. Beazley posted his ninth triumph of the season as he shut out New York on six hits.

At the All-Star Game break, the standings listed Brooklyn as 52–21 and St. Louis as 43–29, eight-and-a-half games behind. But the 1942 Cardinals were a team of destiny. They staged one of the greatest stretch runs in baseball history, winning 34 of their final 43 games. After July 4, Beazley won 14 and lost only two, despite an injury to his pitching thumb. His 21–6 record and 2.13 ERA placed him second in the National League in wins, winning percentage, and ERA. Beazley's performance was instrumental in the Cardinals' nosing out the Dodgers for the pennant with 106 wins, two more than Brooklyn. Only the 1909 Chicago Cubs won as many as 104 games and yet finished second.

When the Yankees won the first game of the World Series, few were surprised. They were, after all, the Yankees. They had won the championship five of the previous six years, failing to appear in the event only in 1940.

On October 1, Sportsman's Park in St. Louis was at capacity with 34,000 fans for the second game of the series. The game started quietly as Beazley disposed of the Yankees in the top of the first without incident. Then St. Louis electrified the sellout crowd as they jumped on Ernie Bonham for two quick runs in the bottom of the inning. Beazley's batterymate, Walker Cooper, provided the key blow. In each of the first five innings, a Yankee reached second base against Beazley, but every time the cool-headed youngster bore down and turned back the Bronx Bombers unscathed. After the first inning, Bonham was equally impressive until after the seventh-inning stretch.

Johnny Hopp led off the seventh by singling to right. Then the St. Louis Swifties, as the 1942 Cards were often called, began running. Hopp broke for second on a hit and run, and Kurowski lined the ball along the left field line. When Keller had trouble catching up with the ball, Hopp scored from first, and Kurowski raced to third with a triple, putting the Cards in front, 3–0.

Southworth, as was his custom, sent Harry Gumbert to the bullpen to warm up as Beazley came out for the top of the eighth. The rookie seemed to scoff at the move as he struck out Rizzuto and induced Rolfe to ground easily to Brown at second. Cullenbine, however, reached first on an infield hit as Brown knocked down his shot but was unable to make the play at first. Cullenbine, in a bit of daring, stole second, making a nifty slide around Brown's attempted tag. Joe DiMaggio singled him home. The faithful in the stands were not concerned. But when King Kong Keller hit Beazley's first pitch onto the right-field pavilion roof to tie the game, the situation was changed. Still Beazley did not crack. He bore down and fanned the dangerous Joe Gordon, the American League's MVP.

Brown opened the bottom of the eighth with a smash to Gordon, who threw him out at first. Terry Moore hit a deep fly to DiMaggio in center. Slaughter brought joy to St. Louis fans when he slashed the first pitch safely to right. Racing for second, he slid hard into the base, losing a portion of his pants on the slide, and then got up and streaked to third when Cullenbine's throw eluded Rizzuto. The game stopped so that Slaughter could change his pants. When Slaughter returned, the heralded rookie, Stan Musial, hitless to this point in the series, stepped to the plate and hit the first pitch safely to center. Slaughter scored standing up, giving the Cards a one-run lead going into the top of the ninth inning.

Would Southworth let young Johnny Beazley come out for the last inning, or would he bring in the veteran Gumbert? The answer to the question came quickly when Beazley strode from the dugout to the mound. The fans gave a resounding roar of approval. Dickey opened the inning with a scratch single. The speedy George Stainback ran for him. Buddy Hassett singled to right, but Slaughter cut down Stainback at third with a great throw. Surprisingly, Southworth kept his resolve to continue with Beazley. Joe McCarthy sent Red Ruffing in to pinch hit. The hard-hitting pitcher drilled a shot deep to right, but Slaughter caught up with it a step in front of the wall. Rizzuto grounded to Marion at short, who threw him out to end the game. Beazley had pitched a complete game victory. The self-assured young Cardinal had allowed the Yankees ten hits but had won, 4–3.

In game three, played October 3 at Yankee Stadium, lefty Ernie White was in complete control of the contest, blanking the Yankees for the first time in a World Series game since 1926, when Pop Haines of the Cardinals had shut them out in game three. White held the Yankees to six singles. The Cardinals scored on Brown's infield out in the third and Slaughter's single in the ninth.

Game four, on October 4, was a high-scoring affair. Mort Cooper again was hit hard by the Yankees. Gumbert relieved him with one out in the sixth and retired one batter, and then was replaced by Lefty Pollett for the third out. Max Lanier came on to restore order in the final three innings and won the game, 9–6, and the Cards now led the Bronx Bombers three games to one. The Yankees had not lost a World Series since the Cards beat them in seven games in 1926, and one would have to go back to 1922 for a Series the Yankees lost in fewer than five games.

The possible final game of the Series was scheduled for October 5 at Yankee Stadium. The baseball world was stunned. The Cardinals were positioned to clinch the world's championship without returning to St. Louis. The pitching matchup for the fifth game was St. Louis's new hero, Johnny Beazley, against the veteran Red Ruffing, who was seeking a record eighth World Series victory. It was the 24-year-old Beazley's first visit to Yankee Stadium, before a crowd of 69,952, only 850 short of the greatest crowd in World Series history.

The contest was marked by remarkable events. The speed and daring of the Cardinals ruffled the veteran Yankees when, in the sixth inning with the Yankees leading, 2–1, Slaughter tied the score on a dash home from third after a short fly ball to Cullenbine in right. A newsreel cameraman complained, "These Cardinals are so fast you can't catch 'em in slow motion."

With the game tied 2–2, Walker Cooper opened the ninth with a single to center. Then rookie third baseman George Kurowski turned on one of Ruffing's inside fastballs and hammered it into the left field seats, putting St. Louis in front, 4–2. But in most respects, the key to the game was the pitching of young Johnny Beazley, who handled the situation with the coolness of a veteran. The critical moment of the game occurred in the fifth inning. The Bronx Bombers loaded the bases with only one out as both Hopp and Brown were guilty of errors. Southworth went to the mound and asked his kid pitcher if he was all right. Beazley replied, "Sure, but, Billy, are you all right?" That was the confidence the Yankees were up against. Beazley got Cullenbine to pop out to Marion at short and then, facing DiMaggio, got the great Yankee Clipper to hit into a force-out at third. With this display of clutch pitching, the Yankees were finished. They got only two hits in the remaining four innings.

Yet, the bottom of the ninth produced more drama. With nobody out and runners on second and third, Cardinal catcher Walker Cooper daringly picked a napping Joe Gordon off second with a strong and accurate throw. With Gordon removed from the bases, Beazley got Gerry Priddy to pop out to Brown at second. The veteran George Selkirk pinch hit for Red Ruffing, and Twinkletoes grounded Beazley's first pitch to second for an easy out. Ruffing never got that eighth World Series win.

Jubilant teammates mobbed the youthful Cardinal as soon as Selkirk was called out. Johnny Beazley had done it again. With exceptional poise and confidence, an exploding fastball, a devastating curveball and a baffling

Johnny Beazley beat the Yankees twice in the 1942 World Series (ROCHESTER *DEMO-CRAT AND CHRONICLE*).

changeup, he had gone the distance to win his second game of the series. Not since Paul Dean in 1934 had a rookie pitcher won two games in a World Series.

Joe Williams, in his column the next day in the New York *World Telegram*, named Beazley "the hero of the series. He pitched against them [the Yankees] as if he were pitching against the Phillies," the perennial door-mats of the National League. Of the critical fifth game, he wrote, "Here was the Yankee power in the big clutch, the moment when every ball carried a $6000 price tag — the reward for the winner — and you would have thought young Beazley, the handshaker, was pitching in a kid's game back of his house. He was that icy cold." Beazley's World Series performance gave him the title of "Two-Win Johnny."

No Rookie of the Year award existed in 1942, but in November, the Chicago baseball writers named the Cardinal World Series hero the most valuable rookie of 1942.

A brilliant pitching career appeared ahead for Beazley. But World War II interfered. He tried to enroll in the Navy's physical fitness program but was rejected, so he enlisted in the Army Air Corps as a mechanic. He attended officer's training school at Miami Beach for 12 weeks, married Carolyn Frey, whom he had met on a blind date, and by March became a second lieu-tenant in the Army Air Force technical training command.

Beazley played baseball for his service post. He realized that pitching in the military was a problem: "I am in excellent physical condition," he said, "but there is a difference between that and baseball condition. I pitch infre-quently now, and I find it is difficult to loosen up. I guess those throwing muscles take special attention."

Had he known how accurate his comment was about the "difference between physical condition and baseball condition" and that "those throw-ing muscles take special attention," he certainly would have exercised greater caution. Ironically, it was in a game for which he was highly motivated to do well, a game against the St. Louis Cardinals, that he failed to warm up properly and severely hurt his arm.

Despite the injury, in September 1945, while pitching in an Hawaii League game as an Army Air Force captain, Beazley showed flashes of his one-time greatness and hurled a no-hit, no-run game. The performance relieved Beazley's concern about his arm.

His unit was shipped from Hawaii to the South Pacific where he was involved in action that imprinted the horrors of war on his mind, a condi-tion that he seemed unable to shake.

Along with most other major leaguers who served during the war, Johnny came marching home in the spring of 1946. He reported to the Car-dinals for spring training. St. Louis was loaded with talent. In an AP poll, 115 of 119 writers selected the Cardinals to run away with the 1946 pennant. The club had an incredible array of pitchers: Red Barrett, Ken Burkhart, Blix Donnelly, George Dockins, Johnny Grodzicki, Howie Krist, Max Lanier,

Fred Martin, Howie Pollett, Max Surkont, Ted Wilks, and Ernie White. On top of that, Red Munger and Alpha Brazle were still with the army in Europe. But Johnny "Two Win" Beazley was the staff headliner.

On March 17, Beazley made his first mound appearance against the Cincinnati Reds in Florida, going three innings and yielding three hits and three walks. He showed plenty of speed and snapped off sharp breaking curves, but he appeared to be forcing his pitches. The stint did little to clear up the status of his ailing right shoulder. Doctors X-rayed the shoulder and discovered that Beazley had a calcified bursa.

Beazley also suffered from severe stomach problems the whole spring, and when he had a flare-up in early April, Manager Eddie Dyer — who had replaced Southworth when Billy moved to Boston to manage the Braves — sent him to St. Louis for observation and possible treatment. "Although Beazley has pitched good enough to have the best spring record of any of our pitchers, other than Fred Martin," Dyer reported, "he has suffered an upset stomach three or four times during the training session."

Dyer, however, remained optimistic, and said he planned to start Beazley opening day against the Pirates.

Faithful to his word, Dyer named Beazley to start the season's opener. A slim crowd of 14,000 showed up at Sportsman's Park for the contest. Beazley pitched poorly and got no decision, allowing six hits in three-and-a-third innings of toil. Plainly, the 1942 Two-Win Johnny had not returned from the war. His arm did not have the snap it did in 1942.

Additionally, the rumor mill said that Beazley's war experiences had impacted on him mentally so that he no longer had a total commitment to baseball. On May 15, 1946, Dan Daniel wrote of Beazley, "The Cardinal right-hander is suffering from war fatigue. He had some harrowing experiences in the South Pacific and doesn't appear to be able to get down to regarding baseball as a serious business."

Beazley appeared in 19 games in 1946 and pitched 103 innings. He won seven and lost five, with a 4.46 ERA.

The pennant race ended in the first tie in baseball history, as St. Louis and Brooklyn both finished with 96–58 records. The Cardinals, always at their best in postseason play, easily beat the Dodgers twice in a best-of-three playoff.

In the World Series, they again faced an outstanding American League team, the Boston Red Sox of Ted Williams. The Series went seven games and belonged to Harry "The Cat" Breecheen, who beat Boston three times while shutting down Ted Williams. Beazley pitched one inning in the fifth game, a contest the Cardinals lost, 6–3. He pitched well the ninth inning, giving up one hit and no runs.

**Johnny Beazley (second from left) in military uniform. His career was strongly
affected by World War II** (NATIONAL BASEBALL HALL OF FAME LIBRARY, COOPERSTOWN,
NY).

Eddie Dyer hoped for a Beazley comeback in 1947. At the beginning of
training camp, the manager was certain that Johnny had rid himself of his
war problems and would again be effective. Before long, however, Beazley
complained that his arm was gone, and he asked Dyer for his unconditional
release.

Dyer was upset. "In the first place, I am convinced there is nothing
wrong with Johnny's arm, and in the second place, the guy is a grand character and deserves a better break," Dyer lamented. "After that impressive little chore in the World Series last October, I was sure Beazley would join Red
Munger among our 1947 effectives. But the other day, Johnny insisted that
he had developed a new kink in his arm, and was finished." Dyer went on to
point out that he had been a pitcher himself and that he understood how it
felt suddenly to get a cutting pain in one's pitching arm. "But," he insisted,
"I have been watching Beazley the last couple of days, and a man whose arm
is gone could not possibly do the things Johnny can accomplish."

On April 17, the Cards sold Beazley to the Boston Braves for cash. Beazley was delighted to be reunited with his old manager, Billy Southworth.

Southworth, in turn, was ecstatic. He believed that Beazley was as loose as ever and that he had the stuff that had made him a star. He planned to start him against the Phils. "If we can get him a one–two run lead," Billy promised, "he will get that first one, the important one, and I will use the whole team to save it for him."

The trade to Boston, however, failed to rejuvenate the World Series hero. He pitched nine times for the Braves in 1947 and won two and lost none. His earned-run average for 28.2 innings was 4.40.

Beazley made token appearances with Boston in 1948 and 1949. In 1948, he pitched in 16 games, mostly in relief, went 0–1, with a 4.50 ERA. In 1949 he pitched two innings in just one game.

In 1949, Beazley also appeared briefly with St. Petersburg as player-manager, and he spent part of the 1950 season with Dallas in the Texas League. Beazley returned to his home in Nashville and became a beer distributor. He was 32 years old. He became involved in Nashville's civic projects and local politics, eventually serving on the Nashville city council in the 1970s.

Beazley died from cancer on April 21, 1990, 38 years and one day after his debut as a starter in 1942. In a sense, he was a war casualty. Had it not been for the war, Beazley might have avoided hurting his shoulder and gone on to a great career. Certainly, he pitched in the military under less than ideal conditions.

For one short but magnificent season, this Cardinal was brilliant.

JOHN ANDREW BEAZLEY

Born Nashville, Tenn., May 25, 1918.   Died Nashville, Tenn., April 21, 1990.   Threw right, batted right.

Year	Team	W–L	Pct.	ERA	G	GS	CG	IP	H	BB	SO	ShO
1937	Leesburg Fla. State	4–3	.571	3.96	9	5	3	59	58	28	34	n/a
1937	Tallahassee Ga.-Fla.	1–7	.125	4.50	n/a	n/a	n/a	74	91	38	29	n/a
1937	Lexington Kitty	2–5	.286	4.50	7	n/a	4	52	48	24	30	n/a
1938	Greenville Cotton State	2–4	.333	n/a	10	n/a	n/a	46	72	31	16	n/a
1938	Abbeville Evang.	6–8	.429	n/a	20	n/a	n/a	113	99	49	71	n/a
1939	New Orleans Southern	n/a	n/a	n/a	n/a	n/a	n/a	n/a	n/a	n/a	n/a	n/a
1939	Montgomery Sou.-East	n/a	n/a	n/a	n/a	n/a	n/a	n/a	n/a	n/a	n/a	n/a

Year	Team	W–L	Pct.	ERA	G	GS	CG	IP	H	BB	SO	ShO
1940	New Orleans Southern	n/a	n/a	n/a	n/a	n/a	n/a	n/a	n/a	n/a	n/a	n/a
1940	Columbus Sou.-Atlan.	5–3	.625	5.17	17	n/a	5	101	111	55	79	n/a
1940	Mobile Sou.-East	4–2	.667	2.04	8	n/a	5	53	41	22	33	n/a
1941	New Orleans Southern	16–12	.571	3.61	44	n/a	n/a	217	210	108	129	n/a
1941	St.L. NL	1–0	1.000	1.00	1	1	1	9	10	3	4	0
1942	St.L. NL	21–6	.778	2.13	43	23	13	215⅓	181	73	91	3
1943–1945	In military service.											
1946	St.L. NL	7–5	.583	4.46	19	18	5	103	109	55	36	0
1947	Bos NL	2–0	1.000	4.40	9	2	2	28.2	30	19	12	0
1948	Bos NL	0–1	.000	4.50	3	2	0	16	19	7	4	0
1949	Bos NL	0–0	.000	0.00	1	0	0	2	0	0	0	0
Major League Totals 6 yrs.		31–12	.721	3.01	76	46	21	374	349	157	147	3

World Series Record

Year	Team	W–L	Pct.	ERA	G	GS	CG	IP	H	BB	SO	ShO
1942	St.L. NL	2–0	1.000	2.50	2	2	2	18	17	3	6	0
1946	St.L. NL	0–0	--	0.00	1	0	0	1	1	0	1	0
Totals		2–0	1.000	2.37	3	2	2	19	18	3	7	0

---

16   THE BIRD

MARK FIDRYCH

"Babe Ruth didn't cause this much
excitement in his brightest day."
PAUL RICHARDS

Phenomenon and phenomenal. Both words describe Mark Fidrych. He
was a phenomenon because he was unique in the history of baseball. He was
phenomenal because once The Bird landed on the mound in Detroit in 1976,
he was virtually unhittable and often unbeatable, winning 19 games while
compiling a league-leading 2.34 earned run average.

Overnight, as the result of Bob Prince and an ABC television broadcast
of a big game with the Yankees on June 28, 1976, attended by 47,855 fans,
he became the "Sweet Bird of Baseball." Don Ohlmeyer, producer of "ABC
Monday Night Baseball" called Fidrych's showing "one of the most exciting
virtuoso performances we've had."

His Tiger teammates called him "The Bird" because he reminded them
of Big Bird, that ridiculous-looking character on *Sesame Street*, a popular
children's television series.

Former *Detroit Free Press* baseball writer Jim Hawkins suggested, "He
looks a little like Harpo Marx, and a lot like Max Patkin."

Whether he was crazy, colorful or just plain exuberant was a matter of
conjecture. One teammate described him simply as "flakier 'n hell."

Mark Fidrych was different. He looked more like a rock star than a
ballplayer. He was loose-limbed and walked with a gawky stride. A curly
hairdo topped his head.

He was irrepressibly enthusiastic about his work. The show began long
before his first pitch. At the beginning of an inning, he flew out of the
dugout, eager to get started with the task of disposing of three enemy batters. But when he got to his perch (the mound), he tidied up a bit before

The Bird manicures the mound in Detroit between innings of a 5–1 nationally televised victory over the New York Yankees on June 28, 1976 (Corbis-Bettman Archives, New York NY).

delivering a pitch, getting on his hands and knees, leveling the dirt, carefully filling in the holes made by the spikes of the opposing pitcher.

"When I'm pitching," he said, "the mound belongs to me. I don't want to step into another guy's groove."

Before each pitch, he audibly encouraged himself and gave direct and pithy instructions to the ball, telling it what to do. "Now you gotta go outside. Outside!" he instructed.

He complimented the ball when he got it back. "Great pitch, way to flow, in the groove."

It was a sight no Detroit fan, or any other, had ever seen before. After each out, he strutted in a circle around the mound, long legs stepping high and head bobbing like a long-legged, long-necked bird searching for food. He applauded and complimented his teammates for making a good play, no matter how routine. If an infielder made a sparkling play, he would briskly walk over and shake that player's hand.

And he consoled his fielders if they messed up. Once slick-fielding third baseman Aurelio Rodriquez dropped a pop-up, putting two Boston Red Sox on base with Rico Petrocelli at the plate. Rodriquez started to throw the ball back to the mound, but the Bird was perched right next to him offering consolation. "Don't worry, don't worry, I'll strike him out," said Fidrych, which he did.

After a winning effort, it was common for Fidrych to say, "Hey, did you see some of that defense they gave me?"

Mark Fidrych loved his work, and he was wide-eyed about being in the major leagues. "I couldn't ask for anything better than being in the big leagues," he chirped. "I've got more spikes than I know what to do with. And I don't even have to buy them. The same with my gloves. It's great."

He shook the hand of everybody in sight and freely autographed anything anyone put in front of him, unlike highly paid ballplayers of a later day who seem to think that their signatures should be worth money.

During his great year of 1976, he was initially paid the minimum salary of $16,500, which appeared to be too little for someone so successful and so popular. Given the skyrocketing players' salaries of the day, it seemed sufficiently paltry to the Michigan Legislature that it entertained a resolution calling on the Tigers to increase the Bird's pay. Some zealous fans started a "Send a buck to the Bird" campaign, and 500 thank-you letters came in with a buck enclosed. The club returned all the money.

Fidrych himself never complained about his paycheck. "I'm making more money right now than my father does," he commented.

He was happy to be playing baseball. He said that his second career choice was pumping gas for the Pierce Gas and Oil Station in Northboro, Massachusetts, and he acknowledged that he was only number two at the station. Despite Fidrych's expressed satisfaction, Detroit gave him a $7,500 bonus on his original contract during the season, for "his swift progress to the majors."

When the eccentric rookie needed money in spring training, instead of pressing the Tiger organization for it, he hung out a sign offering car washes for $1.50. Some of his teammates even pitched in and helped him with the work.

His lifestyle was modest. He had no telephone where he lived, and gave the rationale, "Who would I call?" There was no pretense about him. He was uncomplicated and unmaterialistic. When he became a star, Ford Motor Company offered him the use of a Thunderbird. Fidrych said, "I'd really like to have an old beat-up truck. An old, really beat-up truck. That's me. I'm a truck man." In time, however, he did accept the Thunderbird. There was much of the yokel about him. Stubby Overmire, former Detroit pitcher who managed the Bird in the minors, observed, "He walks like a plow jockey — with one foot in the furrow." His speech was appropriate to his gait. He spoke "yep" as if it were two syllables, and his conversation was well-seasoned with baseball's clubhouse language.

No Big Deal, the Bird's autobiography written with the aid of ghostwriter Tom Clark after the 1976 season, contains samples of Bird-Talk. For example: "I come in, just voom — just throw normal, just say, 'Hey, ground ball, high fly, you'll take all that, just do not get a hit. Make 'em hit what you want, y'know?' And I got in there and I just hung a slider and he just went tccht, thank you. That was it."

The Mark Steven Fidrych story began at Worcester, Massachusetts, on August 14, 1954. While Mark was growing up, it was his father Paul who was the baseball fan. Mark preferred minibikes, motorcycles and cars.

The elder Fidrych taught his son how to play baseball, and the boy dutifully responded to his teaching, but he saw no real future in it. Mark later noted that it was his father who had taught him to smooth out the mound so he "wouldn't slip into some other pitcher's spike marks."

Mark played Little League ball, high school and American Legion baseball. During his senior year at Algonquin High School in Northboro, he was barred from competing because he was too old. The zealous father then enrolled him in a private school, Worcester Academy, where Mark was allowed to play. He was not exactly a big name at Worcester. "I had a losing season," Mark himself reported.

Joe Cusick, then a Detroit scout, saw Mark in high school and began to follow him through prep school. No other major league franchise showed any interest in him, including the nearby Boston Red Sox. Cusick, however, liked Mark's lean and lanky build — six feet, three inches — and his good live fastball.

Detroit listed him seventh on their draft list, but did not take him until the tenth round, probably because they were not worried about losing him to someone else. Mistakes of this sort are often made in the draft.

Fidrych's first stop in the Tigers' minor league chain was at Bristol in the Appalachian League in 1974. He won three games without a loss and struck out 40 batters in 34 innings and compiled a 2.38 earned run average. Coaches noticed that he kept the ball low and fast, mixing in an occasional hard slider to good advantage. It was at Bristol that he was first nicknamed "The Bird" by teammate Jeff Hogan. The label stuck.

In 1975, he hopped from Lakeland, of the Florida State League, where he had a losing 5–9 record and a 3.77 ERA, to Montgomery of the Southern League, where he won two games without a loss and compiled a 3.21 ERA, to Evansville of the American Association, where he went 5–1 with a glittering 1.58 ERA.

Detroit invited him to their spring camp in 1976 as a noncontract player. He arrived clad in faded denims, sneakers, and T-shirt.

His hair was long, curly and unkempt. His alternative attire was cutoff denims and sandals. Appalled by the rookie's appearance, Tigers general manager Jim Campbell took young Fidrych to a store in Lakeland to buy him a couple of suits. Not surprisingly, Fidrych chose two faddish leisure suits.

When salary squabbles delayed spring training for some of the veteran Detroit staff, Manager Ralph Houk started to use the young lad in some of the exhibition games. Before he went out to pitch in his first spring game, he spit tobacco juice all over the front of his uniform. "I wanted the guys to know I chew," he said. Each time Houk sent Fidrych to the mound, tobacco-stained or not, he pitched effectively. He had discovered the formula for pitching success: low, hard and in the strike zone.

"His biggest asset," said Fidrych's catcher, Bruce Kimm, "is that he doesn't make mistakes."

If Fidrych did not get the ball where he wanted it, it was almost never up in the batter's wheelhouse, but low and out of the strike zone. His fastball often was clocked in the low 90s, but he had virtually no curve, in part because he released the ball low and far out from the body. One batter after another hit his low pitches on the ground.

In his first major league start on May 16, the 21-year-old Fidrych flirted with immortality as he held the Cleveland Indians hitless through six innings in a drizzling rain. Despite the moisture, he refused to let the ground crew fix the mound in the sixth inning because of the no-hitter. "Why should I let them mess up the mound when I had a no-hitter going?" he philosophized. He went the distance and settled for a two-hit shutout.

Fidrych lost his second start on May 25 when Luis Tiant and the Boston Red Sox shut out Detroit, 2–0. Then the Bird won seven straight. The seventh win in that streak catapulted him to fame and glory. The game was against the New York Yankees on June 28. A crowd of 47,855 deliriously happy fans witnessed the contest in Tiger Stadium and millions more saw it as ABC's Monday night game of the week.

Hoot Robinson, who owned a bar across the street from the stadium, remarked, "The place hasn't been like this since we won the 1968 World Series."

Fidrych whipped the Yankees, 8–1, on a nifty seven-hitter. He lowered his ERA to 2.05. The fans reacted enthusiastically to Fidrych's antics on the mound. After the final out, the fans would not leave the stadium, but sat chanting, "We want Bird. We want Bird," begging their new-found hero to make a curtain call. Fidrych, who relished the admiration, came back out amidst the roar of the crowd, did his bows, and signed autographs and shook outreached hands.

Mark Fidrych, known as Bird," was a fan favorite (NATIONAL BASEBALL HALL OF FAME LIBRARY, COOPERSTOWN, NY).

Bob Prince, announcing the game for ABC, said, "He's giving me goose bumps, and I've watched 8,000 ball games." Red Foley, baseball writer for the *New York Daily News*, called him "the greatest invention since bottled beer." The game made the Bird a household word.

Although great pitching matchups have often drawn large crowds, seldom has a pitcher pulled in so many fans as Mark Fidrych in 1976. Below are the attendance totals for 10 consecutive games in which the Bird pitched, beginning with the Monday night ABC game.

Date	Game	Attendance
June 28	New York at Detroit	47,855
July 3	Baltimore at Detroit	51,032
July 9	Kansas City at Detroit	51,041
July 20	Detroit at Minnesota	30,425
July 24	Detroit at Cleveland	37,503
July 29	Baltimore at Detroit	44,068
August 3	Detroit at New York	44,909
August 7	Cleveland at Detroit	35,395
August 11	Texas at Detroit	36,523
August 17	California at Detroit	51,822

The average draw for the three road games was 37,612, which almost exceeded the Tigers' average road attendance by 20,000 fans. At home, the difference was about 28,000 fans per game. The Tigers received unusual ticket orders such as, "Send me six tickets for the next game The Bird pitches." The probable date when Fidrych would pitch became valuable information.

For the season, the Bird attracted well over 900,000 fans to his 31 starts, or an average of more than 31,000 per contest. In his 18 starts in Detroit, he attracted 605,677 people. For their 63 other games, the Tigers drew 861,343. The Bird flew high in Detroit in 1976.

Fidrych himself jotted down the attendance figure after each game. Why not keep track of "how many people you pitch in front of?" he explained. Such a record certainly had the potential of enhancing his bargaining position with the club.

Fidrych's pitching matched the size of the crowds. By the All-Star Game, he had a 9–2 record, with a 1.78 ERA, the lowest in the league. He was chosen as the American League starter, the rarest of honors for a rookie. At a pregame press conference, reporters discovered that Fidrych, attired in his customary faded denims and Harpo Marx hairdo, was a talking bird who responded to questions freely.

When asked how he felt, he replied, "No words in the English language can describe what's happening to me now. This is my biggest thrill since I got a mini-bike when I was 14."

Asked if he talked to car engines while he worked at the gas station, he said, "Yeah, I talked to the engines, and if they didn't work, I usually beat on them."

Asked if he was going to study the National League hitters, he laughed off the question: "I don't ask anyone about how to pitch these guys [American Leaguers], so why should I ask about them?"

He was most concerned about hitting. With the designated hitter rule in the American League, Fidrych had not batted all year. He began a search for just the right bat, and finally accepted one from Tigers second baseman Pedro Garcia. He practiced his stance and his swing. He seemed not to appreciate that since the three-inning pitching limit rule was enacted, pitchers rarely batted in All-Star games, especially American League pitchers who have not hit all season.

Fidrych's pitching was less than spectacular. National League hitters sent some of the Bird's pitches soaring around Veterans' Stadium in Philadelphia and they scored twice in the first inning. Fidrych got the side out without a run in the second and then gave way to Catfish Hunter in the third, before he got to bat. The American League lost the game, 7–1, and Fidrych was the losing pitcher. It was the National's fifth consecutive win and thirteenth of the last 14. Fidrych began the second half of the season on an upbeat note. He bested the hard-hitting Oakland A's, 1–0, in 11 innings on July 16. The next time out on July 20, he beat Minnesota, 8–3. The going got a bit rocky after that. The Cleveland Indians knocked him out of the box in less than five innings on July 24, but the Tigers came back to win the game, 5–4. Then on July 29, Fidrych lost a 1–0 heartbreaker to Baltimore. His record stood at 11–3 as July ended.

After a somewhat rocky August, Fidrych bounced back strong enough that by September he was closing in on a 20-win season and looked like a cinch for Rookie-of-the-Year honors, with a chance for the Cy Young Award. Only one Tiger, Harvey Kuenn in 1953, had previously received Rookie-of-the-Year honors. Oren (Kickapoo Ed) Summers, in 1908, was the only Tiger pitcher to win 20 games in his rookie year.

When the final out was made in the 1976 season, the Bird fell one win shy, as he finished 19–9 with a league-leading 2.34 ERA. It is important to note, however, that Fidrych did not start a game until the season was a month old, thereby missing at least five or six starts. Even then, Fidrych led the league in complete games with 24, was tied for fourth in wins, and was fourth in winning percentage at .679. He was not a one-dimensional player, either. He was named to the American League's top-percentage fielding team. Fidrych handled 78 chances flawlessly in 1976.

The Sporting News named him Rookie of the Year, and the National Association of Professional Baseball Leagues honored him as the man of the year. As a reward, Detroit's management gave Fidrych enough of a bonus to bring his income for the season to approximately $60,000.

Topps, the bubble gum baseball card barons, made a colossal goof. They thought so little of Fidrych's chances in the spring that they failed to issue a card for the Tiger rookie pitcher. The Topps organization admitted, "We take pictures of every player in spring training who we feel has a remote shot to make a big-league roster. We underestimated Fidrych, but so did the Tigers. He did not make their media guide."

Just before the end of the season, Fidrych and his father met with Campbell, who offered a three-year contract calling for $55,000 the first season, $75,000 the next, and at least $100,000 for the third year. The elder Fidrych, an assistant principal of a public school in Worcester, looked at the contract and declared it to be "fine." The Bird echoed the reply and signed it.

The younger Fidrych expressed proper appreciation. "I want to play for the Tigers, and they want me," he said. "When I got out of high school, they were the only team that offered me a job." Then he added, "Besides, I have all the money I need."

Fidrych approached his sophomore season fully self-assured. He told anyone who would listen that the "sophomore jinx is irrelevant." He appeared even looser than the year before. His hair was much longer, his dungarees had more holes, and his comments were even more off the wall. Already a legend, his performance in 1977 needed to be sensational to fulfill expectations.

However, physical maladies beset him in March when he ripped cartilage in his knee in spring training by jumping too enthusiastically for a fly ball in the field.

An arthrogram X-ray revealed the injury was severe enough to require surgery. Dr. David Mitchell performed the operation, and Fidrych made what appeared to be a quick comeback from the surgery. In seven weeks, he was back in uniform.

"I thought my arm would go before my legs," the curly-haired hurler muttered.

On May 27, he made his much awaited first mound appearance of the season in Tiger Stadium against the Seattle Mariners. The full house gave him a standing ovation when he sprinted to the mound for the first inning. He pitched reasonably well, but because of a couple of costly errors by center fielder Ron LeFlore and second baseman Tito Fuentes, the Mariners, not the Tigers, prevailed in the game by a 2–1 score.

"I'm just thankful to The Man for letting me out there," the Bird said afterward. "I didn't pitch good. But that's life. I didn't do anything different. Last year I won my first game, 2–1. This year I lost it, 2–1. That's life."

Manager Ralph Houk declared that Fidrych was "over the hump as far as the injury is concerned. If Fuentes and LeFlore hadn't dropped those two balls, it would have been a shutout."

Fidrych lost his second start as well when, on June 1, Cleveland beat him 6–4.

On June 6, he got his first victory. He was so determined that he refused to shave before he faced the California Angels in Anaheim. With feathery stubble on his cheeks, he told reporters, "I gotta look mean. I didn't wash my hair either."

It seemed to work, for he clipped the Angels' wings, 8–0. "I needed a victory," Fidrych exclaimed. "I needed one in my head, you know what I mean?" He used that win as a springboard for winning six straight.

Pitchers, eager to get back to work, often attempt to come back too soon from an injury. Dizzy Dean did that after breaking a toe in the 1937 All-Star game and hurt his arm. Now, 40 years later, Fidrych attempted to come back too soon from his injury. He favored his injured knee and appeared to change his pitching delivery.

Pitching against the Baltimore Orioles on July 4, he took a 2–0 lead into the sixth inning. After two outs, his arm started to "feel weird." The Orioles scored six times before the inning ended, and Baltimore went on to win the game, 6–4.

Fidrych took the mound again on July 12 against the Toronto Blue Jays. He managed to get two outs and then left the game because of a sore shoulder. John Crawford relieved him and pitched brilliantly as he defeated the Blue Jays, 2–1.

In previous performances, Fidrych's arm had "felt funky. This time it just petered out," he reported. "I couldn't even pick my arm up. I knew something was wrong."

He saw several doctors, including Dr. Frank Jobe, a leading orthopedic surgeon in Los Angeles. He got different diagnoses about his problem. The doctors, however, all agreed that he did not need surgery.

"They said I was too young to cut on," Fidrych said. "They suggested trying rehabilitation." Fidrych agreed. The Tigers labeled the problem as tendonitis, and after a week's rest, they placed Fidrych on the disabled list for the season. Mark ended the year with a 6–4 record and a highly respectable 2.89 ERA.

The Bird's wing was pronounced fit after a brief trial in November. When he reported to spring training in 1978, he seemed to throw easily and without pain. But by the end of the spring, the pain had returned. However, the spirited 23-year-old pitcher fought it off, and on opening day, April 7, hurled a five-hit, 6–2 win against the Toronto Blue Jays.

In the fifth inning, the Bird loaded the bases. At that point, he told himself audibly and visibly, "Don't overthrow. Don't overthrow. Keep your rhythm. Throw it down the middle. Let him hit it." His pitch sailed inside to the hitter and struck him out.

From that point on in the game, Detroit's Bird, not the Blue Jays, did the chirping. With two outs in the ninth, he paused to pick up some trash that had blown across the infield, chasing one piece of paper all the way to first base. Then he returned to the mound and got Toronto's Dave McKay to ground back to him for the final out. Fidrych jumped into the air, shaking his fist, shook every teammate's hand and headed for the dugout.

The crowd demanded a curtain call, and the eccentric pitcher flew out of the dugout and doffed his hat. Opening day was complete. The Bird was back on his roost.

The next week, on April 12, he beat Texas, 3–2, on a neat six-hitter.

The third time out, on April 17 against the Chicago White Sox, he experienced tendonitis pain just below his shoulder that was so intense that Detroit put him back on the disabled list. He went four innings in the game, giving up six hits and two runs in a wild contest that Detroit ultimately won, 10–9.

The downhearted Fidrych lamented, "I've gotten my rhythm back, but now I can't put zip on the ball. And I still can't throw without any pain. That's all I ask right now. Just to be able to throw without any pain." He seemed to want surgery on his shoulder. "Surgery doesn't frighten me because I'm told it would be only minor," he said. "There is a cyst of some kind in my shoulder, and that's where the pain is when I throw."

The Tigers, however, sent him to Lakeland for recuperation. The plan was for Fidrych to take medication and treatments to reduce the inflammation and to toss the ball occasionally, testing and strengthening his arm.

Concerned fans wrote and suggested all kinds of home remedies, ranging from going on a vegetable diet to eating nothing but chicken, from wearing three heavy sweatshirts 24 hours a day to applying cow's udder ointment to the shoulder. Perhaps the best advice came from a disgruntled, anonymous fan who simply wanted to know why Fidrych did not learn to throw left-handed. At least 50 chiropractors from all over the country volunteered their services for free.

Meanwhile, Fidrych tried to be patient and worked out with Detroit's Lakeland farm club. All the same, his patience from time to time wore thin. For example, he exclaimed, "It's hell watching your friends play when you want to be out there so much." The Tigers were battling for first place, which bothered Fidrych because he was not contributing. "Just think what 15 or 20 wins would do for us," he said.

Campbell said that the club had not yet considered surgery for Fidrych, but acknowledged that they were rapidly running out of alternatives. Campbell expressed the hope that Florida's hot sun would help the Bird. "If his arm can heal naturally, maybe the hot weather will help. It's just a type of therapy we want to try for awhile," he said.

Fidrych made four appearances for Lakeland, pitching 13 innings with a 1–1 record and 3.46 ERA. His performance was good enough that his spirits were buoyed. However, he did not make it back to Detroit during the season.

The Tigers brought Fidrych along slowly the next spring. He made his first regular-season appearance on May 5 in Minnesota, and he permitted four hits and a couple of runs in four innings. "I felt fine," declared the Bird. "I felt like I could have pitched longer. Maybe I could have gone nine innings, who knows?"

On May 10, he made his first home start of the year against Milwaukee. He went five-and-one-third innings and lost to the Brewers, 5–1. The game was an indication of things to come. After this, he watched most of the games from the sidelines.

In the absence of playing baseball, the Bird began reading the Bible every day. He kept one Bible at home and another in the Tiger clubhouse, and when the team went on the road, he always took one with him. If this behavior indicated anything, it revealed how Fidrych had changed from a few years before when the Tiger rookie had seemed totally self-sufficient.

"I'm not much of a reader," he explained. "I can't start from the beginning and just read. But every day I read one little passage. This way, there's something different every day. It seems like every time I read it, I find a problem I've already had. It explains it. It calms me down." He further explained that he used to relate to God when he was a kid, "So why not try Him again?"

Nonetheless, for the season, Fidrych pitched in four games and was 0–3. His ERA over only 15 innings ballooned to 10.20. Not vintage Mark Fidrych.

In the spring of 1980, his problems persisted. On March 20, he pitched two-and-a-third innings and yielded four runs on five hits against the Philadelphia Phillies. After his 44th pitch, Detroit pitching coach Roger Craig asked Fidrych if he was having arm problems, and Fidrych simply replied, "Yeah." He reported that the top of his triceps muscle in his right arm felt tight and that it prevented him from getting loose. He left the game, and the Phillies went on to win, 10–4.

The medical diagnosis was a strained tricep. As if to convince himself,

Fidrych pointed out that the problem was unrelated to his previous ailment. His spring ERA zoomed to 10.00. Worse yet, when pressed, he acknowledged that the arm misery was in the same spot as before.

The Tigers sent him to Evansville in the American Association for rehab. The Bird criticized manager Sparky Anderson for sending him there and also for not watching his debut for Evansville because it was costing him "pension time." Anderson responded, "I told Mark he was no more important than anyone else. I won't be there when any other Evansville pitcher is starting, so why should I be there when Mark Fidrych pitches?" To Fidrych the message was clear: The Tigers no longer considered him special.

To help him get back to the majors, Fidrych met with Evansville hypnotist Lee Silen. Silen talked to the Bird about his pitching techniques, about his control and his velocity. "We worked on his fears and phobias," Silen said. "Then we got into the confidence factor. Without realizing it, Mark may have had a fear of failure in Detroit."

Fidrych was sufficiently effective in Evansville that Campbell came to watch him pitch. "The most encouraging sign," Campbell said, "is that his arm doesn't hurt. No amount of hypnotism can cure a physical ailment, but maybe Mark's problem has been in the mind and that's what the hypnotist is working on."

In August 1980, the Tigers brought the Bird back to Detroit. He was satisfied that he was ready to pitch for the Tigers because of his work in the minors. He was 6–7 at Evansville with a mediocre 3.93 ERA. "I threw 117 innings at Evansville this year," he said. "It's not like my other comebacks, when I came off the disabled list and never faced any hitters until batting practice."

On August 12, before 50,749 cheering fans, he gave a strong performance against Boston. His zany antics seemed a little less natural than they used to be, but the crowd still loved them. Fidrych lost the game, 5–4, on a homer by Boston's Jim Dwyer.

Notwithstanding, it looked as if Mark Fidrych might be back. Lance Parrish, Detroit's catcher, reported after the game that Fidrych's velocity was not what it once was but that his "breaking ball was probably the best I've seen him throw." Even Sparky Anderson was enthusiastic. "If he pitches like that, he'll pitch every fifth day," the manager announced.

The next time out on August 17 in a 9–3 loss to the Texas Rangers, Fidrych failed to last through the fifth inning, allowing five hits, six runs and three walks, and even Fidrych acknowledged that "it went lousy."

That assessment essentially characterized the rest of the season. He compiled a 2–3 record and a 5.73 ERA in 44 innings of work. The handwriting was on the wall: The Bird's wing was impaired. At the age of 26, he had manicured the Tiger Stadium mound for the last time.

Although released by the Tigers, he hoped for a comeback and spent the next two seasons pitching for Pawtucket in the Boston Red Sox organization. He achieved a moment of glory on July 1, 1982, when he went the distance for Pawtucket in a Class AAA game, outdueling Yankee farm hand Dave Righetti. When Fidrych struck out Butch Hobson to end the game, the home crowd of 9,389 fans in McCoy Stadium went into a frenzy. For 10 minutes, they stood and chanted, "Bird! Bird! Bird!" They refused to leave until the Bird made a curtain call. He faced the bleachers and raised a clenched fist in victory.

Mike Tamburro, the general manager of Pawtucket, called it "the biggest night in the history of our stadium. The scene after the game was like out of a movie."

Righetti and Fidrych, however, went different ways. Righetti went on to a distinguished career with the New York Yankees and pitched the Yanks' first no-hitter since Don Larsen's perfect game in the 1956 World Series. Fidrych, almost a year later to the day, voluntarily retired from professional baseball while the Pawtucket Pawsox were midway through a series with the Tidewater Tides in Virginia. Fidrych realized he no longer was pitching effectively at even a minor league level.

During his stay with Pawtucket, Fidrych pitched in a total of 32 games and won 8 and lost 13. He was 2–5 with a 9.68 ERA in 12 games for the year when he retired in 1983. He himself acknowledged, "It was brutal."

Fidrych returned home to Massachusetts to begin life as a farmer at Bluewater. His 123-acre farm was complete with sheep, pigs and a red barn. The farm, which he purchased with money he made in baseball, bordered his parents' land. Although he felt the farm would keep him busy, he knew he would need to look for steady work because the farm would not fully sustain him. "It's a weight off my shoulders," he said about leaving baseball. "But where am I going to get my next job?"

He did it by doing what he always loved to do: He drove a 10-wheel truck. He installed a telephone answering machine for people to leave messages if they needed hauling.

As a job trucker, he has hauled materials as diverse as asphalt and gunk from septic tanks.

How good was Mark Fidrych? He had that basic quality of effective pitching: excellent control. In 1976, he allowed only 53 walks in 250 innings, an average of 1.91 per game. He also had a low hit-per-inning ratio, giving up 217 hits for an average of 7.81 per nine innings. His ERA was always under

3.00 until 1979, when his injured shoulder prevented him from throwing effectively. Seldom does a young pitcher come along who can keep the ball low and in the strike zone so consistently, at 90 miles an hour, with movement on the pitch. Mark Fidrych did that, and, perhaps most importantly, he rarely made a mistake.

How does Fidrych's 1976 performance at the age of 21 compare to some Hall of Famers who were dominant pitchers? Steve Carlton, the dominant pitcher of the 1970s, at age 21, won three and lost three. Not until age 26 did he win as many as 19 games, going 20–9 in 1971. Bob Gibson, one of the dominant pitchers of the 1960s, was 28 years old before he posted a 19–12 record in 1964. Fireballing Sandy Koufax, at age 21, was only 5–4 in 1957. On the other hand, his fellow fireballer, Bob Feller, the Iowa Boy Wonder of the late 1930s, had won 82 games by the time he turned 22 after the 1940 season.

To opposing hitters, Fidrych appeared more like a vulture than a gentle bird. He was going to be one of baseball's great pitchers until fate, in the form of a shoulder injury, cruelly shot the Bird off his perch on the Tiger Stadium rubber.

That Mark Fidrych's career was so short-lived was unfortunate for baseball. He gave the game a lot of color and a refreshing exuberance at a time when the dominant form of baseball news involved dollar figures. Mark Fidrych put fans in the ballpark, not only because of his antics but also because he was a great pitcher. Perhaps Paul Richards, longtime major league manager and executive, summed it up best when he said, "Babe Ruth didn't cause this much excitement in his brightest day."

A few players thought that perhaps Fidrych was on to something when he talked to the ball, and they felt that they should learn from him. Cuban-born Mike Cuellar of the Baltimore Orioles said he tried it, but, unlike Fidrych, he couldn't get his message across to the ball. "I speak Spanish, and the ball is American," Cuellar reported.

MARK STEVEN FIDRYCH
Born Aug. 14, 1954, Worcester, Mass.   Batted right, threw right.

Year	Team	W–L	Pct.	ERA	G	GS	CG	IP	H	BB	SO	ShO
1974	Bristol Appal	3–0	1.000	2.38	23	0	0	34	24	16	40	0
1975	Lakeland Fla. St	5–9	.357	3.77	17	16	10	117	111	50	73	0
1975	Montgomery, Southern	2–0	1.000	3.21	7	n/a	n/a	14	15	3	11	n/a

Year	Team	W–L	Pct.	ERA	G	GS	CG	IP	H	BB	SO	ShO
1975	Evans-ville, AA	4–1	.800	1.58	6	n/a	n/a	40	27	9	29	n/a
1976	Det AL	19–9	.679	*2.34	31	29	*24	250	217	53	97	4
1977	Det AL	6–4	.600	2.89	11	11	7	81	82	12	42	1
1978	Det AL	2–0	1.000	2.45	3	3	2	22	17	5	10	0
1978	Lakeland Fla St	1–1	.500	3.46	4	4	0	13	6	6	6	0
1979	Det AL	0–3	.000	10.20	4	4	0	15	23	9	5	0
1980	Evans-ville, AA	6–7	.462	3.93	24	18	1	117	123	54	62	0
1980	Det AL	2–3	.400	5.73	9	9	1	44	58	20	16	0
1981	Evans-ville, AA	6–3	.667	5.75	24	9	2	117	111	27	26	0
1982	Pawtucket Inter.	6–8	.429	4.98	20	19	2	139	123	59	51	0
1983	Pawtucket Inter.	2–5	.286	9.68	12	8	0	48	85	37	27	0
Major League Totals 5 yrs.		29–19	.604	3.10	58	56	34	417	397	99	170	5

*Indicates led league

17   IN THE WRONG PLACE

LYMAN BOSTOCK

> "He just wanted to play every day and win."
> DON BAYLOR, TEAMMATE

Baseball is not a violent sport. Of the four major American team sports — baseball, football, basketball and hockey — baseball has the least contact. On occasion a runner slams into a catcher, like Pete Rose did to Ray Fosse in the 1970 All-Star game, or a runner crashes into the shortstop or second baseman while trying to break up a double play. There is the brushback pitch perfected by Sal "The Barber" Maglie that often leads to bench-clearing brawls, which seldom result in injuries. Maglie acquired his nickname because of his uncanny ability to throw close pitches that almost scraped the batter's whiskers. There are also outfielders like Pistol Pete Reiser who crashed into walls, incurring serious injuries.

Still, baseball has the lowest incidence of serious injury of the major sports and death is almost nonexistent within the context of major-league play. In fact, Ray Chapman of the Indians is the only major-league ballplayer to be fatally hurt in a game. Carl Mays, who threw the "pitch that killed," often said, "I won over two hundred games, but what happened to me in August of 1920 is the only thing anyone remembers."

A few ballplayers have taken their own lives. Donnie Moore, the California Angels pitcher who threw the home-run pitch to Dave Henderson in the 1986 league championship series, killed himself on July 18, 1989. In 1940, Willard Hershberger, a promising catcher for the Cincinnati Reds, blamed himself for his team losing a crucial game in late July, and slashed his throat on August 3, 1940. Martin Bergen, catcher for the National League Boston team, killed his wife and two children and then slit his own throat on January 19, 1900. Some people believe that Ed Delahanty of the Philadelphia Athletics, who disappeared on July 2, 1903, killed himself. While traveling on a New York Central train from Chicago to New York, he was disorderly and was ordered off the train on the Canadian side of the Niagara Falls. A week later his body was found.

Another incident in baseball history that fans will never forget involved Eddie Waitkus of the Chicago Cubs. What happened to Waitkus provided the inspiration for Bernard Malamud's *The Natural.*

Waitkus first came up with the Cubs in 1941 to play 12 games, and then went off to war. He returned in 1946 as the Cubs' regular firstsacker, a position he held until he was traded to Philadelphia in 1949. Playing for the Phillies that summer, with his average above the .300 mark by mid–June, he was shot in the chest and almost killed in a Chicago hotel by a young woman he did not even know. The bullet wound ended the season for Waitkus. The episode remains as one of the great mysteries in the history of the game.

Joe Charboneau, Cleveland's glitzy Rookie of the Year in 1980, almost experienced tragedy before he ever got to Cleveland. During the spring, the Tribe, training in Arizona, made a junket to Mexico City for an exhibition game. While there, Charboneau was standing in uniform with the rest of the team outside of a hotel waiting for a bus, when a very unkempt looking man approached Charboneau and asked him where he was from. When Charboneau replied, "California," the man jammed a pen into Charboneau's left side. When the attacker was apprehended, he confessed that he had stabbed Charboneau because he hated all Americans. The Mexican court fined him $2.27 and released him.

Fortunately, the Indians' rookie was not seriously hurt and was in good spirits afterward. "I'm going to try to get a commercial with the Bic people," he quipped. "I can go on TV and say, 'Bic pens are best. It'll even write under blood.'"

Lyman Bostock, star Minnesota and California outfielder in the late seventies who proved to be in the wrong place at the wrong time, was less fortunate than Waitkus and Charboneau and became major league baseball's only homicide victim while in the midst of a career that gained him a huge contract in the early stages of free agency. Other players were murdered after their careers were over, but only Lyman Bostock had a career cut short by murder after he had tasted glory.

Bostock came to the majors in 1975 with the Minnesota Twins as a 24-year-old outfielder. He was well seasoned, having played with Charlotte, Orlando, and Tacoma before being called up by the big club. His full name was Lyman Wesley Bostock, Jr. His father had played in the old Negro American League and was a great hitter. Lyman, Jr., attended college in

California and was a member of an NCAA championship team two years in a row while playing with Cal State Northridge.

In 1972, Bostock signed a contract with the Twins' minor-league team in North Carolina, the Charlotte Twins, and progressed through the Minnesota farm system. His final minor-league stop was with Tacoma in the Pacific Coast League, where he batted .333 in 475 at-bats. Minnesota brought him up in 1975, and he played his first major league game April 8.

The Twins of the mid-seventies were a powerful team, boasting hitters like three-time batting champion Tony Oliva; four-time batting champ Rod Carew; Larry Hisle, acquired from the St. Louis Cardinals; and another strong rookie, Dan Ford. With such talent, the team was expected to challenge the world champion Oakland A's, but injuries and spotty pitching hampered their effort, and the Twins finished fourth, 20 games behind in 1975.

Young Lyman Bostock fought his way into the starting lineup and stayed there. Not only was he rapping the ball with authority, he also played excellent defense. His fly-chasing zeal caused him to miss a month of action after he injured himself by crashing into a fence making a sensational catch of a Bert Campaneris line drive.

But Bostock showed his immaturity, frequently arguing with umpires and walking around the clubhouse as though he were already an established star rather than a rookie. In mid–July, Bostock was batting .215 and was terribly frustrated. He visited an uncle, looking for sympathy, but instead of sympathy, his uncle gave him a stern lecture, admonishing him to quit being a "hot dog" and settle down. Bostock took the advice and his average improved, as did his image. He closed out his rookie year with a .282 average in 98 games played. It appeared that the Twins would have an excellent center fielder, and an All-Star performer, for the next several years.

Developments after the 1974 season were changing the game dramatically. Free agency was emerging. While the owners were battling Marvin Miller and the Players' Union concerning the reserve clause in players' contracts, Catfish Hunter, who had won 25 games as the star hurler for the world champion A's, was declared a free agent after the season as a result of a contract dispute with Oakland owner Charles Finley. A bidding war was waged for the star hurler's services. George Steinbrenner and the New York Yankees won the battle and signed the pitcher to a lucrative contract on December 31, 1974. Although the Red Sox won the pennant in 1975, Hunter hurled 23 victories for the Yanks.

Before the start of the 1976 season, pitchers Dave McNally of Baltimore and Andy Messersmith of Los Angeles were declared free agents, thereby formally initiating the "free agent" era. Baseball would never be the same. The owners retaliated by locking out the players before the start of the 1976 season. Commissioner Bowie Kuhn stepped in to get the season underway. An agreement was finally reached in July when the owners agreed to a provision that any player with six or more years of experience would have the right to declare himself a free agent. The Twins made a serious run at the pennant in 1976, and finished third, five games behind the Kansas City Royals. The seven-year-old expansion franchise won its first of three consecutive Western Division titles. Minnesota led the league in batting, finishing at .274, and they topped the American League in runs scored with 743. The Twins won 85 games, their best record since winning the division in 1970. Pitcher Bill Campbell had a brilliant season, winning 17 and losing only 5; he trailed only Sparky Lyle of New York in saves with 20.

Young Lyman Bostock contributed to the Twins' success. He upped his average from .282 to .323, good enough for fourth in the league, 10 points behind Kansas City's George Brett, who won his first title. The future for the Twins and for Bostock looked bright.

However, free agency had an impact on team rosters. Joe Rudi left the A's for the Angels; Bert Campaneris went from the A's to Texas; and Sal Bando and Rollie Fingers also fled from Charley Finley, the third baseman going to Milwaukee and the star reliever to San Diego in the National League. On November 6, the Twins were jolted when Bill Campbell announced that he had signed with the Boston Red Sox.

Despite the loss of their ace stopper, many writers predicted a championship for Minnesota in 1977 because of the Twins' powerful offense. The club performed to its offensive promise. While the Twins fell far short of the Royals, who won 16 consecutive games in August to best Minnesota by 18 games, the Twins were dominant in hitting, leading the majors with an impressive .282 team average. The Twins scored 867 times that season, which was more than the Big Red Machine in Cincinnati had scored, more than the Yankees in 1977, more than any of the great Oakland teams of the first part of the decade, more than even the powerful 1961 Yankees. The team was led by Rod Carew's .388 average, the highest since Ted Williams hit .406 in 1941. (Williams had also hit .388 in 1957.)

Lyman Bostock, with a strong .336 average, finished second to Carew. He batted in 90 runs while scoring 104. Bostock had arrived as a major-league star. For Bostock it was a showcase year and he was ready to capitalize in his negotiations with Twins owner Calvin Griffith.

The likelihood of Bostock remaining with the Twins was slim. Griffith was known as a tight-fisted owner. He frequently blasted fans in the Twin

Cities for not being loyal, and he often talked about his financial problems. Cal Griffith was the nephew of Clark Griffith, the long-time owner of the Washington Senators who was also known as a tough bargainer. If any owner were to have an exodus of free agent talent, it would be Calvin Griffith. Griffith paid Bostock $20,000 in 1977, a year after he had trailed only three players for the batting title.

Bostock had a season-long battle with Griffith. In early August, Bostock announced, "Now I want to see what I'm worth on the open market. Maybe no one will pay very much for a line drive hitter." One reporter prophetically responded, "Someone probably will." And someone did.

After the season, Bostock waited. He hired an agent, Abdul Jalil. Soon George Steinbrenner's Yankees began wooing Bostock. A November 16, 1977, story in a New York daily said that the Yankees were prepared to offer Bostock $2.9 million for five years, an offer better than the deal they had given Reggie Jackson before the start of the 1977 season. Other teams also expressed interest, notably the Toronto Blue Jays, who along with the Seattle Mariners were the latest expansion teams to join the American League and needed offensive punch. Eventually Toronto, however, dropped out of the bidding. Their director of personnel, Pat Gillick, said, "When the money involved was $1.5 to $2 million, we were able to live with the other factors in the signing of Bostock." But Gillick added that Bostock's demand for a five-year deal for $3 million would pay the costs of operating two full-season Class A farm teams.

A few days later, Bostock signed with the California Angels for a reported annual salary of $400,000 for five years with a $250,000 signing bonus. While this figure did not make Bostock the highest paid of the free agents of 1977, he was among the top five. Teammate Larry Hisle went to Milwaukee for six years for over three million with a $650,000 bonus; Rich Gossage signed a lucrative contract with the Yankees; Oscar Gamble went to San Diego. Of all the deals, Bostock's was the most dramatic since he had received only $20,000 for 1977. Bostock said, "Griffith never got close."

The California fans were expectant as the 1978 season began. Gene Autry's Angels had been in the league since 1961. They had never been serious contenders for a pennant, and the team was going to make a bid through the free agent market. The Angels had added Bobby Grich from Baltimore prior to the 1977 season as well as Don Baylor and Joe Rudi from Oakland. They dealt veteran slugger Bobby Bonds to Chicago for catcher Brian Downing. With the addition of a .300 hitter like Bostock, plus a pitching staff that boasted Frank Tanana, Nolan Ryan, and an excellent stopper in Dave LaRoche, they were ready to challenge the perennial A.L. West winners of

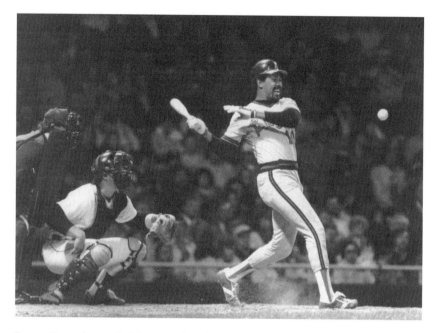

Lyman Bostock, seen lashing out a base hit, was one of the first big-money free agents (Corbis-Bettman Archives, New York, NY).

the late 1970s, the Kansas City Royals. Lyman Bostock opened the 1978 season with the worst slump of his career. He went 2-for-39 for a .051 average for the first ten games of the season. He was so upset by the prolonged slump that he benched himself for a game and threatened to forgo one month's salary. Bostock said, "If I don't do well the rest of April, I'm going to ask Mr. Autry not to pay me for a month."

Despite his poor numbers at the plate, Bostock was outstanding in the field. He called his father in Birmingham to discuss his prolonged slump. Lyman, Sr., drew on his ten years in the Negro leagues and offered his son advice. A few days after the call, Lyman, Jr., began to hit. Early in June, the Angels fired manager Dave Garcia and hired Jim Fregosi. Bostock responded well to this change and began to spark the team. He batted at a .352 clip in June and pushed his average close to .300. He also gained popularity with his teammates, who nicknamed him Abdul Jibber Jabber because of his easygoing, talkative manner. All was well with the young star. He had an owner he respected in Gene Autry; he had a manager who believed in his stardom; and he was with a team that was in a pennant race.

In late September, California played a weekend series against the White Sox in Chicago. Bostock went 2-for-4 in a tough 5–4 loss on September 23.

After the Saturday game, Bostock went to visit relatives. Whenever Bostock was in Chicago, he would go to nearby Gary, Indiana, after games, to visit his two uncles, Edward and Thomas Turner, and take them to dinner and socialize.

Ironically, earlier that season, Bostock had said he was a baseball player in the right place at the right time when he signed a five-year contract with the Angels for nearly $3 million. But on the night of September 23, 1978, he was at the wrong place, at the wrong time.

On the way to dinner, he was in a car that belonged to his uncle, Thomas Turner. Also riding in the car were Mrs. Barbara Smith and her sister, Joan Hawkins. According to Abdul Jalil, Bostock's agent and adviser, the two women in the car were Turner's godchildren. Bostock was seated in back next to Mrs. Smith. Turner, who helped raise the sisters, was driving them to visit relatives in Gary.

Earlier in the day, Barbara Smith's estranged husband, Leonard Smith, had gone to her house and, while there, allegedly threatened her. According to a Gary police official, Smith and his wife had been separated for about two months and he had been stalking her. Divorce proceedings were progressing, but Smith opposed them. That evening, driving alone, Smith spotted the Turner car, pulled up next to it and saw his wife seated in the back next to Bostock. As the cars proceeded through a green traffic signal, Smith pulled out a gun and shot at Barbara, but the bullet missed her and hit Bostock in the right temple. He died from the bullet wound two-and-a-half hours later.

Police Corporal Charles Hicks said later, "Lyman was a victim of circumstances. His [Smith's] intended victim was his wife, not Lyman." He felt that Smith missed his target because both cars were moving when he fired.

Baseball and the California Angels were stunned by the tragedy. The players learned of the murder upon returning to the hotel around midnight. They found Dan Goodwin and Ken Landreau in tears in the lobby. All of Bostock's teammates experienced troubled sleep that fateful night.

The next day, Manager Jim Fregosi locked the dressing room door when the Angels arrived at Comiskey Park for Sunday's game with the White Sox. The players took seats for their typical pregame devotions. An executive with the Fellowship of Christian Athletes conducted the brief service. The executive later said, "It was the hardest thing I've ever done. I read from Romans Chapter VIII, verses 35-39, and made some comments. It [Bostock's death] was senseless and meaningless."

Reactions poured in from across the country. Bostock's close friend,

Larry Hisle, who had signed a long-term contract with Milwaukee but had played with Bostock when they both were with the Twins, was stunned when he learned of the tragedy. He gasped, "How could such a thing happen? I don't know what to say. He was the best friend I had in the game." Hisle was so shattered that he could not bring himself to play and was excused by his manager, George Bamberger.

Gene Autry, owner of the Angels, said he was shocked by the killing. He knew Bostock well and said: "I talked to him a lot of times and saw him practically every game. I always went down to the clubhouse to visit with him and all the team." Autry added, "He was a very, very fine fellow. We were very happy with him."

Teammate Don Baylor called Bostock "a close friend and an outstanding player. It's very shocking — here one day and gone tomorrow. I'll miss his humor. He just wanted to play every day and win." His former Minnesota teammate, Rod Carew, who was on his way to a seventh batting title, said that Bostock was "liked by everybody on the club. I know his wife real well, and all of us share in her grief."

The funeral services were held on Thursday in Los Angeles. There was a standing-room crowd of over 1,000 mourners at the Vermont Square United Methodist Church, and another 500 were outside. Bostock's widow, Youvene, and his mother, Annie, were surrounded by his teammates and Lyman's four brothers. His father was there, as were several players from other teams. Virtually all the teams sent flowers; the Angels' floral display depicted their scoreboard. At age 28, Lyman Bostock, a victim of a meaningless and accidental homicide, was laid to rest.

The outpouring of outrage was present on the editorial pages and sports columns. *Sun-Times* writer Bill Gleason blamed the death on the proliferation of guns. He wrote, "If you were up early Sunday morning, as I was, you heard the radio report of the slaying. Radio could not tell you or me how it had happened. Radio only convinced us that Lyman Bostock was dead. The why is obvious. Lyman Bostock died because we have a nation of gun-toters. This is a fact of city life."

The Sporting News, almost three weeks after the killing, wrote, "Bostock had only begun fulfilling the destiny when he was killed by a gunman he'd never seen." The writer called attention to the irony of Bostock's statement that he made upon signing his contract with the Angels that he had the good fortune "to be in the right place at the right time," but that nine months later, the writer observed, Bostock "was in the wrong place at the wrong time, the apparently unintended victim of a shooting."

And what happened to Leonard Smith? A murder charge was filed against him, but he pleaded innocent by reason of insanity. The court appointed two psychiatrists to examine him and the trial was set for March 12, 1979. Two trials were held. The first resulted in a hung jury, the second in a verdict of not guilty by reason of insanity. Smith was held for a while at the state mental hospital at Logansport, Indiana, but was released on June 20, 1980, when doctors at the Logansport State Hospital filed a request seeking Smith's release after treatment. The Lake County prosecutor, Jack Crawford, said after the release, "Smith has beaten the system and found the way through a loophole."

The public was moved and reacted angrily. The Indiana legislature, to keep such a situation from happening again, enacted legislation that enables juries to find defendants guilty *and* insane. Illinois and Michigan subsequently enacted similar laws. Crawford noted that the new law was directly attributable to the Lyman Bostock case.

The Angels finished second to the Kansas City Royals in 1978, but the next year they finally won the American League West championship. They achieved that pinnacle without Lyman Bostock, Jr., one of the brightest young stars of the decade who was the tragic victim of a homicide.

LYMAN BOSTOCK

Born Nov. 22, 1950, Birmingham, Ala.   Died Sept. 23, 1978, Gary, Ind.   Batted left, threw right.

Year	Team	Pos.	G	AB	R	H	2B	3B	HR	RBI	BB	SB	BA	Slug
1972	Charlotte W. Carolina	OF	57	177	27	52	12	2	0	27	38	5	.294	.384
1973	Orlando Southern	OF	85	297	49	93	18	2	5	37	48	19	.313	.434
1974	Tacoma PC	OF	128	473	73	158	17	2	7	56	59	13	.333	.423
1975	Tacoma	OF	22	92	16	36	5	0	0	13	6	3	.391	.445
1975	Minn AL	OF	98	369	52	104	21	5	0	29	28	2	.282	.366
1976	Minn AL	OF	128	474	75	153	21	9	4	60	33	12	.323	.430
1977	Minn AL	OF	153	593	104	199	36	12	14	90	51	16	.336	.508
1978	Cal AL	OF	147	568	74	168	24	2	5	71	59	15	.296	.379
Major League Totals 4 yrs.			289	851	305	624	102	30	23	250	171	45	.311	.427

18   They Also Tasted Glory

"Spooner was Koufax before Koufax."
VIN SCULLY

The players profiled in this book all tasted glory — some had little sips in single seasons; others had larger careers with notable accomplishments before injuries, sickness or death prevented them from enjoying full careers. One can merely speculate whether full careers for any of these athletes would have resulted in election to the Hall of Fame because, in numerous instances, players who started strong faded to mediocrity despite continued good health. A good example is Gene Bearden.

In 1948, rookie Bearden pitched the Cleveland Indians to a world's championship. He won 20 and lost only seven. He beat Boston in the critical, single playoff game when the Tribe and the Red Sox tied after the 154-game schedule. In the third game of the World Series, Bearden shut out Billy Southworth's Boston Braves, 2–0. He came back in relief to save the decisive sixth game for Bob Lemon.

Bearden was tough to hit because he threw two different knuckleballs, a three-finger and a one-finger, and they both looked like fastballs coming to the plate before they knuckled. In 1948, Bearden's control was so fine that he often threw the knuckleball on a 3-and-0 count.

In the spring of 1949, batters began to move up in the batter's box to hit Bearden's knuckler before it broke. Hitters also learned that if they were patient, they could lay off some of Bearden's better pitches and hit the fastball when he threw it. Bearden began to press and found it difficult to hit the spots with his pitches with the same precision that he had the year before. His effectiveness suffered greatly. Bearden remained in the majors for five years, winning just 25 games, never regaining the form he had demonstrated in 1948.

The players profiled in earlier chapters were not short-term phenoms but were headed for long-term greatness when their careers were ended by injury or illness. Some, like Tony Oliva and Kirby Puckett, were well down the road to the Hall of Fame. Others were felled by misfortune much earlier in their careers, such as Johnny Beasley and Herb Score.

Other lesser known players from baseball's annals were similarly cut down by injury or illness after promising starts. This is especially true of pitchers.

At the turn of the century, Ed Summers, nicknamed the Kickapoo Chief, helped the 1908 Detroit Tigers win the pennant with his sparkling 24–12 record. His 1.64 ERA tied him with Walter Johnson for fourth best in the league; his winning percentage was fourth best in the league; and his win total tied him for second best behind Ed Walsh's 40. In his sophomore season he went 19–9, and in one game he hurled 18 scoreless innings against the Washington Senators, the game ending in a tie. In 1910 rheumatism began to impair his effectiveness, and his record dropped to 13–12. In 1911 he went 11–11, and by 1912 he was back in the minors.

Jack Harper debuted brilliantly with the St. Louis Cardinals in 1901 with a 23–11 season, the second best record in the league. The next year, Harper still pitched in St. Louis but with the Browns, the American League entry, and his record fell to 15 and 11. The Browns, detecting ominous signs in Harper's pitching, shipped him back to the National League to Cincinnati, where Harper's record slipped to 6–8, as he was bothered by bone chip problems in his elbow. But in 1904, Harper made a strong comeback, winning 24 and losing only nine. Six of his wins were shutouts. In 1905, the bone chip problem recurred, and Harper's record fell to 10–13. In 1906, a springtime finger injury prompted the Reds to send Harper to the Chicago Cubs. Despite his elbow woes and his finger injury, Harper held out for more money. Chicago's brass decided that they did not need a sore-armed pitcher who was brash enough to hold out, so they refused to budge. The resulting stalemate ended Harper's brief career.

Perhaps the best pitcher in the early part of the century whose career was shortened by injury was Ferdie Schupp of the New York Giants. Pitching mostly in relief, in 1916 Schupp won 10 and lost three for McGraw's Giants while compiling an 0.90 ERA.

The next year, Schupp won 21 and lost seven, good enough to lead the league in winning percentage. Additionally, the lefthander allowed only 1.91 runs per game, third best in the league, and he led the league in fewest hits per nine innings, 6.68. He also was fourth in the league with six shutouts; third in most strikeouts per nine innings, 4.67; and tied for fifth with 25 complete games. In 1918, Schupp went to war. When he returned, he had lost his effectiveness. The exact nature of his arm injury is uncertain, but he was not the same pitcher he was before he entered the military. The Giants sent him to the Cardinals, for whom he made a one-year comeback, posting a 16–13 season. After that, Schupp faded out of the league.

Was Schupp an outstanding pitcher before he was injured? Many of his Giant teammates provided the answer during the 1917 season by refusing to warm up Schupp because he had so much stuff that they feared his pitches might injure them.

The Monty Stratton story is full of pathos. Stratton came up to the Chicago White Sox in 1936 with outstanding credentials but was disabled by illness most of the season. First, he suffered from tonsillitis; then he had an appendicitis attack. He won five and lost seven in 1936.

His prospects for 1937 seemed bright. Manager Jimmy Dykes thought the strapping righthander might become the ace of a pitching staff that included Thornton Lee, Ted Lyons, Vern Kennedy and Johnny Whitehead, all of whom won ten or more games the year before. Although Stratton's health remained good, he now was plagued by nagging injuries which limited his pitching to 165 innings. He did win 15 and lost only five. He finished second in the American League to the Yankees's Lefty Gomez in earned run average with an impressive 2.40, and second to Johnny Allen of Cleveland with a .750 winning percentage. Moreover, five of Stratton's victories were shutouts.

In 1938, Stratton again was projected as the ace of the White Sox staff, but once more he suffered a minor arm injury that hampered his effectiveness. He did win 15 while losing nine, and anticipated the 1939 season as being the year when his career would reach full bloom. Instead, tragedy struck.

On Sunday afternoon, November 27, 1938, Stratton was hunting rabbits on his mother's farm near Greenville, Texas, when his foot caught a snag on a downhill step toward a creek and the pistol he was carrying accidentally fired a shot into his right leg between the hip and knee, piercing an artery. Stratton's leg was amputated the following day because the bullet had cut off all the blood supply to the lower part of the leg and gangrene had set in. The surgeon, Dr. A.R. Thomasson, said, "Even immediate attention by all the surgeons in the world couldn't have saved the leg. Monty couldn't have hit that artery if he aimed at it. It probably wouldn't happen more than once in a hundred times. It was a case of a leg or a life."

Despite his handicap, Stratton refused to accept the fact that his pitching career was finished. After several years' absence from baseball, Stratton pitched with an artificial leg in the minor leagues in 1945 and 1946. Despite his enthusiasm, his dream of returning to Chicago as a pitcher never was realized.

Metro-Goldwyn-Mayer, however, made Stratton famous when actor Jimmy Stewart portrayed the pitcher in the highly successful 1949 film *The Monty Stratton Story*.

Ernie White arrived in St. Louis in 1941 as one of the best pitchers to come out of the Cardinals' talent-rich minor-league system. In 1938, pitching for Portsmouth in the Middle Atlantic League, White had fanned 18 Johnstown batters in a seven-inning game, tying a league record. In 1939, he had thrown the first no-hit, no-run game in the history of Houston's Buffalo Stadium. In 1940, his 2.25 ERA led the American Association.

White was immediately successful in St. Louis in 1941. At midseason, he put together an eight-game winning streak between July 13 and August 10; he won a game every three-and-a-half days. In one stretch, he got three wins over the Giants in three days. White pitched especially well against the Brooklyn Dodgers, the Cardinals' principal rival for the pennant. White did it with outstanding stuff and control that was so good that it caused Whitlow Wyatt, Brooklyn's mound stalwart, to observe, "Wherever Gus Mancuso would stick his glove, that kid would pop it in there." The Dodgers won the pennant in 1941, but White was sensational for St. Louis. The left-handed rookie was 17–7 with a 2.30 ERA.

White had first hurt his arm at Portsmouth in the game in which he recorded 18 strikeouts. Eager to break the league record, he reached back for a little extra in pitching to the first batter in the eighth inning, injuring his arm. In 1942, the soreness in his arm came back. The Cardinals won the pennant, but White posted only a 7–5 record. He did, however, pitch a big 2–0 win over the Yankees in the third game of the World Series as the Cardinals surprised the favored Yankees, winning the Series in five games.

In 1943, an injury all but ended his career. While backing up a play at third base, White ran into the dugout roof and broke a bone in his shoulder. He returned to baseball after the war with his old manager Billy Southworth of the Boston Braves, but in three-and-a-half years, White never won a game while losing two. A healthy Ernie White was a premier pitcher in an era of strong pitching.

Elmer Riddle posted a brilliant 19–4 record his rookie season in 1941, leading the league in winning percentage, .826, and ERA, 2.24. The next year, he was beset with arm problems, and he struggled to a 7–11 record, but he returned to form in 1943 with a superb 21–11 ledger, leading the league in wins. His arm problems returned in 1944 and he never again approached his early promise. He dropped out of the league in 1950, the victim of a chronic arm condition.

Karl Spooner's story is interesting. In 1951, in his first professional baseball season, spent at Hornell, New York, in the Pony League, Spooner struck out 200 batters and no-hit Bradford. Wildness plagued him and he lingered in the minors, mostly at Pueblo in the Western League. In 1954 he gained control of his fastball to become the sensation of the Texas League, posting a 21–9 record while fanning a league-leading 262 batters. In four minor league seasons, the young lefthander struck out 884 batters in 749 innings, an average of 10.14 per nine-inning game.

Late in 1954, the Dodgers brought Spooner to Brooklyn. He started his first big-league game the day after the Dodgers lost the pennant to the crosstown Giants. Spooner shut out the champion Giants on three hits while whiffing 15, a record for a rookie pitcher. Tom Lasorda, also a rookie on that Dodger team, recalled that during the game as Spooner was mowing down one Giant after another, Dusty Rhodes, pinch hitter deluxe, told Durocher, "If that guy can strike me out, I'll kiss your butt in Macy's window." So the next inning, Durocher sent Rhodes in to hit. Three pitches later, Rhodes was back on the bench and simply said to Durocher, "Where and when?"

A few days later, Spooner shut out the Pirates, striking out 12. The Brooklyn fans began chanting, "The Dodgers should have had Spooner sooner."

On the first day of spring training in 1955, a photographer asked Spooner if he could take his picture, so Spooner picked up a ball and struck a pose. The photographer wanted an action photo. Trying to accommodate him, Spooner lobbed a toss to a catcher. The photographer, however, still was not satisfied and asked the rookie if he could really cut one loose. Spooner obliged without warming up. He heard something pop in his shoulder, and his problems began. He tried to pitch a time or two, but the ache in his shoulder persisted.

Spooner worked 98 innings in 1955, mostly in short relief stints, and he went 8–6 for the year. He started one World Series game against the Yankees but he did not make it through the first inning. It was his last big-league appearance. He struggled in the minor leagues trying to regain his fastball until the spring of 1959 when Spooner finally acknowledged that "the arm was gone." How good was Karl Spooner before injury? Vin Scully summed it up, "Spooner was Koufax before Koufax."

What was the worst trade in baseball history? Anyone from Chicago's North Side will respond, "Lou Brock for Ernie Broglio." Lou Brock, whom the Cubs sent to St. Louis in the deal, went on to a Hall of Fame career with over 3,000 hits; Ernie Broglio, whom the Cubs acquired in the trade, won only 14 games for Chicago in three seasons.

Had Broglio's arm remained sound, the trade would not have been one-sided. After posting a 7–12 record as a Cardinal rookie in 1959, Broglio defied the sophomore jinx in 1960 and pitched as well as anyone in the

Schoolboy Rowe won 62 games in his first three major-league seasons before he hurt his arm. Despite the injury, he had a productive career (NATIONAL BASEBALL HALL OF FAME LIBRARY, COOPERSTOWN, NY).

league. His 21–9 record and .700 winning percentage led the circuit. His superb 2.74 ERA was second best in the league, and his 6.84 hits per nine innings tied Sandy Koufax for the best record.

In 1961, an elbow, which he had first hurt in high school basketball, flared up and reduced his effectiveness to 9–12. But despite occasional pain, he came back with two respectable seasons in 1962 and 1963, going 12–9 and 18–8. After a 3–5 start with St. Louis in 1964, the Cards sent him to the Cubs for Lou Brock.

Broglio never got untracked for Chicago. In November 1964, doctors removed four bone fragments from his elbow and corrected the position of the nerve in the joint. Broglio made valiant efforts to pitch in 1965 and 1966, but his once-bright career came to an end.

From 1975 to 1982, Dennis Leonard of the Kansas City Royals won 130 games, more than any other righthander in baseball. Only Hall of Famer Steve Carlton won more games during that time frame (152). Leonard was the ace of the Kansas City pitching staff in their league championship years of 1976, 1977, 1978 and 1980. Three times he was a 20-game winner. In 1979, an inflammation in his right elbow kept him out for a month and reduced his victory total to 14. In 1981, Leonard was off to one of his best starts, but he won only 13 because of the strike-shortened season.

On May 21, 1982, a line drive off the bat of Buddy Bell of Texas struck Leonard's middle finger on his pitching hand. It was the first of a series of injuries. The big one came on May 23, 1983. While pitching one of his best games, Leonard bore down on a pitch and the tendon in his left knee popped. He battled gamely to return to pitching after four knee operations between 1983 and 1986, but with minimal results. He retired in 1986.

Before Leonard was injured, he was on track toward an outstanding career. He had 130 wins by age 30, a total that exceeds Hall of Famers Carl Hubbell's 110, Warren Spahn's 108, Red Ruffing's 116 and is only three shy of Steve Carlton's 133.

Some pitchers, despite arm problems, have had reasonably good major league careers. Schoolboy Rowe of the Detroit Tigers is a good example. After going 7–4 as a rookie in 1933, Rowe went 24–8 in 1934, the second most wins in the league to Lefty Gomez's 26. He came back with strong 19–13 and 19–10 records in 1935 and 1936, respectively. In 1937, he was kayoed by arm miseries. He returned in 1940 to turn in a glittering 16–3 record. In 1941, his arm problems recurred, and he was sold to Brooklyn in 1942. In 1943, Rowe had a rebirth, winning 14 for the Phillies. The Schoolboy returned after the war to win 11, 14 and 10. Had his pitching not been impaired by arm problems, Rowe might well be in the Hall of Fame.

Mel Parnell of the Boston Red Sox pitched left-handed in Fenway Park, a haven for right-handed batters, yet he ran off six consecutive successful seasons, winning 25 games in 1949 and 21 in 1953. The other years he won 15, 18, 18, and 12. After 1953, he struggled with an elbow problem and won only 12 games in the final three years of his career. In 1956, his final season, he threw the first Red Sox no-hitter in 33 seasons. His career ended with 123 wins and 75 losses, a .621 winning percentage.

Mike Lupica said in *The National Sports Daily* on June 5, 1990: "For two months in '88, you can make a case that Orel Hershiser was the best pitcher who ever lived." Hershiser's march to fame began on August 30, 1988, when he threw four scoreless innings against Montreal. Then he pitched five consecutive shutouts, followed by 10 scoreless innings in a 16-inning game against San Diego to end the season. Hershiser had eclipsed Don Drysdale's major league record of 58 consecutive scoreless innings. The streak was one of the truly great accomplishments in the history of baseball, much like Joe DiMaggio's 56-game hitting streak. Hershiser's record for the season was an outstanding 23–8, and in the four previous seasons, he had posted 60 wins, including a sparkling 19–3 mark in 1985. Hershiser capped the 1988 season by winning two World Series games.

After that spectacular performance in 1988, Hershiser began 1989 by admitting, "I'm in a position for the greatest fall of my life. If I don't win 20 or more games, I'm a failure." The decline started in the very first inning of the season when the Cincinnati Reds scored a run and ended Hershiser's consecutive scoreless innings record. For a superstar, the year was disappointing because he was ordinary, going 15 and 15.

In 1990, an MRI exam revealed damage to his shoulder that required an operation no other major leaguer had ever had before. Dr. Frank Jobe reported, "The shoulder was slipping out of the socket before the operation. What we did was fix the connective tissues and capsule so it doesn't slip out again."

When Hershiser came back to Los Angeles in 1991, he was pretty much a journeyman pitcher. Over the next four years, he won 35 games and lost 37. In 1995, he had a strong year with Cleveland in the American League. He was a mainstay on the Indians' pitching staff that after 41 years finally brought a pennant back to Cleveland. Hershiser posted a 16–6 record during the season, won two games in the playoffs and went 1–1 in the World Series against Atlanta. In 1996, he continued pitching effectively, winning 15 and losing nine. In 1997, he won 14 and lost 6.

The consecutive-scoreless-innings-streak has immortalized Hershiser, and his name will likely be in the record book for a long time, but the shoulder injury will probably keep him out of the Hall of Fame.

Compared to pitchers, there have been fewer star major-league fielders who were stricken down by injuries or illnesses early in their careers. The best that have not been profiled are Dale Alexander, Ray Grimes, Joe Hauser, Charlie Hollocher and Johnny Hodapp.

Orel Hershiser pitched 59 consecutive scoreless innings in 1988, breaking Don Drysdale's major league record by one (National Baseball Hall of Fame Library, Cooperstown, NY).

Dale Alexander was one of the best hitters in baseball while he was in the American League. After a five-year minor league career, Detroit purchased Alexander and Johnny Prudhomme from Toronto in 1929 for $100,000, a spectacular price in those years. Alexander arrived in the AL as an accomplished hitter. His last year at Toronto in the International League he hit .380, knocked out 236 base hits, slammed 49 doubles and 31 homers, scored 110 runs, and batted in 144. His rookie year statistics in the AL were almost as good. He batted .343 for Detroit in 1929, made 215 hits, 33 doubles, eight triples and 25 homers, scored 110 times and batted in 137 runs. No rookie of the year award existed at that time, or Alexander would have won it.

In 1930, Alexander hit .326 with 20 homers. In 1931 he hit for a .325 average, but his home run production dropped to four. In 1932 he was shipped to Boston in mid–June in a trade involving Alexander and Roy Johnson for Earl Webb, who had set a major-league record with 67 doubles in 1931. It was thought that Alexander would prosper in Fenway Park. His batting average did, but not his home run punch. He led the league with a robust .367 average, outdistancing Jimmie Foxx by three points.

In 1933, after a slow start, Alexander hurt his knee. He was given diathermy treatment for the injury in the clubhouse. "It was a new method of treatment, and not much was known about it," Alexander recalled years later. "I noticed my leg felt awfully hot. Anyway, I ended up with third degree burns and a gangrene infection, and I almost lost my leg. I was finished in the majors," Alexander said.

Although few players have hit major-league pitching better than Alexander, he probably was not an all-around Hall of Fame–quality player. "I just didn't have the ability. I couldn't run or field," Alexander himself acknowledged. In 1931, Detroit's manager, Bucky Harris, became so disillusioned with Alexander as a first baseman that he became obsessed with trading him for whatever he could get. The "Ox," as George Stallings dubbed him because of his size, was awkward around the bag. "If only we could get a real fielding first baseman," Harris moaned. To achieve his goal, he acquired Harry Davis, a slick fielder, from Toronto, and sent Alexander to the bench despite his .300 average. Alexander's injury shortened the career of a ballplayer with a .331 lifetime average to only a few seasons.

Ray Grimes of the Chicago Cubs was a premier young hitter in the Babe Ruth era. In 1921 he averaged .321, which tied him for third in the league, and in 1922 he batted .354, slugged .572, and hit 45 doubles, in each case finishing second in the league to Rogers Hornsby. During the season, Grimes set a major league record by batting in at least one run in 17 consecutive games. The next year his problems began. In June, he slipped a disc in his back and never recovered. When he was able to play, he hit well, finishing with a .329 average in 64 games. Grimes played sporadically and finished with the Philadelphia Phillies in 1926. In 433 major league games, he had a .329 average.

Joe Hauser, colorfully nicknamed Unser Choe (Our Joe) by minor-

Dale Alexander won the 1932 AL batting championship before his career was ended by gangrene stemming from a diathermy treatment (NATIONAL BASEBALL HALL OF FAME LIBRARY, COOPERSTOWN, NY).

league fans in his hometown of Milwaukee, was a star performer for Connie Mack the same time as Grimes. In 1922, rookie Hauser hit .323 playing first base for Mack's Athletics. He followed that in 1923 with a .307 average that included 27 doubles, 10 triples, and 16 home runs. In 1924, he banged out 27 home runs, second only to Ruth, and batted in 115 runs. In the field he led AL first basemen in putouts, 1,513, and in double plays, 131. Hauser was headed toward an outstanding career as one of the power hitters of the era, but in 1925 he broke his kneecap and sat out the entire season. He played in 1926, 1928 and 1929, but faded out of the big leagues. In 1930, Hauser became a star in the American Association. He played many years at the Triple A level and became the home run king of minor-league baseball.

Charlie Hollocher was a hard-hitting, slick-fielding shortstop for the Chicago Cubs from 1918–1924. In his rookie year he hit .316, fourth in the league, and led the league in hits (161), at-bats (509), and total bases (202). He was third in stolen bases with 26. He hit .319 in 1920, but illness limited him to 80 games. He was also excellent with the glove, leading National League shortstops in fielding in 1921 and in 1922. Hollocher was the field captain for the Cubs, the mainstay of the infield and the team leader. In 1922, Hollocher hit .340, the best average for a shortstop since Honus Wagner's .354 in 1908.

After Hollocher developed a stomach problem in the spring of 1923 on Catalina Island where the Cubs were training, he returned home to St. Louis for an examination by Dr. Robert Hyland, who sent him to a specialist. Hollocher was advised that he would ruin his health if he returned to baseball that season. But Cubs manager Bill Killifer urged him to rejoin the team, telling him that he did not have to play when he did not feel well. Hollocher yielded, and once in uniform he could not stay off the field. "I played when I should have been at home," Hollocher said. He hit .342 in 66 games.

During the winter, Hollocher tried to regain his health, but failed. He played in only 76 games in 1924. The career of this brilliant shortstop was over. His abdominal problems persisted for life. In 1933 he said, "Now I realize that I made my mistake in playing the 1923 season. But I was of age and guess I can blame only myself." On August 14, 1940, Charles Jack Hollocher shot himself to death with a newly purchased shotgun in his automobile near Lindbergh Boulevard in the St. Louis suburb of Frontenac. Lying near Hollocher's body was a membership card in the Association of Professional Baseball Players.

Another player of the 1920s whom fate dealt a bad hand was Johnny Hodapp of the Cleveland Indians. Hodapp hit .304 in 1927, .323 in 1928 and .327 in 1929, reaching his crest in 1930 with a .354 average, a league-leading 225 hits, and a league-leading 51 doubles. Hodapp also led second basemen in putouts, 403. Late in the 1931 season, Hodapp shattered his knee. He was traded to the White Sox in 1932, hit only .219, and was traded to the Red Sox in 1933, where he played his final year. He hit .312, but he

Both an outstanding hitter and fielder, Charlie Hollocher's career was ended by a chronic stomach problem (NATIONAL BASEBALL HALL OF FAME LIBRARY, COOPERSTOWN, NY).

led AL second baseman in errors with 25. His confidence was ruined by his misfortune, and his career ended.

Other players not discussed started their major league careers with strong performances but were the victims of misfortune. To name a few: Clay Bryant, Bill DeLancey, Chuck Estrada, Wally Bunker, and Wayne Garland. They were not of the same quality as the players featured in this work, however.

Branch Rickey, in a speech delivered to the Executive Club of Chicago, on November 12, 1926, asked the question, "What is the greatest single thing in the character ... of a great baseball player?" He answered, "I think it is the desire to be a great baseball player, a desire that dominates him, a desire that is so strong that it does not admit of anything that runs counter to it, a desire to excel that so confines him to a single purpose that nothing else matters."

Rickey in his talk cited Ty Cobb as having so much desire that he did not wait for breaks to happen — he made his own. The two players since Cobb who perhaps have most resembled the Georgia Peach in their style of play were Jackie Robinson, who integrated baseball, and Pete Reiser, an important performer in this book. The difference between Robinson and Reiser was physical health. Robinson stayed reasonably free from injury and illness and has a plaque bearing his name in Cooperstown. Reiser does not. Call it luck, destiny, fate or misfortune, the injuries to Pete Reiser, resulting greatly from his Cobb-like desire and abandon, kept him from achieving baseball's highest goal, enshrinement in the Hall of Fame. Like all the other players in this book, he tasted glory, but only briefly. It is hoped that the pages of this book rekindle the luster of their careers.

INDEX